MONUMENT TO JUNIPERO SERRA IN GOLDEN GATE PARK
"His memory still rests like a benediction over the noble
State which he rescued from savagery."

# SPANISH AND INDIAN PLACE NAMES OF CALIFORNIA

*THEIR MEANING AND THEIR ROMANCE*

BY

## NELLIE VAN DE GRIFT SANCHEZ

AUTHOR OF

"THE LIFE OF MRS. ROBERT LOUIS STEVENSON"
SPANISH ARCADIA", ETC.

SAN FRANCISCO
## A. M. ROBERTSON
MCMXXX

*TO MY SON*

## AN ACKNOWLEDGMENT

The author wishes to express appreciation of generous assistance given in the preparation of this book by Dr. Herbert E. Bolton and Dr. A. L. Kroeber, of the University of California; Dr. John C. Merriam and Dr. C. Hart Merriam, Smithsonian Institution; and numerous correspondents throughout the state. Indebtedness is also acknowledged to the Bancroft Library at the University of California and to the many writers from whose works quotations have been freely used.

"NONE CAN CARE FOR LITERATURE IN ITSELF WHO DOES NOT TAKE A SPECIAL PLEASURE IN THE SOUND OF NAMES; AND THERE IS NO PART OF THE WORLD WHERE NOMENCLATURE IS SO RICH, POETICAL, HUMOROUS, AND PICTURESQUE AS THE UNITED STATES OF AMERICA. . . . THE NAMES OF THE STATES AND TERRITORIES THEMSELVES FORM A CHORUS OF SWEET AND MOST ROMANTIC VOCABLES; . . . THERE ARE FEW POEMS WITH A NOBLER MUSIC FOR THE EAR; A SONG-FUL, TUNEFUL LAND; AND IF THE NEW HOMER SHALL ARISE FROM THE WESTERN CONTINENT, HIS VERSE WILL BE ENRICHED, HIS PAGES SING SPONTANEOUSLY, WITH THE NAMES OF STATES AND CITIES THAT WOULD STRIKE THE FANCY IN A BUSINESS CIRCULAR."

ROBERT LOUIS STEVENSON.

# PLACE NAMES OF CALIFORNIA

## TABLE OF CONTENTS

PLACE NAMES OF CALIFORNIA

THEIR MEANING AND ROMANCE

## LIST OF ILLUSTRATIONS

# PLACE NAMES OF CALIFORNIA

# SPANISH AND INDIAN PLACE NAMES
## OF CALIFORNIA

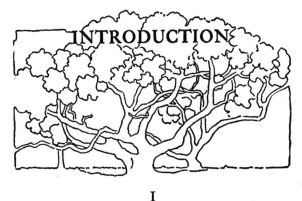

# INTRODUCTION

## I

This volume has been prepared in the hope that it may serve, not only as a source of entertainment to our own people, but also as a useful handbook for the schools, and as a sort of tourist's guide for those who visit the state in such numbers, and who almost invariably exhibit a lively interest in our Spanish and Indian place names.

We of California are doubly rich in the matter of names, since, in addition to the Indian nomenclature common to all the states, we possess the splendid heritage left us by those bold adventurers from Castile who first set foot upon our shores. Nor let it be thought that these Spanish pioneers were mere rough sailors, without culture or education. Spain sent out her best as missionaries, such men as Serra, Palou, Lasuén, Durán, and, in fact, all that devoted band who left home and a promising future to come to

1

darkest America to save the souls of the heathen. Francisco Palou wrote the first book ever written in California, entitling him to be regarded as the father of all our literature. As for the Indians, the place names in their language are the only heritage left by that unfortunate race to show that they were the original owners of the land, and as such they should be preserved. In these names the spirit of our romantic past still lives and breathes, and their sound is like an echo coming down the years to tell of that other day when the savage built his beehive huts on the river-banks, and the Spanish caballero jingled his spurs along the Camino Real.

And in what manner, it may well be asked, have we been caring for this priceless heritage,— to keep it pure, to preserve its inspiring history, to present it in proper and authentic form for the instruction and entertainment of "the stranger within our gates," as well as for the education of our own youth? As the most convincing answer to this question, some of the numerous errors in works purporting to deal with this subject, many of which have even crept into histories and books for the use of schools, will be corrected in these pages.

In the belief that the Spanish and Indian names possess the greatest interest for the public, both "tenderfoot" and native, they will be

dealt with here almost exclusively, excepting a very few of American origin, whose stories are so involved with the others that they can scarcely be omitted. In addition, there are a number that appear to be of Anglo-Saxon parentage, but are in reality to be counted among those that have suffered the regrettable fate of translation into English from the original Spanish. Of such are Kings County and River, which took their names from *El Río de los Santos Reyes* (the River of the Holy Kings), and the Feather River, originally *El Río de las Plumas* (the River of the Feathers).

In the search for the beginnings of these names through the diaries of the early Spanish explorers and other sources, a number of curious stories have been encountered, which are shared with the reader in the belief that he will be glad to know something of the romance lying behind the nomenclature of our "songful, tuneful" land.

It is a matter of deep regret that the work must of necessity be incomplete, the sources of information being so scattered, and so often unreliable, that it has been found impossible to trace all the names to their origin.

Indian words are especially difficult; in fact, as soon as we enter that field we step into the misty land of legend, where all becomes doubt and uncertainty. That such should be the case is inevitable. Scientific study of the native Cali-

3

fornian languages, of which there were so many as to constitute a veritable Babel of tongues among the multitude of small tribes inhabiting this region, was begun in such recent times that but few aborigines were left to tell the story of their names, and those few retained but a dim memory of the old days. In view of the unsatisfactory nature of this information, stories of Indian origin will be told here with the express qualification that their authenticity is not vouched for, except in cases based upon scientific evidence. Some of the most romantic among them, when put to the final test of such investigation, melt into thin air. In a general way, it may be said that Indian names were usually derived from villages, rather than tribes, and that, in most cases, their meaning has been lost. As for pronunciation, since there are no fixed rules for Indian names, and they do not always follow the Spanish rules, it will not be attempted in this book except in well-known cases.

In the case of Spanish names, we have a rich mine in the documents left behind by the methodical Spaniards, who maintained the praiseworthy custom of keeping minute accounts of their travels and all circumstances connected therewith. From these sources the true stories of the origin of some of our place names have been collected, and are retold in these pages, as

4

far as possible, in the language of their founders. Unfortunately, the story can not always be run to earth, and in such cases, the names, with their translation, and sometimes an explanatory paragraph, will appear in a supplementary list at the end of the volume. The stories have been arranged in a series of groups, according to their geographical location, beginning with San Diego as the most logical point, since it was there that the first mission was established by the illustrious Junipero Serra, and there that the history of California practically began. The arrangement of these groups is not arbitrary, but, in a general way, follows the course of Spanish Empire, as it took its way, first up the coast, then branching out into the interior valley, and climbing the Sierra.

Some of the stories may appear as "twice-told tales" to scholars and other persons to whom they have long been familiar, but are included here for the benefit of the stranger and the many "native sons" who have had no opportunity to become acquainted with them.

A few words in regard to the methods of naming places customary among the Spanish explorers may help the reader to a better understanding of results. The military and religious members of the parties were naturally influenced by opposite ideas, and so they went at it

in two different ways. The padres, as a matter of course, almost invariably chose names of a religious character, very often the name of the saint upon whose "day" the party happened to arrive at a given spot. This tendency resulted in the multitude of *Sans* and *Santas* with which the map of our state is so generously sprinkled, and which are the cause of a certain monotony. Fortunately for variety's sake, the soldiers possessed more imagination, if less religion, than the padres, and were generally influenced by some striking circumstance, perhaps trivial or humorous, but always characteristic, and often picturesque. In many cases the choice of the soldiers has out-lived that of the fathers.

Broadly speaking, it may be said that names were first applied to rivers, creeks or mountains, as being those natural features of the country most important to the welfare, or even the very existence, of the exploring parties. For instance, the *Merced* (Mercy) River was so called because it was the first running water encountered by the party after having traversed forty miles of the hot, dry valley. Then, as time passed and the country developed, towns were built upon the banks of these streams, frequently receiving the same names, and these were often finally adopted to designate the counties established later in the regions through which their waters

flow. In this way Plumas County derived its name from the Feather River, originally *El Río de las Plumas,* and Kings County from *El Río de los Reyes* (the River of the Kings). This way of naming was, however, not invariable.

It sometimes happens that the name has disappeared from the map, while the story remains, and some such stories will be told, partly for their own interest, and partly for the light they throw upon a past age.

Of street names of Spanish and Indian origin there is such a multitude that their story would make another book. Hence only a few of the most important will be mentioned in the Final Index.

The frequent repetition of the same names in different parts of the state has made it impracticable to locate them all geographically, but the definition in one case usually applies to all bearing the same name, although the circumstances of the naming may be different.

Among our Spanish names there is a certain class given to places in modern times by Americans in a praiseworthy attempt to preserve the romantic flavor of the old days. Unfortunately, an insufficient knowledge of the syntax and etymology of the Spanish language has resulted in some improper combinations. Such names, for instance, as *Monte Vista* (Mountain or Forest

7

View), *Loma Vista* (Hill View), *Río Vista* (River
View), etc., grate upon the ears of a Spaniard,
who would never combine two nouns in this
way. The correct forms for these names would
be *Vista del Monte* (View of the Mountain),
*Vista de la Loma* (View of the Hill), *Vista del
Río* (View of the River), etc. Between this class
of modern Spanish names, more or less faulty
in construction, given by "Spaniards from Kan-
sas," as has been humorously said, and the real
old names of the Spanish epoch about which a
genuine halo of romance still clings, there is an
immense gulf. Yet, notwithstanding that these
modern names are lacking in historical interest,
some of the most important are included for the
benefit of tourists and others who may wish to
know their meaning.

In the numerous quotations used in this book,
the language of the original has generally been
retained, with no attempt to change the form of
expression. In spite of the most conscientious
efforts to avoid them, unreliability of sources,
particularly through the well-meant but often
untrustworthy accounts of old residents, may
cause some errors to find their way into these
pages; for these the author hopes not to be held
responsible.

## II

First comes the name of *California* herself, the *sin par* (peerless one), as Don Quixote says of his Dulcinea. This name, strange to say, was a matter of confusion and conjecture for many years, until, in 1862, Edward Everett Hale accidentally hit upon the explanation since accepted by historians.

Several theories, all more or less fanciful and far-fetched, were based upon the supposed construction of the word from the Latin *calida fornax* (hot oven), in reference either to the hot, dry climate of Lower California, or to the "sweat-houses" in use among the Indians. Such theories not only presupposed a knowledge of Latin not likely to exist among the hardy men who first landed upon our western shores but also indicate a labored method of naming places quite contrary to their custom of seizing upon some direct and obvious circumstance upon

which to base their choice. In all the length and breadth of California few, if any, instances exist where the Spaniards invented a name produced from the Latin or Greek in this far-fetched way. They saw a big bird, so they named the river where they saw it *El Río del Pájaro* (the River of the Bird), or they suffered from starvation in a certain canyon, so they called it *La Cañada del Hambre* (the Canyon of Hunger), or they reached a place on a certain saint's day, and so they named it for that saint. They were practical men and their methods were simple.

In any case, since Mr. Hale has provided us with a more reasonable explanation, all such theories may be passed over as unworthy of consideration. While engaged in the study of Spanish literature, he was fortunate enough to run across a copy of an old novel, published in Toledo sometime between 1510 and 1521, in which the word *California* occurred as the name of a fabulous island, rich in minerals and precious stones, and said to be the home of a tribe of Amazons. This novel, entitled *Las Sergas de Esplandián* (The Adventures of Esplandián), was written by the author, García Ordóñez de Montalvo, as a sequel to the famous novel of chivalry, *Amadís of Gaul,* of which he was the translator. The two works were printed in the same volume. Montalvo's romance, although of

10

small literary value, had a considerable vogue among Spanish readers of the day, and that its pages were probably familiar to the early explorers in America is proved by the fact that Bernal Díaz, one of the companions of Cortés, often mentions the Amadís, to which the story of Esplandián was attached. The passage containing the name that has since become famous in all the high-ways and by-ways of the world runs as follows: "Know that on the right hand of the Indies there is an island called *California*, very near to the terrestrial paradise, which was peopled by black women, without any men among them, for they were accustomed to live after the manner of Amazons. They were of strong and hardened bodies, of ardent courage and of great force. The island was the strongest in the world, from its steep rocks and great cliffs. Their arms were all of gold and so were the caparisons of the wild beasts they rode."

It was during the period when this novel was at the height of its popularity that Cortés wrote to the King of Spain concerning information he had of "an island of Amazons, or women only, abounding in pearls and gold, lying ten days journey from Colima." After having sent one expedition to explore the unknown waters in that direction, in the winter of 1533, an expedition that ended in disaster, he went himself and

11

planted a colony at a point, probably La Paz, on the coast of Lower California. In his diary of this expedition, Bernal Díaz speaks of California as a "bay," and it is probable that the name was first applied to some definite point on the coast, afterward becoming the designation of the whole region. The name also occurs in Preciado's diary of Ulloa's voyage down the coast in 1539, making it reasonable to suppose that it was adopted in the period between 1533 and 1539, whether by Cortés or some other person can not be ascertained.

Dr. Chapman, in his *History of California*, asserts his belief that the name was applied by Fortún Jiménez on the occasion of his discovery of the peninsula in 1533-1534.

Bancroft expresses the opinion that the followers of Cortés may have used the name in derision, to express their disappointment in finding a desert, barren land in lieu of the rich country of their expectation, but it seems far more in keeping with the sanguine nature of the Spaniards that their imaginations should lead them to draw a parallel between the rich island of the novel, with its treasures of gold and silver, and the new land, of whose wealth in pearls and precious metals some positive proof, as well as many exaggerated tales, had reached them.

An argument that seems to clinch the matter

12

of the origin of the name is the extreme improbability that two different persons, on opposite sides of the world, should have invented exactly the same word, at about the same period, especially such an unusual one as *California.*

As for the etymology of the word itself, it is as yet an unsolved problem. The suggestion that it is compounded of the Greek root *kali* (beautiful), and the Latin *fornix* (vaulted arch), thus making its definition "beautiful sky," may be the true explanation, but even if that be so, Cortés or his followers took it at second hand from Montalvo and were not its original inventors.

Professor George Davidson, in a monograph on the *Origin and the Meaning of the Name California,* states that incidental mention had been made as early as 1849 of the name as occurring in Montalvo's novel by George Ticknor, in his *History of Spanish Literature,* but Mr. Tickner refers to it simply as literature, without any thought of connecting it with the name of the state. This connection was undoubtedly first thought of by Mr. Hale and was discussed in his paper read before the Historical Society of Massachusetts in 1862; therefore the honor of the discovery of the origin of the state's name must in justice be awarded to him. Professor Davidson, in an elaborate discussion of the possible etymology of the word, expresses the

opinion that it may be a combination of two Greek words, *kallos* (beauty) and *ornis* (bird), in reference to the following passage in the book: "In this island are many griffins, which can be found in no other part of the world." Its etymology, however, is a matter for further investigation. The one fact that seems certain is its origin in the name of the fabulous island of the novel.

A curious discovery has recently been made of the occurrence of the name Califerne, referring to an unknown heathen country, in *The Chanson de Roland,* the famous epic poem commemorating the exploits of the legendary hero Roland in the wars conducted by Charlemagne. This poem is very ancient, the first mention of it occurring in 1066, and, considering Montalvo's predilection for works of chivalry, it is possible that he read this song, that his fancy was attracted by the name Califerne, and that, with a change in the spelling to make it more euphonious and more Spanish in form, he adopted it for his mythical island of pearls and gold. There is no positive evidence, however, that the two words, California and Califerne, are identical, and the resemblance may be purely accidental.

A new link in the chain of evidence has recently been uncovered by a French investigator

which possibly connects the name of *Califerne,*
as used in the *Chanson,* with the designation of
a great fortified city actually existing in Northern Africa in ancient times—*kalaa-iferne.* This
would reveal the source from which the name
originally came—so ancient that the city bearing
it was supposed to have been built by a race of
giants.

It is hoped that researches now going on in
Spain under the auspices of the Native Sons of
the Golden West may at some future time clear
up this whole subject. Recent investigations by
Henry Raut Wagner lead him to believe the
name may have been first applied by an expedition to the peninsula in 1541 or 1542 under command of Francisco de Bolaños. In the meantime
it may well suffice for the fortunate heritors of
the splendid principality now known as *California* that this charming name became affixed to it
permanently, rather than the less "tuneful" one
of *New Albion,* which Sir Francis Drake applied
to it, and under which cognomen it appears on
some English maps of the date.

## EL MAR PACIFICO

### (The Peaceful Sea)

Though the great sea which washes her long shore from end to end can scarcely be called a part of California, yet the two are so inseparably connected that as well may one speak of David without Jonathan, of Damon without Pythias, as of California without her age-old companion, the Pacific Ocean.

On that memorable day, September 26, 1513, when Balboa gazed in triumph across the glittering expanse of heaving waters spread out before him, he called it the South Sea, for, from his stand on the isthmus, it lay to the south of him. Moreover, as the Spaniards had called the Atlantic Ocean the North Sea because it washed the northern shore of the Isthmus of Panamá, it was natural to call the ocean bathing the southern shore the South Sea. And so it was known until seven years later, when the Portuguese navigator, Fernao de Magalhaes (Magellan), made his famous passage through the strait which now bears his name. Magellan, a Portuguese of noble family, who had quarreled with the King of Portugal, entered the service of the King of Spain, and the voyage upon which he set

16

MISSION OF SAN ANTONIO DE PALA, FOUNDED IN 1816

"Many a romantic tale has been told about the 'bells of Pala.'"

out with several ships in the year 1519 was undertaken with the express and particular purpose of finding a southern passage to the "spice islands," so that ships might make the return voyage from them without the necessity of unloading. That there was some vague knowledge of the existence of a strait connecting the two oceans previous to this time is believed by historians, but, so far as the records show, it is to Magellan that the credit for its actual passage is due. His own account of the voyage is unfortunately missing, but in his company there was a volunteer, one Antonio Pigafetta, a nobleman of Venice, who has left a detailed record of the entire journey around the world. After a long and tempestuous voyage, during which many troubles and vicissitudes were suffered, the fleet arrived opposite the Atlantic mouth of the strait, and Magellan judged, by the strong current rushing out of it, and the large number of skeletons of dead whales seen on the shore, that it led to the other sea. So great was his confidence that he gave orders for a festival of rejoicing on all the ships. Sailing through the strait, past lofty mountains laden with snow, of which Pigafetta says, "I think that there is not in the world a more beautiful country or better strait than this one," on the afternoon of November 28, 1520, they came

17

out into the other sea, where, he says: "We disembouched from the strait in order to enter the great sea, to which we later gave the name of Pacific." Further on he says: "During three months and twenty days we ran in an open sea for fully four thousand leagues. It was well named Pacific, for during this time we met with no storm." They suffered greatly, however, from the lack of fresh food and water, being reduced to living on old biscuit decayed to powder and full of grubs, and drinking water that was "yellow and stinking." They ate ox hides which they soaked four or five days in the sea and then "put them on the embers and so ate them." They also ate "the sawdust of wood, and rats, and, moreover, not enough of them were to be got." As a consequence of this wretched diet they became afflicted with scurvy, and suffered so much that nineteen of them died, besides a giant Patagonian whom they had on board. This was but part of the price paid by those brave adventurers who led the way to that magnificent body of water which has become the highway between East and West, and which, besides being the brightest jewel in California's crown of beauty, has been the means of pouring untold riches into her lap—the Pacific Ocean, so named by Magellan and his hardy companions. It is not to be forgotten, however, that Magellan

18

and his crew gained their experience of this great ocean in that part of it where storms are infrequent. Later navigators complained of the inappropriateness of the name when they found themselves lashed by the fury of the terrific tempests which sometimes rage across its vast surface in more northern latitudes. The Italian traveler, Gemelli Careri, who made the voyage from Manila to Acapulco in 1697-1698, said: "The Spaniards and other geographers have given this the name of the Pacific Sea . . . but it does not suit with its tempestuous and dreadful motion, for which it ought rather to be called the Restless."

## IN AND ABOUT SAN DIEGO

### III

Like many other places in California, *San Diego* has had more than one christening. The first was at the hands of Juan Rodríguez Cabrillo, who discovered the harbor in 1542, and named it *San Miguel* (St. Michael). Cabrillo was a Portuguese in the Spanish service, who was sent to explore the coast in 1542 by Viceroy Mendoza. "He sailed from Natividad with two vessels, made a careful survey, applied names that for the most part have not been retained, and described the coast somewhat accurately as far as Monterey. He discovered 'a land-locked and very good harbor,' probably San Diego, which he named San Miguel. 'The next day he sent a boat farther into the port, which was large. A very great gale blew from the west-southwest, and south-southwest, but the port being good, they felt nothing.' On the return from the north the party stopped at La Posesión,

where Cabrillo died on January third, from the effects of a fall and exposure. No traces of his last resting-place, almost certainly on San Miguel near Cuyler's harbor, have been found; and the drifting sands have perhaps made such a discovery doubtful. To this bold mariner, the first to discover her coasts, if to any one, California may with propriety erect a monument." —(Bancroft's *History of California*.)

Then, in 1602, came Sebastián Vizcaíno, who changed the name from San Miguel to San Diego. He was "sent to make the discovery and demarcation of the ports and bays of the Southern Sea (Pacific Ocean)," and to occupy for Spain the California isles, as they were then thought to be. From the diary of Vizcaíno's voyage we get the following account of his arrival at San Diego: "The next day, Sunday, the tenth of the said month (November), we arrived at a port, the best that there can be in all the Southern Sea, for, besides being guarded from all winds, and having a good bottom, it is in latitude 33½. It has very good water and wood, many fish of all sorts, of which we caught a great many with the net and hooks. There is good hunting of rabbits, hares, deer, and many large quail, ducks and other birds. On the twelfth of the said month, which was the day of the glorious San Diego, the admiral, the priests,

21

the officers, and almost all the people, went on shore. A hut was built, thus enabling the feast of the Señor San Diego to be celebrated."

A party sent out to get wood "saw upon a hill a band of 100 Indians, with bows and arrows, and many feathers upon their heads, and with a great shouting they called out to us." By a bestowal of presents, friendly relations were established. The account continues: "They had pots in which they cooked their food, and the Indian women were dressed in the skins of animals. The name of *San Diego* was given to this port." Thus, it was the bay that first received the name, years afterwards given to the mission, then to the town. During the stay of Vizcaino's party the Indians came often to their camp with marten skins and other articles. On November 20th, having taken on food and water, the party set sail, the Indians shouting a vociferous farewell from the beach *(quedaban en la playa, dando boces)*.

A long period of neglect of more than 160 years then ensued. The Indians continued to carry on their wretched hand-to-mouth existence, trapping wild beasts for their food and scanty clothing, fishing in the bountiful ocean, and keeping up their constant inter-tribal quarrels unmolested by the white man. Several generations grew up and passed away without a

22

MISSION OF SAN DIEGO DE ALCALA, FOUNDED IN 1769

"The first one of the chain of missions founded by the illustrious Junípero Serra."

reminder of the strange people who had once been seen upon their shores, except perhaps an occasional white sail of some Philippine galleon seen flitting like a ghost on its southward trip along the coast.

Then the Spaniards, alarmed by reports of the encroachments of the Russians on the north, waked up from their long sleep, and determined to establish a chain of missions along the California coast. Father Junípero Serra was appointed president of these missions, and the first one of the chain was founded by him at San Diego in 1769. The name was originally applied to the "Old Town," some distance from the present city. The founding party encountered great difficulties, partly through their fearful sufferings from scurvy, and partly from the turbulent and thievish nature of the Indians in that vicinity, with whom they had several lively fights, and who stole everything they could lay their hands on, even to the sheets from the beds of the sick. During one of these attacks, the mission buildings were burned and one of the padres, Fray Luís Jaime, suffered a cruel death, but all difficulties were finally overcome by the strong hand of Father Serra, and the mission was placed on a firm basis. Its partially ruined buildings still remain at a place about six miles from the present city.

23

To return to the matter of the name, the titular saint of this bay, and later of the mission and town, was the canonized Franciscan monk, San Diego de Alcalá. This mild and gentle saint was a humble lay brother in a monastery of Alcalá in Andalusia. He lived from 1400 to 1463, and was canonized rather for his pious life and the miracles wrought through him before and after his death than for any high position held by him. Through his intercession the Infante Don Carlos was healed of a severe wound. An interesting story of a miracle said to have been performed by this saint runs as follows: "In Seville a boy, fleeing from punishment at the hands of his mother, concealed himself inside of an oven and fell asleep there. The mother, not dreaming that the boy was in the oven, filled it with wood and lighted it. Awakened with the heat of the flames, he cried for help, but the fire was now raging and it was too late to save him. The afflicted mother, desperate with grief, ran into the streets shrieking like an insane person. Providence granted that San Diego should be passing at that moment. After consoling her and sending her to pray at the altar of Our Lady, he went with a great crowd and opened the oven. Wonder of wonders! Although the wood was almost all consumed, the boy came out safe and sound."

24

In the translation of the name itself—Diego—it is rather curious that although all dictionaries give it as James, ecclesiastics render San Diego as Saint Didacus. This saint was a lay brother of the Order of Friars Minor. He was chiefly noted for his care of the sick, and his biographers record the miraculous cure of many whom he attended. His feast day occurs on the 12th of November.

## CORONADO BEACH

The name of Coronado Beach, the long spit of land forming the outer shore of the harbor of San Diego, is said to have been suggested by the Coronado Islands near it. These islands were not, however, named in honor of the famous explorer, Francisco Vásquez de Coronado, as many have supposed, but for Los Quatro Martires Coronados (the four crowned martyrs), whose feast occurs on November 8th. The name finally took the shorter form of Coronados, and its resemblance to that of the great conquistador led to some confusion.

## SAN LUIS REY

*San Luís Rey de Francia* (St. Louis King of France), is the name of the mission situated in a charming little valley about forty miles north

of San Diego and three miles from the sea. It was founded June 13, 1798, by Padres Lasuén, Santiago and Peyri, and its ruins may still be seen upon the spot. A partial restoration has been made of these buildings and they are now used by the Franciscans. The exact circumstances of its naming have not come to light, but we know of its patron saint that his holiness was such that even Voltaire said of him: "It is scarcely given to man to push virtue further." Born at Poissy in 1215, the son of Louis VIII and Blanche of Castile, he became noted for his saintliness, and twice led an army of Crusaders in the "holy war."

## PALA

*Pala,* often misspelled *palo,* through an accidental resemblance to the Spanish word *palo* (stick or tree), is situated some fifteen miles or more to the northeast of San Luís Rey, and is the site of the sub-mission of San Antonio de Pala, founded in 1816 by Padre Peyri as a branch of San Luís Rey. This mission was unique in having a bell-tower built apart from the church, and many romantic stories have been told about the "bells of Pala." It was located in the center of a populous Indian community, and it happens, rather curiously, that the word itself has a significance both in Spanish and Indian, meaning in

26

Spanish "spade" and in Indian "water." The Reverend George Doyle, pastor at the mission of San Antonio de Pala, writes the following in regard to this name: "The word 'Pala' is an Indian word, meaning in the Cupanian Mission Indian language, 'water,' probably due to the fact that the San Luís Rey River passes through it. The proper title of the mission chapel here is San Antonio de Padua, but as there is another San Antonio de Padua mission chapel in the north, to distinguish between the two some one in the misty past changed the proper title of the Saint, and so we have 'de Pala' instead of 'de Padua.' Some writers say Pala is Spanish, but this is not true, for the little valley in no way resembles a spade, and the Palanian Indians were here long before the Franciscan padres brought civilization, Christianity and the Spanish language."

*Pala,* in this case, is almost certainly Indian, and originates in a legend of the Luiseños. According to this legend, one of the natives of the Temécula tribe went forth on his travels, stopping at many places and giving names to them. One of these places was a canyon, "where he drank water and called it *pala,* water."—*(The Religion of the Luiseño Indians,* by Constance Goddard Dubois, in the Univ. of Cal. Publ. of Arch. and Ethn.)

## SAN JUAN CAPISTRANO

*San Juan Capistrano* (St. John Capistrano), was at one time sadly mutilated by having its first part clipped off, appearing on the map as *Capistrano,* but upon representations made by Zoeth S. Eldredge it was restored to its full form by the Post Office Department. A mission was founded at this place, which is near the coast about half way between San Diego and Los Angeles, by Padres Serra and Amurrio, November 1, 1776, the year of our own glorious memory. While on the other side of the continent bloody war raged, under the sunny skies of California the gentle padres were raising altars to the "Man of Peace."

The buildings at this place were badly wrecked by an earthquake on December 8, 1812, yet the ruins still remain to attest to the fact that this was at one time regarded as the finest of all the mission structures.

Its patron saint, St. John Capistrano, was a Franciscan friar who lived at the time of the crusades, and took part in them. A colossal statue of him adorns the exterior of the Cathedral at Vienna. It represents him as having a Turk under his feet, a standard in one hand, and a cross in the other.

## SUPPLEMENTARY LIST

There remain some names in the San Diego group of less importance, yet possessing many points of interest, which will be included in the following list, with an explanation of their meanings, and their history wherever it has been possible to ascertain it.

*Agua Tibia* (warm water, warm springs), is in San Diego County. For some reason difficult to divine, this perfectly simple name has been the cause of great confusion in the minds of a number of writers. In one case the almost incredibly absurd translation of "shinbone water" has been given. It may be thought that this was intended as a bit of humor, but it is greatly to be feared that the writer mixed up the Spanish word *tibia,* which simply means "tepid, warm," with the Latin name of one of the bones of the lower leg, the *tibia.* In another case the equally absurd translation "flute water" has been given. Where such a meaning could have been obtained is beyond comprehension to any person possessing even a slight knowledge of the Spanish language. *Agua Tibia* is no more nor less than "warm water," applied in this case to warm springs existing at that place. This extreme case is enlarged upon here as an example of the gross

29

errors that have been freely handed out to an unsuspecting public in the matter of our place names. There are many more of the same sort, and the authors of this inexcusable stuff have been accepted and even quoted as authorities on the subject. Those of us who love our California, in other words all of us, can not fail to be pained by such a degradation of her romantic history.

*Ballena* (whale) is in San Diego County at the west end of Ballena Valley, and as it is a good many miles inland its name seems incongruous, until we learn from one of its residents that it was so called in reference to a mountain in the valley whose outline along the top is exactly the shape of a humpbacked whale.

"This place has probably no connection with Ballenas, a name applied to a bay in Lower California on account of its being a favorite resort of the Humpback whale."—(Mr. Charles B. Turrill.)

*Berenda,* in Merced County, is a misspelling of Berrendo or Berrenda.

*Berrendo* (antelope). A writer whose knowledge of Spanish seems to be wholly a matter of the dictionary, confused by the fact that the definition given for *berrendo* is "having two colors," has offered the fantastic translation of *El Río de los Berrendos* as "The River of the two Colors." Although the idea of such a river, like

a piece of changeable silk, may be picturesque, the simple truth is that the word berrendo, although not so defined in the dictionaries, is used in Spanish America to signify a deer of the antelope variety and frequently occurs in that sense in the diaries. Miguel Costansó, an engineer accompanying the Portolá expedition of 1769, says: *"Hay en la tierra venados, verrendos* (also spelled *berrendos), muchos liebres, conejos, gatos monteses y ratas* (there are in the land deer, antelope, many hares, rabbits, wild-cats and rats)."* On August 4th this party reached a place forty leagues from San Diego which they called *Berrendo* because they caught alive a deer which had been shot the day before by the soldiers and had a broken leg. Antelope Creek, in Tehama County, was originally named *El Río de los Berrendos* (The River of the Antelopes), undoubtedly because it was a drinking place frequented by those graceful creatures, and Antelope Valley, in the central part of the state, must have received its name in the same way.

*El Cajón* (the box), about twelve miles northeast of San Diego, perhaps received its name from a custom the Spaniards had of calling a deep canyon with high, box-like walls, *un cajón* (a box).

*Caliente Creek* (hot creek) is in the northern part of San Diego County.

31

*Campo* (a level field), also sometimes used in the sense of a camp, is the name of a place about forty miles east-southeast of San Diego, just above the Mexican border. *Campo* was an Indian settlement, and may have been so called by the Spaniards simply in reference to the camp of Indians.

*Cañada del Bautismo* (glen of the baptism), so called from the circumstance that two dying native children were there baptised by the padres, as told in the diary of Miguel Costansó, of the Portolá expedition in 1769. Death, when it came to the children of the natives, was often regarded as cause for rejoicing by the missionaries, not, of course, through any lack of humanity on their part, but because the Indian parents more readily consented to baptism at such a time, and the padres regarded these as so many souls "snatched from the burning."

*Carriso* (reed grass) is the name of a village and creek in San Diego County. The grass called carriso is a sort of cane, and, like the cane, it contains a certain amount of sugar in the sap of its stem. This had been discovered by the Indians before the coming of the whites, and from this sap they manufactured a sort of sugar which they traded to the Mexicans for other articles.

*Chula Vista* (pretty view) is the name of a

ARCHWAY AT CAPISTRANO
"At one time regarded as the finest of all the mission structures."

town near the coast, a few miles southeast of San Diego. *Chula* is a word of Mexican origin, meaning pretty, graceful, attractive. "This name was probably first used by the promoters during the boom of 1887."

*La Costa* (the coast), a place on the shore north of San Diego.

*Coyote Valley,* situated just below the southern border of the San Jacinto Forest Reservation. *Coyote,* the name of the wolf of Western America, is an Aztec word, originally *coyotl.*

*Cuyamaca* is probably derived from the land grant of that name, which in turn took its name from the Cuyamaca Mountain, which, according to the scientists, was so called in reference to the clouds and rain gathering around its summit. Mr. T. T. Waterman, instructor in Anthropology at the University of California, says the word is derived from two Indian words, *kwe* (rain) and *amak* (yonder), and consequently means "rain yonder." The popular translation of it as "woman's breast" is probably not based on fact. There was an Indian village of that name some miles northwest of San Diego.

*Descanso* (rest) is the name of a place northeast of San Diego, so called by a government surveying party for the reason that they stopped here each day for rest.

*Dulzura* (sweetness) is the name of a place

33

but a few miles north of the Mexican border line. What there was of "sweetness" in the history of this desolate mining camp can not be discovered.

*Encinitas* (little oaks) is a place on the coast about twenty miles northwest of San Diego.

*Escondido* (hidden), a place lying about fifteen miles from the coast, to the northeast of San Diego. It is said to have been so named on account of its location in the valley. A place at another point was called *Escondido* by the Spaniards because of the difficulty they experienced in finding the water for which they were anxiously searching, and it may be that in this case the origin of the name was the same.

*La Jolla,* a word of doubtful origin, said by some persons to mean a "pool," by others to be from *hoya,* a hollow surrounded by hills, and by still others to be a possible corruption of *joya,* a "jewel." The suggestion has been made that La Jolla was named from caves situated there which contain pools, but until some further information turns up this name must remain among the unsolved problems. There is always the possibility also that *La Jolla* means none of these things but is a corruption of some Indian word with a totally different meaning. More than one place in the state masquerades under an apparently Spanish name which is in

reality an Indian word corrupted into some Spanish word to which it bore an accidental resemblance in sound. *Cortina* (curtain) is an example of this sort of corruption, it being derived from the Indian *Ko-tina*.

*Laguna del Corral* (lagoon of the yard). *Corral* is a word much in use to signify a space of ground enclosed by a fence, often for the detention of animals. In one of the diaries an Indian corral is thus spoken of: "Near the place in which we camped there was a populous Indian village; the inhabitants lived without other protection than a light shelter of branches in the form of an enclosure; for this reason the soldiers gave to the whole place the name of the *Rancheria del Corral* (the village of the yard)." There are other *corrals* and *corralitos* (little yards) in the state.

*Linda Vista* (charming or pretty view) is the name of a place ten or twelve miles due north of San Diego.

*Point Loma* (hill point). *Loma* means "hill," hence Point Loma, the very end of the little peninsula enclosing San Diego bay, is a high promontory.

*De Luz* (a surname), that of a pioneer family. The literal meaning of the word *luz* is "light.

*Del Mar* (of or on the sea), the name of a

35

place on the shore about eighteen miles north of San Diego.

*La Mesa* (literally "the table"), used very commonly to mean a "high, flat table-land." *La Mesa,* incorrectly printed on some of the maps as one word, *Lamesa,* lies a few miles to the northeast of San Diego.

*Mesa Grande* (literally "big table"), big table-land, is some distance to the northeast of San Diego.

*El Nido* (the nest), is southeast of San Diego, near the border.

*Potrero* (pasture ground), is just above the border line. There are many *Potreros* scattered over the state.

*La Presa* (the dam or dike). *La Presa* is a few miles east of San Diego, on the Sweetwater River, no doubt called *Agua Dulce* by the Spaniards.

*Los Rosales* (the rose-bushes), a spot located in the narratives of the Spaniards at about seventeen leagues from San Diego, and two leagues from Santa Margarita. Nothing in the new land brought to the explorers sweeter memories of their distant home than "the roses of Castile" which grew so luxuriantly along their pathway as to bring forth frequent expressions of delight from the padres. This particular place we find mentioned in the diary of Miguel Cos-

MISSION OF SAN GABRIEL ARCANGEL, FOUNDED IN 1771, SHOWING INDIAN HUTS IN THE FOREGROUND

"Its flocks and herds once covered the country for many miles around."

tansó, as follows: "We gave it the name of *Cañada de los Rosales* (glen of the rose-bushes), on account of the great number of rose-bushes we saw."

*Temécula,* the name of a once important Indian village in the Temécula Valley, about thirty-five miles south of Riverside. Its inhabitants suffered the usual fate of the native when the white man discovers the value of the land, and were compelled to leave their valley in 1875, and remove to Pichanga Canyon, in a desert region.

*Tijuana,* a place on the border between California and Mexico, whose chief claim to fame, or notoriety, is the opportunity that it offers for gambling and other sorts of dissipation to persons who find things too tame on the northern side of the line. The name, variously spelled Tiwana, Tijuana, and Tiguana, is Indian in origin, its meaning unknown. It has been said to mean "by the sea," but this theory has not been verified. For years the name was corrupted into Tia Juana, Spanish for "Aunt Jane," but it has finally been restored to its original Indian form.

# LOS ANGELES AND HER NEIGHBORS

## IV

*Los Angeles* (the angels). In the diary of Miguel Costansó, date of August 2, 1769, we read: "To the north-northeast one could see another watercourse or river bed, which formed a wide ravine, but it was dry. This watercourse joined that of the river, and gave clear indications of heavy floods during the rainy season, as it had many branches of trees and debris on its sides. We halted at this place, which was named *La Porciúncula*. Here we felt three successive earthquakes during the afternoon and night."

This was the stream upon which the city of Los Angeles was subsequently built and whose name became a part of her title. Porciúncula was the name of a deserted chapel near Assisi which became the abode of St. Francis de Assisi after the Benedictine monks had presented him, about 1211, with the little chapel which he

called, in a pleasant way, *La Porciúncula* (the small portion). By order of Pius V, in 1556 the erection of a new edifice over the Porciúncula chapel was begun. Under the bay of the choir is still preserved the cell in which St. Francis died, while a little behind the sacristy is the spot where the saint, during a temptation, is said to have rolled in a brier-bush, which was then changed into thornless roses.—(Catholic Encyclopedia.) In this story there is a curious interweaving of the history of the names of our two rival cities, San Francisco in the north and Los Angeles de Porciúncula in the south.

Continuing their journey on the following day, the Portolá party reached the Indian ranchería (village) of *Yangna,* the site chosen for the pueblo established at a later date. Father Crespi writes of it thus: "We followed the road to the west, and the good pasture land followed us; at about half a league of travel we encountered the village of this part; on seeing us they came out on the road, and when we drew near they began to howl, as though they were wolves; we saluted them, they wished to give us some seeds, and as we had nothing at hand in which to carry them, we did not accept them; seeing this, they threw some handfuls on the ground and the rest in the air."

August 2d being the feast day of *Nuestra*

*Señora de los Angeles,* as the Virgin Mary is often called by the Spaniards, this name was given to the place.

The actual founding of the pueblo did not occur until September 4, 1781, when Governor Neve issued the order for its establishment upon the site of the Indian village Yangna. It is said that the Porciúncula River, henceforth to be known as the Los Angeles, at that time ran to the east of its present course. The name of the little stream was added to that of the pueblo, so that the true, complete title of the splendid city which has grown up on the spot where the Indian once raised his wolf-like howl is *Nuestra Señora la Reina de los Angeles de Porciúncula* (Our Lady the Queen of the Angels of Porciúncula).

The social beginnings of Los Angeles were humble indeed, the first settlers being persons of mixed race, and the first houses mere hovels, made of adobe, with flat roofs covered with asphalt from the springs west of the town.

## EL RANCHO LA BREA

*La Brea* (the asphalt) has been retained as the appropriate designation of the ranch containing the famous asphaltum beds near Los Angeles. Ever since the days of the Tertiary

Age, the quaking, sticky surface of these beds has acted as a "death trap" for unwary animals, and the remains of the unfortunate creatures have been securely preserved down to our times, furnishing indisputable evidence of the strange life that once existed on our shores. Fossils of a large number of pre-historic and later animals have been taken out, aggregating nearly a million specimens of bird and animal life, many of them hitherto unknown to science. Among them are the saber-tooth tiger, gigantic wolves, bears, horses, bison, deer, an extinct species of coyote, camels, elephants, and giant sloths. Remains are also found of mice, rabbits, squirrels, several species of insects, and a large number of birds, such as ducks, geese, pelicans, eagles and condors.

Among the most remarkable of these fossils are the saber-tooth tiger and the great wolf. Specimens of the wolf have been found which are among the largest known in either living or extinct species. This wolf differs from existing species in having a larger and heavier skull and jaws, and in its massive teeth, a conformation that must have given it great crushing power. The structure of the skeleton shows it to have been probably less swift, but more powerful than the modern wolf, and the great number of bones found indicate that it was exceedingly

common in that age. One bed of bones was uncovered in which the number of saber-tooth and wolf skulls together averaged twenty per cubic yard. Altogether, the disappearance of these great, ferocious beasts from the California forests need cause no keen regret.

Next to the large wolf the most common is the saber-tooth tiger, of which one complete skeleton and a large number of bones have been found. The skeleton shows the animal to have been of about the size of a large African lion, and its most remarkable characteristic was the extraordinary length of the upper canine teeth, which were like long, thin sabers, with finely serrated edges. These teeth were awkwardly placed for ordinary use, and it is thought by scientists that they were used for a downward stab through the thick necks of bulky creatures, such as the giant sloth. There is also an unusual development of the claws, possibly to make up for the loss of grasping power in the jaws, resulting from the interference of the long saber teeth. It appears from the state of many of the fossils that these teeth were peculiarly liable to fracture, and accidents of this sort may have led to the extinction of the species, the animal thus perishing through the over-development of one of its characteristics.

Fossils of the extinct horse and bison are com-

mon and a smaller number are found of camels, deer, goats, and the mammoth. The bison were heavy-horned and somewhat larger than the existing species of buffalo. The camel, of which an almost complete specimen has very recently been taken out by Professor R. C. Stoner, of the University of California, was much larger than the present day species. Since the above was put in type, a human skeleton has been taken from the vicinity of the La Brea bed. Whether this skeleton belongs with the La Brea deposits, and what its comparative age in relation to other human remains may be, are matters now being investigated by scientists.

The preponderance of meat-eating animals in the La Brea beds has attracted the attention of scientists, who believe that these creatures were lured to the spot in large numbers by the struggles and cries of their unfortunate prey caught in the sticky mass of the tar. In this way, a single sloth or other creature may have been the means of bringing retribution upon a whole pack of wolves. — (Notes taken from an article in the Sunset Magazine of October, 1908, entitled *The Death Trap of the Ages,* by John C. Merriam, Professor of Paleontology in the University of California.)

The manner in which this great aggregation of animals came to a tragic end in that long-

past age is exemplified in the way that birds and other small animals are still occasionally caught in the treacherous asphalt and there perish miserably, adding their bones to those of their unhappy predecessors.

The La Brea beds furnish one of the richest fields for paleontological research to be found anywhere in the world and it may be said, that with her great Sequoias in the north, and her reservoir of pre-historic remains in the south, California stands as a link between a past age and the present.

The tarry deposit itself has its own place in history, for it appears that the first settlers of Los Angeles were alive to the practical value of this supply of asphaltum lying ready to their hands, and used it in roofing their houses. Even the Indians, little as is the credit usually given them for skill in the arts and crafts, recognized the possibilities of this peculiar substance, and used it in calking their canoes.

## LOS OJITOS

The story of *Los Ojitos* (literally "little eyes"), but here used in the sense of "little springs," situated about two leagues from Santa Ana, indicates that the pleasures of social intercourse were not altogether lacking among the Califor-

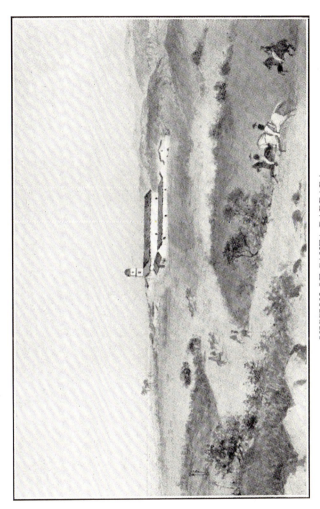

MISSION OF SANTA BARBARA

" * * * its broad steps are deeply worn by the feet of many generations of worshipers."

nia Indians. In the diary of Miguel Costansó, of
the date of their arrival at this place, he writes:
"We found no water for the animals, but there
was sufficient for the people in some little
springs or small pools, in a narrow canyon close
to a native village. The Indians of this village
were holding a feast and dance, to which they
had invited their relatives of the *Río de los
Temblores* (River of the Earthquakes, or Santa
Ana)." During this time the travelers experienced a series of earthquakes lasting several days.

*Ojo de agua* was commonly used by the Spaniards to mean a spring, but during the eighteenth
century it was frequently used in America in the
sense of a small stream of water rather than a
spring.

## SANTA ANA

On the day, Friday, July 28, 1769, of the arrival
of the Portolá expedition at the stream now
called the *Santa Ana,* which takes its rise in the
San Bernardino Mountains, and empties into the
ocean at a point southeast of Los Angeles, four
severe earthquakes occurred. Speaking of this
circumstance in his diary, Father Crespi says:
"To this spot was given *El Dulce Nombre de
Jesús de los Temblores* (The Sweet Name of
Jesus of the Earthquakes), because of having
experienced here a frightful earthquake, which

was repeated four times during the day. The first, which was the most violent, happened at one o'clock of the afternoon, and the last about four o'clock. One of the *gentiles* (unbaptized Indians), who happened to be in the camp, and who, without doubt, exercised among them the office of priest, no less terrified at the event than we, began, with horrible cries and great demonstrations, to entreat Heaven, turning to all points of the compass. This river is known to the soldiers as the *Santa Ana*." This was one of the rare cases where the usual method of naming was reversed, and the soldiers chose the name of the saint. St. Anna was the mother of the Virgin and her name signifies "gracious."

In the diary of Father Font, companion of Captain Anza in his second expedition, this reference occurs: "The river of Santa Ana was so called because the expedition under Commander Portolá reached it on the day of Santa Ana, and he gave it this name."

In the account of Captain Pedro Fages, of the same expedition, the natives on this stream are described as having light complexions and hair, and a good appearance, differing in these particulars from the other inhabitants of that region, who were said to be dark, dirty, undersized and slovenly. This is not the only occasion when the Spaniards reported finding Indians of light com-

46

plexions and hair in California. One account speaks of a red-haired tribe not far north of San Francisco, and still another of "white Indians" at Monterey, but, judging by the light of our subsequent knowledge of these aborigines, the writers of these reports must have indulged in exaggeration.

On the southern bank of the Santa Ana, not far from the coast, is the town of the same name, and further inland its waters have made to bloom in the desert the famous orange orchards of Riverside.

## SANTA MONICA

*Santa Mónica,* situated at the innermost point of the great curve in the coast line just west of Los Angeles, was named in honor of a saintly lady whose story is here quoted from Clara Erskine Clement's *Stories of the Saints:* "She was the mother of St. Augustine, and was a Christian, while his father was a heathen. Mónica was sorely troubled at the dissipated life of her young son; she wept and prayed for him, and at last sought the advice and aid of the Bishop of Carthage, who dismissed her with these words, 'Go in peace; the son of so many tears will not perish.' At length she had the joy of beholding the baptism of St. Augustine by the Bishop of Milan."

47

Santa Mónica is venerated as the great patroness of the Augustinian nuns, and might well be placed at the head of the world-wide order of "Anxious Mothers."

## SANTA CATALINA

*Santa Catalina,* the beautiful island off the coast of Southern California, was named by Vizcaíno in honor of St. Catherine, because its discovery occurred on the eve of her feast day, November 24, 1602. In the diary of the voyage we get an interesting description of the island and its aboriginal inhabitants: "We continued our journey along the coast until November 24, when, on the eve of the glorious Santa Catalina, we discovered three large islands; we took the one in the middle, which is more than twenty-five leagues in circumference, on November 27, and before dropping anchor in a good cove which was found, a great number of Indians came out in canoes of cedar-wood and pine, made of planking well joined and calked, and with eight oars each and fourteen or fifteen Indians, who looked like galley-slaves. They drew near and came on board our vessels without any fear whatever. We dropped anchor and went on shore. There were on the beach a great number of Indians, and the women received us

MISSION OF SANTA INEZ, FOUNDED IN 1804

"Its patron saint is St. Agnes, one of the four great virgin martyrs of the Latin Church."

with roasted sardines and a fruit cooked in the manner of sweet potatoes."

Mass was celebrated there in the presence of 150 Indians. The people were very friendly and the women led the white men by the hand into their houses. The diary continues: "These people go dressed in the skins of seals; the women are modest but thievish. The Indians received us with embraces and brought water in some very well-made jars, and in others like flasks, that were highly varnished on the outside. They have acorns and some very large skins with long wool . . . apparently of bears . . . which serve them for blankets."

The travelers found here an idol, "in the manner of the devil, without a head, but with two horns, a dog at the feet . . . and many children painted around it." The Indians readily gave up this idol and accepted the cross in its stead.

St. Catherine, patroness of this island, was one of the most notable female martyrs of the Roman Catholic church. We are told that she was of royal blood, being the daughter of a half-brother of Constantine the Great. She was converted to Christianity, and became noted for her unusual sanctity. She was both beautiful and intellectual, and possessed the gift of eloquence in such a high degree that she was able to confound fifty of the most learned men appointed

by Maximin to dispute matters of religion with her. The same Maximin, enraged by her refusal of his offers of love, ordered that she be tortured "by wheels flying in different directions, to tear her to pieces. When they had bound her to these, an angel came and consumed the wheels in fire, and the fragments flew around and killed the executioners and 3000 people. Maximin finally caused her to be beheaded, when angels came and bore her body to the top of Mt. Sinai. In the eighth century a monastery was built over her burial place."—*(Stories of the Saints.)* Santa Catalina is the patroness of education, science, philosophy, eloquence, and of all colleges, and her island has good reason to be satisfied with the name chosen by Vizcaíno.

## LAS ANIMAS BENDITAS

Of *Las Animas* (the souls), which lay between San Gabriel and the country of the Amajaba (Mohave) Indians, we find the story in Fray Joaquín Pascual Nuez's diary of the expedition made in 1819 by Lieutenant Gabriel Moraga, to punish the marauding Amajabas, who had murdered a number of Christian natives. This name was also used as the title of a land grant just south of Gilroy.

The Moraga party arrived at a point "about a

league and a half from Our Lady of Guadalupe of Guapiabit. We found the place where the Amajabas killed four Christians of this mission (San Gabriel), three from San Fernando, and some *gentiles* (unbaptized Indians). We found the skeletons and skulls roasted, and, at about a gun-shot from there we pitched camp. The next day, after mass, we caused the bones to be carried in procession, the cross in front, Padre Nuez chanting funeral services, to the spot where they had been burned. There we erected a cross, at the foot of which we caused the bones to be buried in a deep hole, and then we blessed the sepulchre. We named the spot *Las Animas Benditas* (The Blessed Souls)." May they rest in peace!

## SAN GABRIEL

*San Gabriel,* the quaint little town lying nine miles east of Los Angeles, is the site of the Mission *San Gabriel Arcángel* (St. Gabriel Archangel), founded September 8, 1771, by Padres Cambón and Somera. This mission was placed in a fertile, well-wooded spot, in the midst of a large Indian population, who, under the instruction of the padres, became experts in many arts, such as sewing, weaving, soap-making, cobbling, etc. Their flocks and herds increased to such an extent that they covered the country for many miles around.

51

The patron saint, San Gabriel, was the second in rank of the archangels who stand before the Lord. Whenever he is mentioned in the Bible, it is as a messenger bearing important tidings, and he is especially venerated as having carried to the Virgin the message that she was to become the mother of Christ.

San Gabriel (man of God) has a place in several religions. To the Israelites he was the angel of death; according to the Talmud he was the prince of fire and ruled the thunder. He set fire to the temple of Jerusalem; appeared to Daniel and Zacharias; announced to Mary the birth of Christ, and dictated the Koran to Mahomet. The last-named prophet describes him very fully, mentioning among other things 500 pairs of wings, the distance from one wing to another being 500 days journey. His day in the church calendar is March 18th.—(Hubert Howe Bancroft.)

Father Font says in his diary of the Anza expedition: "San Gabriel de los Temblores (Saint Gabriel of the earthquakes) was so called because the earth trembled on the day when they reached that spot."

## SAN FERNANDO

It was in the valley of *San Fernando* (St. Ferdinand), a short distance northwest of Los

MISSION OF SAN MIGUEL, FOUNDED IN 1797

"It once had its work-shops and little factories where good padres taught the Indians useful arts."

Angeles, that the mission pertaining to the latter place was established, September 8, 1797, by Padres Lasuén and Dumetz. The Camulos Rancho, the home of Ramona, the heroine of Mrs. Helen Hunt Jackson's romance, was once included in the lands of this mission.

St. Ferdinand, King of Spain, in whose honor this place was named, was a notable warrior, as well as a saint, and he succeeded in expelling the Moors from Toledo, Córdova and Seville. He is said also to have been a patron of the arts, and to have been the founder of the cathedral at Burgos, celebrated for the beauty of its architecture. But more than for such attainments, he is remembered for his tenderness toward the poor and lowly of his people. When urged to put a tax upon them in order to recruit his army, he replied: "God in whose cause I fight, will supply my need. I fear more the curse of one poor old woman than a whole army of Moors."—*(Stories of the Saints.)*

## TEMESCAL

*Temescal* (sweathouse), in Riverside County, although a place of no great importance in itself, is interesting in that its name recalls one of the curious customs widely prevalent among the natives of the Southwest. The word itself is of

Aztec origin, and was brought to California by the Franciscans.

The *temescal* is thus described by Dr. A. L. Kroeber, in the University of California Publications in Archaeology and Ethnology: "At the Banning Reservation a sweat-house is still in use. From the outside its appearance is that of a small mound. The ground has been excavated to the depth of a foot or a foot and a half, over a space of about twelve by seven or eight feet. In the center of this area two heavy posts are set up three or four feet apart. These are connected at the top by a log laid in their forks. Upon this log, and in the two forks, are laid some fifty or more logs and sticks of various dimensions, their ends sloping down to the edge of the excavation. It is probable that brush covers these timbers. The whole is thoroughly covered with earth. There is no smoke hole. The entrance is on one of the long sides, directly facing the space between the two center posts, and only a few feet from them. The fireplace is between the entrance and the posts. It is just possible to stand upright in the center of the house. In Northern California the so called sweat-house is of larger dimensions, and was pre-eminently a ceremonial or assembly chamber."

Dr. L. H. Bunnell, in his history of the discovery of the Yosemite Valley, gives us some

interesting details of the use of the sweat-house among the Indians of that region: "The remains of these structures were sometimes mistaken for *tumuli,* being constructed of bark, reeds or grass, covered with mud. It (the sweat-house) was used as a curative for disease, and as a convenience for cleansing the skin, when necessity demands it, although the Indian race is not noted for cleanliness. I have seen a half-dozen or more enter one of these rudely constructed sweat-houses through the small aperture left for the purpose. Hot stones are taken in, the aperture is closed until suffocation would seem impending, when they would crawl out, reeking with perspiration, and with a shout, spring like acrobats into the cold waters of the stream. As a remedial agent for disease, the same course is pursued, though varied at times by the burning and inhalation of resinous boughs and herbs. In the process of cleansing the skin from impurities, hot air alone is generally used. If an Indian had passed the usual period of mourning for a relative, and the adhesive pitch too tenaciously clung to his no longer sorrowful countenance, he would enter and re-enter the heated house until the cleansing had become complete. The mourning pitch is composed of the charred bones and ashes of the dead relative or friend. These remains of the funeral pyre, with the charcoal, are pulver-

55

ized and mixed with the resin of the pine; this hideous mixture is usually retained upon the face of the mourner until it wears off. If it has been well-compounded, it may last nearly a year; although the young, either from a super-abundance of vitality, excessive reparative powers of the skin, or from powers of will, seldom mourn so long. When the bare surface exceeds that covered by the pitch, it is not a scandalous disrespect in the young to remove it entirely, but a mother will seldom remove pitch or garment until both are nearly worn out."

This heroic treatment, while possibly efficacious in the simple ailments by which the Indians were most often afflicted, usually resulted in a great increase of mortality in the epidemics of smallpox following upon the footsteps of the white man. One traveler speaks of a severe sort of intermittent fever, to which the natives were subject, and of which so many died that hundreds of bodies were found strewn about the country. Having observed that the whites, even when attacked by this fever, rarely died of it, he was inclined to ascribe the mortality among the natives to their great cure-all, the *temescal*.

A number of places in the state bore this name, among them a small town lying between the sites now occupied by the flourishing cities of Oakland and Berkeley. Its citizens became

discontented with the undignified character of the name, and changed it to Alden.

## SAN BERNARDINO

*San Bernardino* is the name of a county in the southeastern part of California, whose broad expanse is mainly made up of volcanic mountains, desert plains and valleys without timber or water.

The name was first given to the snow-capped peak, 11,600 feet high, lying about twenty miles east of the city of San Bernardino, which is situated sixty miles east of Los Angeles, in the fruit and alfalfa region. The name of this town is one of the most regrettable examples of corruption that have occurred in the state, having passed from its original and sweetly flowing syllables through the successive stages of *San Berdino, Berdino,* until finally reaching the acme of vulgarity as *Berdoo,* by which appellation it is known to its immediate neighbors. If ideas of romance, of pleasant-sounding words, and of fidelity to history make no appeal to our fellow-Californians, let them read again the quotation from Stevenson given above, and learn that a romantic nomenclature may sometimes be a valuable financial asset.

*San Bernardino* (St. Bernardinus), the patron saint of the places bearing his name, is particu-

larly remembered as the founder of the charitable institution known in Spanish as *Monte de Piedad* (hill of pity), and in French as *Mont de Piété,* municipal pawnshops where money was loaned on pledges to the poor. These pawnshops are still conducted in many Spanish towns, in America as well as in Europe.

## SUPPLEMENTARY LIST

*Abalone Point,* some miles to the southeast of San Pedro Bay, was no doubt so named from the abundance of the great sea snails called *abalone,* whose iridescent shells, the abandoned dwellings of the dead animals, almost comparable in beauty to the mother-of-pearl, once covered the beaches of the California coast with a glittering carpet. The word "once" is used advisedly, for, with our usual easy-going American negligence we have permitted these creatures of the sea, valuable for their edible meat as well as for their exquisitely colored shells, to be nearly destroyed by Chinese and Japanese fisheries. That the flesh of the abalone formed a useful part of the food supply of the Indians is evidenced by the large number of shells to be found in the mounds along the shore. In the living state the abalone clings to the rocks on the shore, and its grip is so tenacious that more than one

unfortunate person, caught by the foot or hand between the shell and the rock, has been held there while death crept slowly upon him in the shape of the rising tide. There is another Abalone Point on the northern coast.

*Agua Caliente* (literally "hot water"), generally used in reference to hot springs. Of these there are many in the state, one on the Indian Reservation southeast of Riverside. Agua Caliente was originally a land grant.

*Alamitos* (little cotton woods), from *álamo,* a tree of the poplar family indigenous to California. There are several places bearing this name in the state, one a short distance northeast of Santa Ana.

*Aliso* (alder tree) is the name of a place on the Santa Fé Railroad, south of Los Angeles, near the shore, and was probably named for the *Rancho Cañada de los Alisos.* It is probably modern.

*Azusa* is the name of a place in Los Angeles County, twenty miles east of Los Angeles, and was originally applied to the land grant there. It is an Indian place name of a lodge, or ranchería, the original form being *Asuksa-gna,* the *gna* an ending which indicates place.

*Bandini* (a surname) is the name of a place a short distance southeast of Los Angeles, on the Santa Fé Railroad. The founder of this family was José Bandini, a mariner of Spanish birth,

who came to California with war supplies, and
finally settled at San Diego. His son, Juan Bandini, was a notable character in the history of the
state. He held several public offices, took part in
revolutions and colonization schemes and finally
espoused the cause of the United States. Bancroft gives the following resumé of his character:
"Juan Bandini must be regarded as one of the
most prominent men of his time in California.
He was a man of fair abilities and education, of
generous impulses, of jovial temperament, a most
interesting man socially, famous for his gentlemanly manners, of good courage in the midst of
personal misfortunes, and always well-liked and
respected; indeed his record as a citizen was an
excellent one. In his struggles against fate and
the stupidity of his compatriots he became absurdly diplomatic and tricky as a politician. He
was an eloquent speaker and a fluent writer."
Members of the Bandini family still occupy positions of respect and influence in the state and
have made some important additions to its historical literature.

*Bolsa* (pocket), a term much in use with the
Spaniards to signify a shut-in place. Bolsa is in
Orange County, twelve miles north by west of
Tres Pinos, and was probably named from the
land grant, *Rancho de las Bolsas*.

*Cabezón* (big head) is the name of a place

MONTEREY IN 1850

"We arrived at this port of Monterey on the sixteenth of December, 1602, at seven o'clock
in the evening."—(Sebastián Vizcaíno)

southeast of Colton. It was probably named for a large-headed Indian chief who lived there at one time and who received this name in pursuance of an Indian custom of fitting names to physical peculiarities. This name is improperly spelled on some maps as Cabazon.

*Cahuenga,* named for a former Indian village, is important as the scene of the signing, on January 13, 1847, by Andrés Pico and Frémont, of the papers of capitulation giving the United States possession of California.

*Cahuilla,* the name of an Indian tribe, probably "Spanishized" in its spelling from Ka-we-a. The valley and village of this name are situated in the San Jacinto Forest Reserve, southeast of Riverside, and received their name from a tribe who lived, in 1776, on the northern slopes of the San Jacinto Mountains. The word *Cahuilla* is of uncertain derivation.

*Calabazas* (squashes, or gourds) is northwest of Los Ángeles. The name refers to the wild gourds that grow in that locality.

*Casa Blanca* (white house) is a short distance west of Riverside, on the Santa Fé Railroad, so called from a large white ranch house once in conspicuous view from the railroad station.

*Casco* (skull), shell or outside part of anything. El Casco is situated about twelve miles

east of Riverside. Its application here has not been ascertained.

*Conejo* (rabbit) is the name of a number of places in the state, one of them in the Santa Mónica Mountains, another in the Central Valley, on the Santa Fé road.

*Cucamonga* is an Indian name, derived from a village in San Bernardino County, forty-two miles by rail east of Los Angeles. It was originally applied to the land grant at that place.

*Duarte,* a surname.

*Las Flores* (the flowers). At this place there was once a large Indian village, called in the native language *ushmai,* the place of roses, from *ushla,* rose.

*Garvanza* (chick-pea). Garvanza is a corrupt word, possibly corrupted from *garbanzo* (chick-pea). The town name is a modern one, given not by Spaniards but by tenderfeet, and there is no known reason for its application.

*Hermosa* (beautiful) is the name of a town in San Bernardino County, and of a beach in Los Angeles County; also of a mine in Nevada County.

*Indio,* the Spanish word for "Indian," is the name of a place in Riverside County, near Colton.

*La Joya* (the jewel).

*Laguna* (lagoon).

*La Mirada* (the view).

*Los Molinos* (the mills, or mill-stones), a name applied to a place east of San Gabriel by the Moraga party of 1819, who went out from the mission on a punitive expedition against the Amajaba (Mohave) Indians. Padre Nuez, who accompanied the party, says: "On the return we passed by a place where there was plenty of water, below a hill of red stone, very suitable for mill-stones." The same name, probably for similar reasons, was applied to other places in the state, among them one in Sonoma County, and Mill Creek in Tehama County, originally called *El Río de los Molinos* (The River of the Mill-stones).

*Montalvo* (a surname), the name of a place in Ventura County, near Ventura. This name is interesting as being the same as that borne by the author of *Las Sergas de Esplandián,* in which the fabulous island of *California* plays a leading part.

*Murietta* (a surname), the same as that of the noted bandit, Joaquín Murietta, who once terrorized California with his depredations. The town of Murietta, however, was not named in honor of this gentleman of unsavory memory, but for Mr. J. Murietta, who is still living in Southern California.

*Los Nietos* (literally "the grandchildren"), but

in this case a surname, that of the Nieto family. *Los Nietos* was a land grant taken up by Manuel Nieto and José María Verdugo in 1784.

*Pasadena,* said to be derived from the Chippewa Indian language. The full name is said to be *Weoquan Pasadena,* and the meaning to be "Crown of the Valley." Let no man believe in the absurd story that it means "Pass of Eden." Professor Kroeber says: "No unsophisticated and very few civilized Indians would think of calling any place the 'crown of the valley.' The phrase has all the appearance of having been coined by an American out of Indian or imaginary Indian terms."

*Prado* (meadow). "The Prado" is also the name of a famous promenade in the city of Madrid. In the present instance it is a modern name applied without much regard for its fitness.

*Puente* (bridge), in Los Angeles County, was taken from the name of the land grant, *Rancho de la Puente.*

*Pulgas Creek* (fleas creek).

*Redondo Beach* (round beach), a well-known seaside resort near Los Angeles, is usually supposed to have received its name from the curved line of the shore there, but the fact that a land grant occupying that identical spot was called *Sausal Redondo* (round willow-grove), from a

MISSION OF SAN LUIS OBISPO, FOUNDED IN 1772

" * * * in a smiling vale, which was once the haunt of great troops of bears."

clump of willows growing there accounts for its name.

*Rivera,* the name of a street in San Francisco, is in honor of Captain Rivera y Moncada, military governor of California in 1773-5. He was killed in the Yuma Massacre of 1781. There is also a town named Rivera in Los Angeles County.

*Rodéo de las Aguas* (gathering of the waters), a name once given to the present site of La Brea Rancho, near Los Angeles, perhaps because there is at that point a natural amphitheatre which receives the greater portion of the waters flowing from the neighboring mountains and the Cahuenga Pass.

*San Clemente* (St. Clement), the name of the island fifteen miles south of Santa Catalina. The saint for whom this island was named "was condemned to be cast into the sea bound to an anchor. But when the Christians prayed, the waters were driven back for three miles, and they saw a ruined temple which the sea had covered, and in it was found the body of the saint, with the anchor round his neck. For many years, at the anniversary of his death, the sea retreated for seven days, and pilgrimages were made to this submarine tomb."—*(Stories of the Saints.)*

*San Jacinto* (St. Hyacinth) was a Silesian nobleman who became a monk, and was noted

65

for his intellectual superiority, as well as for his piety. San Jacinto is the name of a town in Riverside County, thirty miles southeast of Riverside, in the fruit region, and of the range of mountains in the same county.

*San Juan Point* (St. John Point).

*San Matéo Point* (St. Matthew Point).

*San Onofre* (St. Onophrius) was a hermit saint whose chief claim to sanctity seems to have been that he deprived himself of all the comforts of life and lived for sixty years in the desert, "during which time he never uttered a word except in prayer, nor saw a human face."

*San Pedro* (St. Peter) is on San Pedro Bay, twenty-six miles south of Los Angeles. St. Peter was a fisherman of Capernaum who left his home to follow Christ and preach His Gospel. He and St. Paul are called "the two princes among the apostles." Much discussion has raged around the question of the place and circumstance of St. Peter's death, but Catholic authorities regard it as beyond doubt that he was martyred at Rome, though the exact spot there is not certain. According to the Scriptures the name Peter signifies "a rock." "Thou art Peter, on this rock have I founded my church." (Matthew, 16-18.) It seems probable, however, that San Pedro Bay was not named in honor of the apostle St. Peter, but for St. Peter the martyr,

Bishop of Alexandria, who was martyred in the year 311. The fact that Vizcaíno first sighted the bay on November 26th, the feast day of the Alexandrian saint, leads to this supposition.

*Saticoy* was the name of a former Chumash Indian village on the lower part of Santa Paula River, in Ventura County, about eight miles from the sea. The present town of Saticoy is on the Santa Clara River, in Ventura County, near Ventura.

*Serra* (a surname), probably given in honor of the celebrated founder of the California missions.

*El Toro* (the bull).

*Trabuco Canyon* (literally blunderbuss canyon). This name originated in the circumstance that the men in the first expedition under Captain Anza lost a *trabuco* (a short, wide-mouthed gun) in this canyon.—Diary of Father Font.

*Valle Verde* (green valley), incorrectly spelled on the map as *Val Verde.*

*Valle Vista* (valley view) is in Riverside County, five miles northwest of San Jacinto. This name is modern and incorrect in construction.

*Verdugo* was named for the Verdugo family, the owners of the *Rancho San Rafael,* northeast of Los Angeles and near the base of the Verdugo

Mountains. José María Verdugo was one of the grantees of the Nietos grant in 1784.

*Vicente Point* (Point Vincent). This point was named in 1793 by George Vancouver, the English explorer, in honor of Friar Vicente Santa María, "one of the reverend fathers of the mission of Buena Ventura."

MISSION OF SAN CARLOS BORROMEO, FOUNDED IN 1770

"Under its altar lies buried all that is mortal of its venerable founder, Junípero Serra."

# IN THE VICINITY OF SANTA BARBARA

## V

*Santa Bárbara,* the charming little town that dreams away its existence among the flowers of its old gardens, on the shore of the sheltered stretch of water formed by the islands lying to the seaward, was named for a noble lady of Heliopolis, the daughter of Dioscorus. She became converted to Christianity, and was in consequence cruelly persecuted and finally beheaded by her own father. "The legend that her father was struck by lightning in punishment for this crime probably caused her to be regarded by the common people as the guardian saint against tempest and fire, and later, by analogy, as the protectress of artillery-men and miners."—(Catholic Encylopedia.) For this reason her image was placed over the doors of

powder magazines, and her name came at last to be applied to the magazines themselves, which are known to the Spanish people as *santabárbaras*. Thus is explained the apparent incongruity between the name of the gentle saint and the places for storage of the instruments of savage war. The channel between the mainland and the chain of islands was entered by Vizcaíno in 1602, on the 4th day of December, which is the feast day of Santa Bárbara, and for this reason the name was bestowed upon it.

At the time of the arrival of the Spaniards the shores of the Santa Bárbara channel probably supported a denser native population than any other part of the state. The gracious climate and never-failing food supply furnished by the generous waters of the ocean, enabled the Indians to live at ease.

When Cabrillo entered the channel in 1542, he reported that: "A great number of Indians issued from the bushes, yelling and dancing, and making signs, inviting us to come on shore. They laid down their bows and arrows and came to the vessel in a good canoe. They possessed boats, large enough to carry twelve or fourteen men, well-constructed of bent planks and cemented with bitumen."

These Indians were of a higher order of intelligence than those farther north, and were

skilled in some of the arts, including the making
of excellent pottery. They were expert fisher-
men, using nets for the purpose, and often eating the fish raw. They wore their hair long, tied
up with long cords, to which many small dag-
gers of flint, wood and bone were attached. They
had some notion of music, using a primitive sort
of flute, or whistle, made of the hollow bones of
birds. They lived in conical houses, which were
covered well down to the ground.

When Father Serra passed that way, more
than two centuries later, he found the same conditions of population, counting as many as
twenty populous villages along the channel. He
was moved to bitter tears of grief over the delay
in establishing a mission where so rich a harvest
of souls lay ready to his hand. He died before
this dearest wish of his heart was accomplished,
yet Santa Bárbara may justly claim the honor
of his presence at her birth, for he took part in
the establishment of the presidio, which oc-
cured in 1783, three years before the building of
the mission. In Palou's *Life of Serra* he describes that occasion thus: "The party traveled
along the coast of the channel, in sight of the
islands which form it, and when they judged it
to be about half way, about nine leagues from
San Buenaventura, they stopped and selected a
site for the presidio, in sight of the beach, which

there forms a sort of bay, furnishing anchorage for ships. On this beach there was a large village of *gentiles*. Here the cross was raised, Father Serra blessed it and the land, and held mass. The following day they began to cut wood for the building of the chapel, the priest's house, officials' houses, cuartel, *almacenes* (storehouses), houses for families of married soldiers and the stockade."

The mission, which is still in an excellent state of preservation, was not established until December 4, 1786, although Serra looked upon that location as the most desirable in California, and spent the last years of his life in constant efforts to urge on the authorities to the work. That his hopes were realized to the full after his death, and that large numbers of natives, as well as the succeeding white parishioners, knelt before the altar dedicated to the gentle Santa Bárbara, is evidenced by the deeply worn marks of several generations of feet to be seen in the wide flight of steps at the entrance.

A legend has long gone the rounds that Santa Bárbara is unique among the missions in having within her gardens, hidden behind their secluding walls, a "holy of holies," where no woman's foot is permitted to press the sacred soil. As a matter of fact, this convent varies in no wise from others in the particular of prohibiting the

entrance of persons of the opposite sex, male or female as the case may be, into their inner cloisters.

*San Buenaventura Mission,* at the town now called Ventura, stands near the southeastern end of the Santa Bárbara channel. It was the last work of the great Serra, and was founded March 31, 1782, by the venerable president himself and Father Cambón. Palou gives us a detailed account of this event in his *Life of Serra:* "March 26th, the whole party, the largest ever engaged in the founding of a mission, soldiers, settlers, and their families, muleteers, etc., but only two priests, Padres Serra and Cambón, set out . . . They went on to the head of the channel, a site near the beach, on whose edge there was a large town of *gentiles* (unbaptized Indians), well built of pyramidal houses made of straw. They raised the cross, erected an arbor to serve as chapel, made an altar and adorned it. On the last day of March they took possession and held the first mass. The natives assisted willingly in building the chapel, and continued friendly, helping to build a house for the padre,—all of wood. The soldiers began to cut timbers for their houses, and for the stockade. They also went to work at once to conduct water by ditches from a neighboring stream, to bring it conveniently near the houses, and to serve to

irrigate crops. By means of a neophyte, brought from San Gabriel, they were able to communicate with the natives, and to let them know that their only purpose in coming here was to direct their souls to Heaven."

The patron of this mission was originally named Giovanni Fidanga. When a child he fell very ill, and was taken by his mother to St. Francis to be healed. When the saint saw him recovered he exclaimed: "O buena ventura!" whereupon his mother dedicated him to God by the name of *Buenaventura* (good fortune). It is a pity that a name of such happy augury should be mutilated by the amputation of its first part, the town and county now appearing as *Ventura*.

## ASUNCION

In the diaries of the Spanish pioneers, a distinct impression is conveyed that the California Indians, so far from being morose and taciturn, as their brothers in other parts of the United States are often portrayed, were rather a merry lot, and received the white men everywhere in their long journey up the coast, with music, feasting and the dance. In fact, we run across a complaint now and then that their hospitality was sometimes so insistent that their guests suf-

fered from loss of sleep, the serenading being kept up during the entire night.

Their music, no doubt of the most primitive sort, was produced by means of a "small whistle, sometimes double, sometimes single, about the size and length of a common fife. It was held in the mouth by one end, without the aid of the fingers, and only about two notes could be sounded on it."—(Bancroft, from Cal. Farmer.)

Along the Santa Bárbara channel the festivities in honor of the strangers were especially lively. At *Asunción* (Assumption), a point on the coast five leagues below Carpintería, they enjoyed a reception of which we read in Costansó's diary of the Portolá expedition of 1769, date of August 14th: "We reached the coast, and came in sight of a real town, situated on a tongue or point of land, right on the shore, which it dominated, seeming to command the waters. We counted as many as thirty large and capacious houses, spherical in form, well built and thatched with grass. We judged there could not be less than four hundred souls in the town. These natives are well built and of a good disposition, very agile and alert, diligent and skillful. Their handiness and ability were at their best in the construction of their canoes, made of good pine boards, well joined and calked, and of a pleasing form. They handled

75

these with equal skill, and three or four men go
out to sea in them to fish, for they will hold
eight or ten men.  They use long, double-bladed
paddles, and row with indescribable agility and
swiftness.  All their work is neat and well finished, and what is most worthy of surprise is
that to work the wood and stone they have no
other tools than those made of flint . . . . We
saw, and obtained in exchange for strings of
glass beads, and other trinkets, some baskets or
trays made of reeds, with different designs;
wooden plates, and bowls of different forms and
sizes, made of one piece, so that not even those
turned out in a lathe could be more successful.
They presented us with a quantity of fish, particularly the kind known as *bonito;* it has as
good a flavor as that caught in the tunny-fish-
eries of Cartegena de Levante, and on the coasts
of Granada.  We gave it the name of *La Asunción de Nuestra Señora* (the Assumption of Our
Lady), because we reached it on the eve of that
festival."

## EL BAILARIN

*El Bailarín* (the dancer). This spot, one league
from Carpintería, was named in honor of a
nimble-footed Indian, who cheered the weary
travelers on their way, as thus told by Father
Crespi, in his diary of the Portolá expedition:

INTERIOR OF THE QUADRANGLE AT SAN CARLOS MISSION

"Here the daily life of the mission was carried on."

"This place was named through the notable fact of an Indian having feasted us extraordinarily two leagues beyond (always coasting the seashore), where there is a large town on a point of land on the same shore; which Indian was a robust man of good form, and a great dancer; through respect for him we called this town, of which our friend was a resident, *El Pueblo del Bailarín* (the Town of the Dancer)."

*Ranchería del Baile de las Indias* (Village of the Dance of the Indian Women). As a rule, the women seemed to take no part in the dances, but Costansó tells of one occasion when they joined in the festivities: "They honored us with a dance, and it was the first place where we saw the women dance. Two of these excelled the others; they had a bunch of flowers in their hands, and accompanied the dance with various graceful gestures and movements, without getting out of time in their songs. We called the place the *Ranchería del Baile de las Indias*."

This place was about five leagues from Point Pedernales.

## CARPINTERIA

*Carpintería* is the name of a little cluster of houses near the shore about ten miles east of Santa Bárbara. It lies in a region once densely populated with natives of very "gentle and mild

77

disposition." The story of its naming is told by Father Crespi, of the Portolá party: "Not very far from the town we saw some springs of asphaltum. These Indians have many canoes, and at that time were constructing one, for which reason the soldiers named this town Carpintería (carpenter shop), but I baptized it with the name of *San Roque*."

## MONTECITO

*Montecito* (little hill or little wood) is the name of a small village about six miles from Santa Bárbara. The country in this vicinity, through its extraordinary charm of climate and scenery, has attracted a large number of very rich people, whose splendid country houses, in bizarre contrast, now occupy the self-same spots where the Indians once raised their flimsy huts of straw. In the church archives Montecito is mentioned as the place chosen for the site of the mission, about three quarters of a league from the presidio of Santa Bárbara, making it evident that the present Montecito was not the place to which the name was originally given. In California *monte* was more often used to mean a wood rather than a hill, so in this case Montecito probably meant a small grove of trees.

## SANTA CRUZ ISLAND

While traversing the shore of Santa Bárbara channel, the Portolá expedition of 1769 took time to make trips to the islands and bestow names upon them. The island of Santa Cruz received its name from a rather trivial circumstance. By some chance the padres lost there a staff which bore a cross on the end. They gave it up as irretrievably lost, so were the more pleased when the Indians appeared the following day to restore it. From this they gave the island the name of *Santa Cruz* (Holy Cross).

## RANCHERIA DE LA ESPADA

Of the *Ranchería de la Espada* (village of the sword), Captain Fages, of the Portolá expedition says: "Two and a half leagues northwest of Point Conception, another glen is found with a population of twenty hearths, with 250 Indians, more or less. The natives of the settlement here are extremely poor and starved, so that they can scarcely live, being without canoes, in rugged land, and short of firewood. While here a soldier lost his sword, leaving it carelessly fastened, so that they took it from his belt. But the Indians who saw this theft themselves ran in pursuit of the thief, and deprived him of the

article in order that its owner might recover it."
From this the place received the name of the
*Ranchería de la Espada,* and the little story is
still commemorated in the name of Espada
Landing.

## MATILIJA

*Matilija Creek* and *Matilija Springs,* in Ventura County, derive their name from an Indian
village, one of those mentioned in the mission
archives. The name is best known as applied to
the Matilija poppy, that flower of the gods which
has its native habitat along the banks of the
creek. This giant poppy, by reason of its extraordinary size and delicate beauty, has a just
claim to be called "queen of all California's wild
flowers," as the Sequoia is king of her trees. It
is a perennial plant, of shrubby character, and
grows wild in the southern part of the state,
from the Santa María River southward, extending into Lower California, where it spreads over
large areas. It flourishes in particular luxuri-
ance in the Matilija canyon, but the popular idea
that that spot was its only habitat is erroneous.
The shrub reaches a height of eight or ten feet,
has gray-green foliage, and bears splendid, six-
petaled white flowers, often six or seven inches
in diameter, "of a crepe-like texture, pure
glistening white, with bright yellow centers." "It

ON THE SHORE NEAR LA PUNTA DE LOS CIPRESES

"The home of those wonderful trees, twisted into a thousand
fantastic shapes by their age-long struggle
with the ocean winds."

not only grows in fertile valleys, but seeks the seclusion of remote canyons, and nothing more magnificent could be imagined than a steep canyon-side covered with the great bushy plants, thickly covered with the enormous white flowers."—(Miss Parsons, quoted by J. Burt Davy, in *Bailey's Cyclopedia of American Horticulture.*)

## POINT PEDERNALES

Captain Fages, of the Portolá party, says of this place: "Going two leagues through high land, and with a good outlook over the sea coast, a flowing stream appears, with very good water, and near it a poor settlement of only ten houses, probably numbering about sixty inhabitants, crowded together. We stopped at the place near where a strip or point of land extends to the sea. There we gathered a multitude of flints, good for fire-arms, and so this place is called *Los Pedernales* (the flints)."

Point Pedernales still remains as the name of "that point of land extending into the sea," a few miles north of Point Conception.

## CAMULOS

*Camulos,* also spelled *Kamulas,* was the name of an Indian village near San Buenaventura. This village is among those mentioned in the

mission archives, and is noted as the home of Ramona, the heroine of Mrs. Helen Hunt Jackson's romance. The meaning of the word *Camulos,* according to Professor A. L. Kroeber, is "my fruit."

## SUPPLEMENTARY LIST

*Los Alamos* (the cottonwoods) is in Santa Bárbara County, northwest of Santa Bárbara. The *álamo* is a species of poplar tree indigenous to California and widely spread throughout the state.

*Argüello Point* is on the coast of Santa Bárbara County, just south of Point Pedernales. Argüello is a surname, that of a pioneer family, of which José Darío Argüello was the founder. "For many years Don José was the most prominent, influential and respected man in California."—(Bancroft.) *Argüello Point* was named by Vancouver in honor of the Spanish governor.

*El Cojo* (the lame one). This place, near Point Conception, was so named by the Spaniards because they saw here an Indian chief who was lame.

*Point Concepción,* the point at the southwestern extremity of Santa Bárbara County, was so named in reference to the "immaculate conception" of the Virgin.

*Los Dos Pueblos* (the two towns) is on the coast a few miles west of Santa Bárbara. On October 16, 1542, the Cabrillo expedition anchored opposite two Indian villages here, and named the place *Los Dos Pueblos.* "Although these villages were separated only by a small stream, their inhabitants were of a different race and language, those on one side being short, thick and swarthy, and on the other tall, slender and not so dark. The depth of the kitchen refuse at the site of these two towns indicates that these Indians had lived here since the Christian era and were contemporary with the mound builders."—*(History of Santa Bárbara County.)*

Bancroft, however, has little faith in the extraordinary antiquity ascribed to the Indian remains found at this place, and says in regard to them: "There was a tendency at first, as is usual in such cases, to ascribe the channel relics to a pre-historic race, but nothing indicating such an origin has ever been found there."

*Gaviota* (seagull) is on the shore a few miles west of Santa Bárbara. Father Crespi mentions having given this name to another place further down the coast: "We reached an estuary, on whose border stood a ranchería of fifty-two huts, with three hundred people. For having killed a sea-gull here, the soldiers called this place *La Gaviota,* but I named it *San Luís Rey*

*de Francia."* As *San Luís Rey* it has remained on the map.

*Gaviota Pass* is an important gap in the Santa Inez range.

Every one who has crossed the bay of San Francisco in the winter season must have rejoiced in the sight of the flying convoy of those beautiful creatures, the *gaviotas,* by which each ferry-boat is accompanied.

*Goleta* (schooner) is the name of a village in Santa Bárbara County, seven miles west of Santa Bárbara.

*Guadalupe.* This name is Spanish-Arabic, but in Mexico it may represent certain Aztec sounds. Guadalupe is strictly the name of a picture, but was extended to the church containing the picture and to the town that grew up around it. It is a name held in the deepest reverence by every Mexican, for Our Lady of Guadalupe is the patron saint of that country. There is a delightfully romantic story of her first appearance which runs as follows: On a certain day long ago, fixed exactly as Saturday, December 9, 1531, a poor Indian neophyte named Juan Diego was hurrying down Tepeyac Hill to hear mass in Mexico City. Suddenly the Blessed Virgin appeared to him and gave him a message for Bishop Zumárraga, asking that a temple be built to her where she stood. The Bishop asked for

MISSION OF SANTA CLARA, FOUNDED IN 1777

"The special symbol of the sweet St. Clara is the lily, peculiarly appropriate for the ever-blooming Santa Clara Valley."

a sign that she was the true mother of God. The Indian returned, and the Virgin told him to gather roses in his cloak and take them to the Bishop. This he did, and when the cloak, made of poor sack cloth, was unrolled, the roses fell out and a life-size figure of the Virgin was seen imprinted on it. From that day Our Lady of Guadalupe was made an object of veneration, and was adopted as the patroness of Mexico. The church dedicated to her worship in the vicinity of the City of Mexico has become a shrine for pilgrims, and its interior is crowded with offerings of all sorts made in gratitude to the saint by votaries who believe themselves to have been saved from peril by sea and land through the saint's intervention. Outside of it may be seen the famous "Sails of Guadalupe," a representation in stone of the sails of a ship, which was erected by some sailors in expression of their gratitude for rescue from a shipwreck.

The name is a great favorite among Mexicans, not only to designate places, but also as a Christian name for both men and women. In California there is the town of Guadalupe near the northern border of Santa Bárbara County, and the river bearing the same name in Santa Clara County, originally called by the Spaniards *El Río de Nuestra Señora de Guadalupe,* no doubt

because it was discovered on her feast day, December 12th. The story of the naming of this stream is given by Father Font in his diary of the Anza expedition of 1776: "We set out from the Arroyo de San Mateo at a quarter past seven in the morning, and at four in the afternoon halted on the other side of a river which we called El Río de Guadalupe. It has its outlet in the extremity of the port, and for about a league above its mouth is very deep, on account of its waters being backed up and without current.

*Lompoc* is one of the names of Indian villages taken from the mission archives. It is situated fifty miles northwest of Santa Bárbara, on the Southern Pacific Railroad.

*Nojoqui,* in Santa Bárbara County, was presumably the name of an Indian village.

*Los Olivos* (the olives) is in Santa Bárbara County, on the Coast Line Railroad.

*La Piedra Pintada* (the painted rock) is about eighty miles from Santa Bárbara. Here there was a stone wigwam, forty or fifty yards in diameter, whose walls were covered with paintings in the form of halos and circles, with radiations from the center.—*(History of Santa Bárbara County.)*

*Punta Gorda* (fat or broad point) is one of the points of land running into the sea from the

Santa Bárbara Coast. Its name indicates its shape.

*Punta de las Ritas* (point of the rites), perhaps refers to some religious ceremony held upon that spot.

*La Purísima Concepción* (the immaculate conception) was the third of the channel missions. It was founded on the south bank of the Santa Inez River, then called the Santa Rosa, on December 8, 1787. The site is in Santa Bárbara County, near the town of Lompoc, and a short distance from the coast. Although it was the most modest of all the missions in its architecture and dimensions, it had a very stirring history. In 1812 a terrific earthquake, said to be the most violent that has ever occurred in California, reduced the church building and the houses of the Indians to ruins. The earth opened in several places, emitting water and black sand, and torrents of rain caused floods in the river which completed the ruin. The fathers were undismayed, however, and went immediately to work to replace the first buildings, which were of adobe, with more solid structures of stone. The next disaster was a revolt of the natives in 1824, during which the Indians used the church as a fort. They erected palisades, cut loopholes in the walls of the church and other buildings, and mounted one or two rusty old cannon.

When the attacking party appeared on the scene
they were met by a lively fire from the natives
inside the church, but their marksmanship was
so poor that little execution was done. The revolt was soon put down, and affairs at the mission resumed their old peaceful course, until, in
1844, an epidemic of smallpox broke out and
caused the death of the greater portion of
the Indians. In 1845 the mission estate, excepting the church buildings, was sold to John
Temple by Governor Pico for a paltry sum, and
its old time glories were soon a thing of the
past. Its ruins still stand, interesting and picturesque, but a silent and melancholy reminder of
its former prosperous days.

*Rincón Point* (corner point) is one of the
many points of land running out from the Santa
Bárbara Coast.

*Point Sal* was named for Hermenegildo Sal,
who was one of the prominent figures in the
early history of Southern California. He was a
Spanish soldier who came to this coast in 1776
with Anza and his party of colonists. Sal filled
many important military offices. This point was
named by Vancouver for this official, who was
at one time comandante of the presidio of San
Francisco, in return for signal courtesies shown
by him in 1792, when he permitted Vancouver
to go to the mission of Santa Clara, this being

the first occasion when this part of Spanish America was penetrated by any foreigner.

*Sal Si Puedes* (get out if you can). Several places in the state, one in the Santa Cruz Mountains, another in Santa Bárbara County, received this name, so eloquent of the rough road that the Spaniards sometimes had to travel. Captain Argüello, in his diary of the expedition of 1821, refers to his struggle in getting out of a certain canyon in these terms: "On account of its difficult situation it was named *Montaña de Maltrato y Arroyo de Sal si Puedes*" (mountain of ill-treatment and creek of get out if you can).

*Santa Inez* (St. Agnes) is the name of a river in Santa Bárbara County which rises in the Coast Rrange and flows into the Pacific Ocean about ten miles north of Cape Conception. The town of the same name is situated on this river. The Mission Santa Inez was founded September 17, 1804, by Padres Tapis, Calzada and Gutierrez. It flourished for a time, but was greatly damaged by an earthquake in 1812, was rebuilt and damaged again by the Indians in the revolt of 1824, and its partially ruined buildings still remain to tell of a vanished past. Its patroness, St. Agnes, was one of the four great virgin martyrs of the Latin Church. She was a Roman maiden of great beauty, and was condemned to death by the sword, by the Prefect Sempronius,

in revenge for her refusal to marry his son, on
the ground that she was "already affianced to a
husband whom she loved, meaning Jesus." Before causing her death Sempronius attempted to
procure her dishonor by having her conveyed to
a house of infamy, "but when she prayed to
Christ that she might not be dishonored, she
saw before her a shining white garment which
she put on with joy, and the room was filled
with great light."

*Santa María* (St. Mary), so named in honor of
the mother of Christ, is in Santa Bárbara
County, near the Santa María River.

*Santa Paula* (St. Paula) is in Ventura County,
thirty-five miles west of San Fernando, on the
Southern Pacific Railroad. "St. Paula was a
noble Roman matron, a pupil and disciple of St.
Jerome. Though descended from the Scipios
and the Gracchi, and accustomed to luxurious
self-indulgence, she preferred to follow her
saintly teacher to Bethlehem and devote herself
to a religious life. She built a monastery, a
hospital, and three nunneries at Bethlehem."—
*(Stories of the Saints.)*

*Serena* (serene), a place on the shore near
Santa Bárbara, whose placid charm well befits
its name. Judging by its form this name must

90

be modern, as Spaniards do not use an adjective standing alone as a place name.

*Ventura* (fortune), a town near the southeastern end of the Santa Bárbara channel.

# THE SAN LUIS OBISPO GROUP

## VI

*San Luís Obispo* (St. Louis the Bishop). Travelers on the Coast Line, whose attention is attracted to the smiling vale where the pretty town of *San Luís Obispo* nestles in the hollow of the hills, about eight miles from the ocean and ninety to the northwest of Santa Bárbara, will doubtless be pleased to learn something of its history. So peaceful is the aspect of the valley at this time that it comes rather as a surprise to read, in the diaries of the Portolá expedition of 1769, stories of fierce fights with bears, which then haunted this place in such numbers that the explorers gave it the name of *La Cañada de los Osos* (the glen of the bears). From Father Crespi we get some account of the numbers and ferocity of these animals: "In this glen we saw troops of bears, which have the ground ploughed up and full of scratches which they make in search of the roots that form their food. Upon these roots, of which there are many of a good savor and taste, the *gentiles* (unbaptized In-

THE PALO COLORADO (REDWOOD TREE)
"First observed and named by Gaspar de Portola."

dians) also live. The soldiers, who went out to hunt, succeeded in killing one bear with gunshots, and experienced the ferocity of these animals. Upon feeling themselves wounded they attack the hunter at full speed, and he can only escape by using the greatest dexterity. They do not yield except when the shot succeeds in reaching the head or heart. The one that the soldiers killed received nine balls before falling, and did not fall until one struck him in the head."

Captain Fages, of the same expedition, gives a similar account " . . . . a spacious glen with a rivulet of very good water . . . . In said glen they saw whole herds of bears, which have ploughed up all the ground, where they dug to seek their livelihood from the roots that it produces. They are ferocious brutes, and of very difficult hunting, throwing themselves with incredible speed and anger upon the hunter, who only escapes by means of a swift horse. They do not yield to the shot unless it be in the head or heart."

Miguel Costansó, of the same party, says: "In the afternoon, as they had seen many tracks of bears, six soldiers went out hunting on horseback, and succeeded in shooting one bear. It was an enormous animal; it measured fourteen palms from the sole of the feet to the top of its

head; its feet were more than a foot long; and is must have weighed over 375 pounds. We ate the flesh and found it savory and good."

At a later date, when the mission at Monterey was in serious danger of a famine, Captain Fages called to mind the experiences in the *Cañada de los Osos,* and headed a hunting expedition to that region for the purpose of securing a supply of bear meat. The party succeeded in killing a considerable number of the animals, and were thus able to relieve the scarcity at Monterey. The name of *Los Osos* (the bears) is still applied to a valley in the vicinity of San Luís Obispo.

Finding this spot highly suitable for a settlement, in the matters of climate, arable land, and water, points always carefully considered by the padres, the mission of *San Luís Obispo de Tolosa* (St. Louis the Bishop of Toulouse) was established by Padre Serra, September 1, 1772, in *La Cañada de los Osos*. In the usual course of events, the name of the mission was extended to the town and finally to the county.

The story of the patron saint of this mission runs as follows: "St. Louis of Toulouse was the nephew of St. Louis, King of France, and son of the King of Naples and Sicily. Like his kingly uncle-saint, he was piously reared by his mother. When he was but fourteen, his father, being

made prisoner by the King of Aragon, gave Louis and his brother as hostages. He became wearied of everything but religion, and in 1294, when he was made free, he gave all his royal rights to his brother Robert, and became a monk of the Order of St. Francis. He was then twenty-two years old. Soon he was made Bishop of Toulouse; and he set out, bare-footed and clothed as a friar, to take his new office. He went into Provence on a charitable mission, and died at the castle of Brignolles, where he was born. He was first buried at Marseilles, then removed to Valencia, where he was enshrined. His pictures represent him as young, beardless, and of gentle face. He has the fleur-de-lis embroidered on his cope, or on some part of his dress. The crown which he gave away lies at his feet, while he wears the mitre of a bishop."
—*(Stories of the Saints.)*

## SAN MIGUEL

*San Miguel* (St. Michael), situated about forty-seven miles northeast of San Luís Obispo, is the site of Mission San Miguel, founded July 25, 1797, by Padres Lasuén and Sitjar. It is said that "the lands of this mission extended from the Tulares on the east to the sea on the west, and from the north boundary of the San Luís

Obispo district to the south line of San Antonio. It had its work-shops and little factories where the good padres taught the Indians the useful arts. Its property was confiscated in 1836, and sold at auction in 1846."

St. Michael, in whose honor this mission was named, "is regarded as the first and mightiest of all created spirits. He it was whom God commissioned to expell Satan and the rebellious angels from Heaven. His office now is believed to be two-fold, including that of patron saint of the Church on earth, and Lord of the souls of the dead; presenting the good to God and sending the evil and wicked away to torment." In pictures St. Michael is always represented as young and beautiful, sometimes as the Lord of souls in pictures of death, sometimes in armor as the conqueror of Satan.

## PASO DE ROBLES

*Paso de Robles* (pass of the oaks), known far and wide for its hot sulphur springs, where the sick of many lands find surcease from their pain, is situated twenty-nine miles north of San Luís Obispo. It was named for the reason indicated by Father Crespi, who says: " . . . . in a valley in the hollow of the Santa Lucía Mountains, called *Los Robles,* for the great abundance

96

MISSION OF SAN JUAN BAUTISTA, FOUNDED IN 1797

"Although twice attacked by Indians and damaged by earthquakes in 1800, it is still
moderately well preserved."

of these trees with which it is populated."

It should be explained that the *roble* is not the evergreen, or live-oak, which is called *encino*. At Leland Stanford Jr. University the names of these two species of oaks have been rather poetically used for the students' dormitories,—Encina Hall for the men, and Roble Hall for the women.

## SUPPLEMENTARY LIST

*Arroyo Grande* (big creek), a village in San Luís Obispo County, fifteen miles southeast of San Luís Obispo.

*Atascadero* (boggy ground, quagmire).

*Avenal* (a field sown with oats).

*Buchón* (big craw) is the name of the point on the coast directly opposite the town of San Luís Obispo, and has a significance not altogether agreeable. The Spanish soldiers called the place *Buchón* from an Indian in the neighborhood who was the unfortunate possessor of an enormous goitre, which was so large that it hung down upon his breast.

*Cañada del Osito* (glen of the little bear), so called because some Indians from the mountains offered the Spaniards a present of a bear cub.

*Cayucos* is the name of a village in San Luís

Obispo County, eighteen miles northwest of San Luís Obispo. The word *cayuco* is probably Indian in origin, and is used in different senses in different parts of America. In Venezuela it means a small fishing boat, built to hold one person, while in Cuba is means "head." As this place is on the shore, it was probably named in reference to Indian fishing skiffs.

*Cholame* (the name of an Indian village).

*Cuesta* (hill, mount, ridge, also family name).

*Esteros* (estuaries, creeks into which the tide flows at flood time).

*Estero Point* (estuary point).

*Estrella* (star).

*López* (a surname).

*Morro* (headland, bluff). Morro is the name of a hamlet in San Luís Obispo County, on the shore, twelve miles northwest of San Luís Obispo. See Final Index.

*Nacimiento* (birth). This word is generally used by the Spaniards in the sense of the birth of Christ; but it also means headwaters of a river, and may be used here in reference to Nacimiento Creek, in the southern part of Monterey County.

*Los Osos* (the bears).

*Piedras Blancas* (white stones, or rocks), the name of a point on the coast.

*Pismo,* an Indian word said to mean "place of fish," but this definition is not based upon scientific authority.

*Pozo* (well, or pool) is the name of a village in San Luís Obispo County.

*San Simeón* (St. Simeon) is the name of a village in San Luís Obispo County, on the shore twenty miles south of Jolón. It has a good harbor. St. Simeon, the patron saint of this place, was one of the apostles, and is called "the Prophet" because he was the translator of the book of Isaiah in which is made the prophecy, "Behold a virgin shall conceive."

St. Simeon Stylites, who set the fashion of the pillar-hermits, spent almost half of the fifth century on the summit of a column sixty feet in height, drawing up his meager food and water in a pail which he lowered for the purpose. This peculiar and apparently senseless mode of life has been partially justified by the reflection that the notoriety he thus gained brought curious crowds of pagans about his pillar, to whom he was enabled to preach the Christian doctrine. It is said that he converted many thousands of the nomadic Saracen tribes to Christianity.

*Santa Lucía* (St. Lucy) is the name of a section of the coast range of mountains in the central part of the state. St. Lucy is the protectress

against all diseases of the eye, and is the patroness of the laboring poor.

*Santa Margarita* (St. Margaret) is the name of a town in San Luís Obispo County, on the Southern Pacific Railroad. St. Margaret is the patroness who presides over births.

THE CITY OF YERBA BUENA (SAN FRANCISCO IN 1846–47)

" * * * so called in reference to the profuse growth of that charming little vine about the locality."

# IN THE
# NEIGHBORHOOD OF
# MONTEREY

## VII

*Monterey. "Llegamos á este puerto de Monterey á 16 de Diciembre, 1602 á las siete de la noche"* (We arrived at this port of Monterey on the sixteenth of December, 1602, at seven o'clock in the evening).—From the diary of Sebastián Vizcaíno.)

When Vizcaíno sailed into the beautiful blue bay of Monterey, and looked about him at the ring of hills, dark with the dense growth of pines covering them from summit to base, he became at once enamored with the place, and wrote enthusiastically to his Spanish Majesty concerning it. In a letter of the date of May 23, 1603, he says: "Among the ports of most importance which I found was one in latitude 37, which I named Monterey. As I wrote to your majesty from there on the twenty-eighth of September of the said year, it is all that can be desired for the convenience and seaport of the ships of the Philippine line, whence they come

101

to explore this coast. The port is sheltered from all winds, and has on the shore many pines to supply the ships with masts of any size that they may wish, and also live-oaks, oaks, rosemary, rock-roses, roses of Alexandria, good hunting of rabbits, hares, partridges and flying birds of different sorts. The land is of mild temperature, and of good waters, and very fertile, judging by the luxuriant growth of the trees and plants, for I saw some fruits from them, particularly of chestnuts and acorns, larger than those of Spain; and it is well-populated with people, whose disposition I saw to be soft, gentle, docile, and very fit to be reduced to the Holy Church. Their food is of many and various seeds that they have and also wild game, such as deer, some of which are larger than cows, also bears, and cattle and buffalo, and many others. The Indians are of good body, white of countenance, and the women somewhat smaller, and well-favored. Their dress is of the people of the beach, of the skins of seals, of which there are an abundance, which they tan and prepare better than in Spain."

At first thought it would seem that Vizcaíno must have been in error about finding buffalo at Monterey, but investigation shows that in 1530 those animals "ranged through what is now New Mexico, Utah, Oregon, Washington, and

British Columbia."—*(Handbook of American Indians.)* Oregon is not so far away but that scattering herds may have wandered as far as Monterey, and that Vizcaíno actually saw them there. It has been suggested, also, that he may have mistaken the tracks of the great elk for those of buffalo. In calling the Indians "white," he was, no doubt, speaking comparatively. According to the diaries of the Spaniards, the natives of different sections varied considerably in complexion. What he meant by "chestnuts" can only be conjectured, since that tree is not indigenous to Monterey, but it is possible that the nut of the wild buck-eye, which resembles the chestnut in size and shape, may have been mistaken for it by the Spaniards.

Vizcaíno named the port in honor of Gaspar de Zúñiga, Count of Monterey, at that time Viceroy of Mexico. The word itself, whose literal meaning is "the King's wood," or "the King's mountain," since *monte* may be used in either sense, was formerly spelled Monterrey, Monterey, or Monte Rey.

When Father Serra arrived at Monterey in 1770, he decided to make it the headquarters of all the California missions, and it was here that the rest of his life was spent, excepting the periods of absence required in visiting the other missions, and in one visit to Mexico. Very

103

shortly after the landing of the party in a little cove at the edge of the present town, it was decided that not enough arable land existed at that point for the support of the mission, so the religious establishment was removed to Carmel Bay, while the Presidio and its chapel remained at Monterey.

The Mission *San Carlos Borroméo* (St. Charles Borroméo) was founded June 3, 1770, at Monterey, and in the following year was removed to the banks of the Carmelo River. This church, now in an excellent state of repair, through the efforts of the late Father Angelo Casanova, is distinguished above all the others, "for under its altar lies buried all that is mortal of the remains of its venerable founder, Junípero Serra."

Its patron saint, St. Charles Borroméo, belonged to a noble family of Lombardy. Being a second son, he was dedicated to the church at a very early age, and soon rose to distinction, receiving the cardinal's hat at twenty-three. The death of his elder brother placed the family fortune at his disposal, but he gave it all in charity, reserving for himself merely enough for bread and water, and straw on which to sleep. In public he gave feasts, but never partook of them himself. At the time of the plague in Milan, when all others fled from the city, he

104

remained to attend the sick. His remains repose in a rich shrine in that city.

Visitors to Monterey often confuse the parish church in the town with the Old Mission, which is situated some miles to the south in the valley of the Carmel River. The one in the town, San Carlos de Monterey, was built and conducted by the fathers for the benefit of the soldiers of the presidio, while the one in the valley, San Carlos de Carmel, was the Mission for the Indians. The latter, of course, is the veritable Old Mission. Both churches were rebuilt of stone at the same time, the work beginning in 1793 and occupying some years. The object in having the two churches at some distance from each other was to prevent disturbances between the soldiers and the Indians. The church in the town is in good repair and is still in use for regular services. Most of the relics have been taken to it from the Old Mission.

## SAN ANTONIO

At *San Antonio* (St. Anthony), in Monterey County, twenty miles from Kings City, Father Serra established the mission of San Antonio de Padua, July 14, 1771. In connection with its establishment, Palou tells a story that brings out one of the most marked characteristics of the

venerable founder,—his ardent enthusiasm:
"They [the founding party] departed for the
Santa Lucía Mountains, taking priests for the
new mission, the required escort of soldiers, and
all necessaries. Twenty-five leagues south-southeast from Monterey, they arrived at the hollow
of this ridge, where they found a great *cañada,*
which they called *Robles* (oaks), from the great
number of those trees. Finding a level plain in
the same *cañada,* bordering on a river which
they called *San Antonio,* and which they thought
to be a good site, for the good flow of water,
even in the dry month of July, which could be
conducted to the lands without difficulty, all
agreed upon the choice of this spot. Serra ordered the mules to be unloaded, and the bells to
be hung up on the branch of a tree. As soon as
they were hung up, he began to ring them, cry-
ing out, 'Ho! Gentiles, come, come to the Holy
Church, come to receive the faith of Jesus
Christ!'" One of the other priests remonstrated
with him, saying it was idle to ring the bells in
the absence of the gentiles, but Serra said, "Let
me ring, let me relieve my heart, so that all the
wild people in this mountain range may hear!"
It happened that some natives were attracted by
the ringing of the bells, and came to witness the
first mass, which Serra regarded as a good
augury.

106

St. Anthony of Padua, the patron of this place, was a Portuguese by birth, who entered the Franciscan Order. He went as a missionary to the Moors, but was compelled by illness to return to Europe, where he had great success in Italy and France as a preacher. Among many miracles accredited to him is the one thus related: "When preaching at the funeral of a very rich man, St. Anthony denounced his love of money, and exclaimed, 'His heart is buried in his treasure chest; go seek it there and you will find it.' The friends of the man broke open the chest, and to their surprise, found the heart; they then examined his body and found that his heart was indeed wanting."—*(Stories of the Saints.)*

## POINT CYPRESS

*La Punta de los Cipreses* (Point Cypress) is the home of those wonderful trees, twisted and gnarled into a thousand fantastic shapes by their age-long struggle against the ocean winds, which furnish yet another proof of the part played by California in the preservation of the rare and the unique, for this species of coniferous tree is said to be confined to that region, not occurring in any other part of the world.

The following interesting paragraph on these trees is quoted from *The Trees of California,* by

Willis Linn Jepson, Asst. Professor of Dendrology in the University of California: *"Cupressus Macrocarpa* is limited to two localities on the ocean shore at the mouth of the Carmel River near Monterey. The Cypress Point grove extends along the cliffs and low bluffs from Pescadero Point to Cypress Point, a distance of two miles, reaching inland about one-eighth of a mile. The Point Lobos grove is much smaller. The trees are scattered over the summits of two headlands, and cling to the edges of the cliffs, where on account of the erosive action of the ocean, they are occasionally under-mined and fall into the sea. Monterey Cypress is most interesting for its remarkably restricted natural range and the exceedingly picturesque outlines characteristic of the trees growing on the ocean shore. As a result of their struggle with violent storms from the Pacific Ocean which break on the unprotected cliffs and headlands of Cypress Point and Point Lobos, they present a variety and singularity of form which is obviously connected with their exposed habitat, and lends a never-failing interest to these two narrow localities. Of the highly picturesque trees, the most common type is that with long irregular arms. Such trees recall most strikingly the classical pictures of the Cedars of Lebanon. Monterey Cypress is of course a genuine cypress and Lebanon Cedar

MISSION OF SAN FRANCISCO DE ASIS, COMMONLY CALLED MISSION DOLORES

"It stood unharmed through the earthquake and fire of 1906 which laid low all
its proud modern neighbors."

a genuine cedar; the two do not even belong to the same family of conifers. Yet the popular story that the two are the same makes so strong an appeal to the imagination of the tourist at Monterey that the guides and promoters in the region will doubtless never cease to disseminate it. As a consequence the error goes into the daily press and the magazines, and is evidently destined to flourish in perennial greenness under the guise of fact. The wide dissemination of this fiction is all the more remarkable in that in the case of all other unique features of the state, such as the Sequoias and the Yosemite, our Californians have evinced a remarkable pride in their possession, without thought of inventing a duplication of them elsewhere. . . . . . . The matter of the age of these trees has been much exaggerated. It is a tree of rapid growth, and the older specimens are probably not more than 200 or 300 years old."

The above paragraph, quoted from a writer acknowledged to be one of the best authorities on the trees of California, is given here in full, in the hope of correcting these two common errors concerning the Monterey Cypress,—the one that it is identical with the Cedar of Lebanon, the other, an exaggerated notion of the great age of some of the trees. As Professor

Jepson justly remarks, the truth in this case is a greater matter for pride than the fiction.

## POINT PINOS

*La Punta de Pinos* (the point of pines) is situated a few miles from Monterey, just beyond Pacific Grove. It is one of the most picturesque points on the coast, and is the location of one of the government light-houses.

## SALINAS

When the Portolá expedition of 1769 arrived at the Salinas River, they made the first of the series of errors which caused them to pass by the bay of Monterey without recognizing it, for they mistook this stream for the Carmel. The *Salinas* (salt marshes), so called for the chain of salt-water ponds lying along its course, was known by various names before a permanent one became attached to it, appearing at different times as *El Río Elzeario, Santa Delfina,* and *El Río de Monterey.*

The town of Salinas is the county seat of Monterey County and is situated about eighteen miles east of Monterey, in the heart of an important agricultural, dairying, and sugar-beet district.

## SOLEDAD

*Soledad* (solitude), in Monterey County, 143 miles southeast of San Francisco, is described as

"a very dry plain, with few trees, swept by fierce winds and dust storms in summer." No wonder they called it *Soledad,*—Lonesometown!

Yet those same dry plains proved to be of sufficient fertility to warrant the establishment, in 1791, of the mission of *Nuestra Señora de la Soledad,* freely translated as "Our Lady of Sorrows," which became the center of a large and prosperous Indian community. The buildings of the mission have now fallen into almost complete decay.

In the diary of Father Font, companion of Captain Anza in his second expedition to California, in 1776, this mention of the origin of the name of Soledad occurs: "At the end of about six leagues is the place called La Soledad, which they told me was so called because in the first expedition under Portolá they asked an Indian what its name was and he replied 'Soledad,' or something that sounded like that."

## PAJARO

*Pájaro* (bird), a town in Monterey County, on the Pájaro River, which rises on the slope of the Coast Range, and flows westerly, falling into Monterey Bay, derives its name from a circumstance told in the diary of the faithful Father Crespi: "We saw in this place a bird, which the

111

*gentiles* (unbaptized Indians) had killed and
stuffed with straw, and which appeared to some
[of the party] to be a royal eagle; it was measured from tip to tip of the wings, and was found
to measure eleven palms (nine feet and three
inches) for which reason the soldiers called the
place *El Río del Pájaro.*" The scream of the
eagle may still be heard in the more remote
parts of the Santa Cruz Mountains, where the
great birds are occasionally seen circling far
over head, or perched in the tops of the tallest
trees.

## SANTA CRUZ

*Santa Cruz* (holy cross), the well-known seaside resort lying at the northern hook of the
great curve that forms Monterey Bay, was
named by the Portolá expedition, as thus described by Father Crespi: "We camped on the
north side of the river [San Lorenzo], and we
had a great deal of work to cut down trees to
open a little passage for our beasts . . . . . Not
far from the river we saw a fertile spot where
the grass was not burnt, and it was a pleasure
to see the pasture and the variety of herbs and
rose-bushes of Castile." The next day they
moved on again, and the diary continues: "After
proceeding about five hundred steps, we passed
a large stream of running water, which has

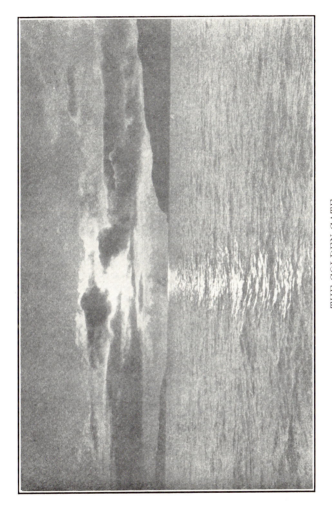

THE GOLDEN GATE

" * * * called by the Indians Yulupa, (the place where the sun plunges into the sea)"

its source among some high hills and passes through some great table-lands of good soil, that may easily be irrigated by the waters of the said creek. This creek was named *Santa Cruz*."

A mission was established at this place by Padres Salazar and López, September 25, 1791, but the buildings finally fell into a ruinous condition, and were removed to give place to the modern church which now stands upon the original site.

## SAN JUAN BAUTISTA

*San Juan Bautista* (St. John the Baptist) has suffered mutilation by the dropping of its last part, and usually appears as *San Juan*. San Juan is a small town in San Benito County, in a fertile valley on the San Benito River, forty-four miles southeast of San José. At this place the mission of San Juan Bautista was founded, June 24, 1797. Although this mission passed through some strenuous experiences, and was twice attacked by the Indians, and somewhat damaged by repeated earthquakes in 1800, it is still moderately well preserved, and shelters within its hallowed walls a large and interesting collection of relics of the old mission days. An interesting circumstance at this mission is the presence in the floor tiles of hardened foot-prints of wild animals— foxes and others. These prints were left in the

soft tiles by prowling animals at the time of the building of the missions, showing the primitive conditions of that day.

## SUPPLEMENTARY LIST

*Agua Amargosa* (bitter water), a place in San Benito County now known by its English translation, "Bitter Water," and so called from mineral springs.

*Año Nuevo* (new year) is the name of a prominent cape running out from the shore of Santa Cruz County, where one of the coast light-houses is situated. It received its name from the day of its discovery.

*Arroyo Seco* (dry creek). The Arroyo Seco, rising in the Santa Lucía Range and flowing northeasterly into the Salinas River, is probably the most remarkable example of terrace formation to be found among the streams of the state.

There are other Arroyo Secos in the state, one near Los Angeles which is very striking in its color effects.

*Blanco* (white) is a town in Monterey County. The name turns out to be historical, given by the Portolá expedition of 1769 in reference to the white clay seen in the neighborhood. Father Crespi says in his diary, "Because the earth there had a whitish color, this place was called *Real Blanco* (white camp)." The story that it is

114

a translation of the name of a man named White is pure invention.

*Cañada Segunda* (second canyon).

*Carmelo.* This word, although not Spanish in origin, being derived from the Hebrew Kar-mel (a garden or garden-land), is interesting as one of the oldest names bestowed by Spanish explorers in California, and important as the name of the river on whose banks stands the most famous of the missions, San Carlos Borroméo. The river, which flows through a valley so fertile and lovely that its name of "garden-land" well befits it, was named by Vizcaíno in 1602 in honor of the Carmelite friars who accompanied the expedition and who chanced to be the first to observe the river. The paragraph in Vizcaíno's original narrative runs as follows: "A river of very good water but little depth, whose banks are well peopled with black poplars, very tall and smooth, and other trees of Castile; and which descends from high white mountains. It was called *El Río de Carmelo,* because the friars of this order discovered it."

*Cerro del Venado* (hill of the deer).

*Chualar* is a village in Monterey County, in the Salinas valley, 128 miles southeast of San Francisco. The *chual* is a wild plant of California,—pig-weed or goose-foot,—and *chualar* is a spot abounding in chual plants.

115

*Corral* (yard, enclosed place). On October 11, 1769, the Portolá party stopped at a place about a league from the Pájaro River, where they constructed a fence between a lake and a low hill, in order to keep the animals secure at night without the need of many watchmen. Palou, in his *Life of Serra,* says: "The first expedition called this place the *Corral,* on account of having built there, with some sticks nailed together, a pasture in the manner of a yard, in order to keep the animals safe at night. This was of great assistance, for there were so many sick that there were not enough [people] to guard the animals." In different parts of the state there were many *Corrals* and *Corralitos* (little yards). Sometimes the enclosing fence was made of stones, when more convenient, and the enclosure was then called *Corral de Piedra* (stone corral); sometimes a barricade of earth was thrown up, and it was then called *Corral de Tierra* (earth corral). *Corral de Tierra* is the name of a wellknown ranch near Monterey. In the days of old, many a joyous *merienda* (picnic) and barbecue was held at the Corral de Tierra Rancho. *Corralitos* (little corrals) is in Santa Cruz County, fourteen miles east of Santa Cruz.

*Gabilán,* also spelled *Gavilán* (hawk), is the name of the long mountain ridge, a branch of

the Coast Range, which extends through the counties of Monterey and San Benito.

*Gonzales* (a surname). This place is in Monterey County, in the Salinas Valley, seventeen miles southeast of Salinas.

*Gorda* (fat, thick).

*Las Grullas* (the cranes). In the diaries of the Portolá expedition, date of October 7, 1769, we read: "We pitched our camp between some low hills near a pond, where we saw a great number of cranes, the first we had seen on this journey." This was about four leagues from the Pájaro River.

*Jolón,* a word of doubtful origin, which has been variously explained. It is thought by some persons to be a corruption of Jalón, a proper name, but old Spanish residents say it is an Indian word, meaning "valley of dead oaks."

*Llanada* (a plain, level ground). This place is in San Benito County.

*Laureles* (laurels). *Los Laureles* is the name of a ranch near Monterey. The wild laurel is a shrub common to many parts of the state.

*Lobos* (wolves), generally used on this coast in the sense of *lobo marino* (sea-wolf, or seal). There is a *Punta de Lobos* (seal point) near Monterey which is noted for the bold grandeur of its ocean scenery, as well as for its seals.

*Loma Prieta* (dark hill) is the name of a peak

117

in the Santa Cruz Mountains. Its dark form, shaped like a truncated cone, stands out against the sky and may be seen from a long distance.

*Moro Cojo* (literally "lame Moor") is the name of a well-known ranch in Monterey County. The Spaniards were in the habit of using *moro* to mean anything black, and in this case, according to old residents, the ranch was named for a lame black horse that ran wild there.

*Natividad* (nativity of Christ) is the name of a town in Monterey County, about one hundred miles southeast of San Francisco.

*Paicines* is in San Benito County. This is a word of doubtful origin, and many theories have been advanced to account for it. The most probable is that given by an Indian woman, a resident of the place, who says it was the name of an Indian tribe. The word is also sometimes spelled *Pajines*. See *Tres Pinos*.

*Panocha* is in San Benito County. This is a word applied to crude sugar, or syrup, somewhat resembling sorghum. Probably modern.

*Paraíso Springs* (paradise springs) is a health resort in Monterey County.

*Pleito* (quarrel, argument, lawsuit). This place is in Monterey County. It has not been possible to ascertain the application of its name.

*Potrero* (pasture). There were many *potreros* scattered about the state.

118

*Puentes* (bridges). This place, two leagues from the San Lorenzo River, was reached by the Portolá party October 18, 1769, and the reason for its naming is explained by Miguel Costansó: "These canyons contained running water in very deep ditches, over which it was necessary to lay bridges of logs, covered with earth and bundles of sticks, so that the pack animals could cross. The place was called *Las Puentes."*

*San Benito* (St. Benedict) was named in honor of the founder of the great order of Benedictines. San Benito Creek was named in 1772 by Father Crespi, and the name was eventually applied to the county. The town of San Benito is on the Salinas River, sixty miles southeast of Monterey. It is said of St. Benedict that he became a hermit at the age of fifteen and fled to the wilderness, where he lived on bread and water. While there he was tempted by the remembrance of a beautiful woman he had seen in Rome, and to overcome his wish to see her again "he flung himself into a thicket of briers and thorns, and rolled himself therein until he was torn and bleeding. At the monastery of Subiaco they show roses, said to have been propagated from these briers."

*San Lucas* (St. Luke) is in Monterey County, sixty miles southeast of Salinas. St. Luke was the disciple of Paul, who speaks of him as "Luke, the beloved physician," but tradition re-

ports him to have been an artist, and that he always carried with him two portraits, one of the Savior and the other of Mary. Doubtless for this reason he is regarded as the patron of artists and academies of art.

*Sur* (south). Point Sur (south point), on the coast south of Monterey, is a bold promontory where a light-house was placed by the government, in consequence of the frequent occurrence of shipwrecks there. The Sur River runs through a region remarkable for the wild picturesqueness of its scenery, and for the strange tales told of happenings among its early inhabitants.

*Toro* (bull) is the name of a ranch near Monterey, said to have been so called after a wild bull.

*Tres Pinos* (three pines), a place in San Benito County, one hundred miles southeast of San Francisco. Postmaster Black, of Tres Pinos, gives us the following history of the naming of this place: "The name was originally applied to what is now known as *Paicines,* but when the railroad came to this place they appropriated the name of Tres Pinos, hence it has no significance as applied to this town. The name was given the stopping-place now known as Paicines because of three pines alleged to have grown on the banks of the Tres Pinos creek near that place. Paicines, then Tres Pinos, was the scene

of the Vasquez raid and murders in the early '70's."

*Uvas* (grapes), the name of a town and creek in the Santa Cruz Mountains, no doubt so called from the abundance of wild grapes found in that locality.

# THE SANTA CLARA VALLEY

## VIII

*Santa Clara.* When the Spaniards passed through this valley, they were not slow to recognize in it one of those favored spots on the earth's surface where climate and soil unite to produce the highest results. So here they founded two missions, one at Santa Clara, and one at San José. Santa Clara County was named by the first legislature of California, which first thought of calling it San José County, but finally decided to name it for the mission.

*Santa Clara* (St. Clara) stands in one of the most fertile valleys in California, which is equivalent to saying in the whole world, and is about forty-six miles south-southeast of San Francisco. The mission was founded by Padres Peña and Murguia, January 12, 1777. The buildings now standing are mainly modern, but a small portion of the original structure being incorporated in them. The ceiling over the sanctuary is original, and a small part of the adobe buildings. Since

this writing the mission buildings have been destroyed by fire and again restored.

Clara de Asís, the sweet saint for whom this mission was named, was the daughter of a nobleman. Her beauty and wealth brought her many offers of marriage, all of which she refused, preferring to devote herself to a religious life. She became the founder of the order of Franciscan nuns, known as the "Poor Clares," to which many noble ladies attached themselves. After reaching the ripe age of sixty years Saint Clara's health began rapidly to decline, and she died in an ecstatic trance, believing herself called to Heaven by angelic voices. Her special symbol is the lily, peculiarly appropriate for the patroness of the ever - blooming Santa Clara Valley.

## SAN JOSE

*San José* (St. Joseph) enjoys the distinction of having been the first civic pueblo planted in the state by the Spaniards, although when we read the complaints of the padres concerning the highly undesirable character of its first settlers, recruited mainly from the criminal classes of Sonora, the distinction would seem to be of rather a doubtful sort.

Spurred on by the old bogie of their fear of foreign invasion, the Spanish government de-

cided to establish colonies of white settlers, believing that their hold upon the country would be rendered more secure by this means. The pueblo of San José de Guadalupe, founded November 29, 1777, by Lieutenant José Moraga, then in command at San Francisco, under orders from Governor Neve, was originally located on a site about a mile and a quarter distant from the present city, but was removed in 1797, in consequence of the discovery that the low-lying ground of its first location was often submerged during the winter rains. The people of the pueblo were compelled to travel a distance of three miles to attend mass at the Santa Clara Mission, and in order to make this journey more agreeable, Father Maguín de Catalá laid out the *alameda* between the two places, planting a fine avenue of willow trees which once comforted the wayfarer with their grateful shade. The original trees have now practically all disappeared and others have taken their places in part. The old alameda has vanished.

Not until 1797 was the mission of San José founded, on a spot some fourteen miles distant from the pueblo. The padres had no keen desire to place the missions in close proximity to the pueblos, fearing the evil influence on the Indians of a bad class of white men, besides other inevitable complications, such as the mixing up

124

of cattle. Father Engelhardt, in his *History of the California Missions,* tells the story of the founding of the Mission San José thus: "Here, on Trinity Sunday, June 11, 1797, Father Lasuén raised and blessed the cross. In a shelter of boughs he celebrated Holy Mass, and thus dedicated the mission in honor of the foster-father of Christ, St. Joseph."

The old church was unfortunately so shattered by an earthquake in 1868 that it was torn down and replaced by a wooden edifice.

It should be made clear that two missions were established here, Santa Clara and San José, and that the latter was not at San José, as some maps represent it, but some fourteen miles distant from the town.

## PALO ALTO

*Palo Alto* (high stick, or tree), in Santa Clara County, sixteen miles northwest of San José, once a stock farm where blooded horses were raised, now best known as the site of the Leland Stanford Junior University, is said to have received its name from a tall redwood tree on the *San Francisquito* (little St. Francis )creek. This tree stands just a few feet from the railroad bridge near Palo Alto station, and is said by old residents to have originally been in the form of a twin tree, one of the twins having been cut

down. The trees of this species received the name *Palo Colorado* (red stick, or tree) from the Portolá party, whose attention was attracted by their uncommon size and the peculiar reddish color of the wood, and the honor of their discovery may justly be awarded to Gaspar de Portolá, since he seems to have been the first white man to make report of having seen them.

This place was named by the Anza expedition of 1775-1776, and it seems rather strange that no mention is made in the diaries of the fact that the tree was a twin. Father Pedro Font, who accompanied the expedition, says: "From a slight eminence I here observed the lay of the port from this point and saw that its extremity lay to the east-southeast. I also noticed that a very high spruce tree, which is to be seen at a great distance, rising up like a great tower, from the *Llano de los Robles,*—it stands on the banks of the *Arroyo de San Francisco;* later on I measured its height—lay to the southeast." Further on in the diary he says: "Beside this stream is the redwood tree I spoke of yesterday: I measured its height with the graphometer which they lent me at the mission of San Carlos, and according to my reckoning, found it to be some fifty yards high, more or less, the trunk was five yards and a half in circumference at the base, and the soldiers said that there were still larger

126

ones in the mountains." This description of Father Font's gives rise to a strong suspicion that the tree now so highly venerated is not the original Palo Alto from which the place takes its name. The name was first applied to a land grant.

## LA SALUD

*La Salud* (health). In the name of this place, not far from the San Lorenzo River, reached by the Portolá party on October 22, there is a reference to one of the heaviest of the afflictions from which the Spaniards suffered during their journey up the state,—serious sickness and many deaths from scurvy. To their great surprise, after a wetting received during a heavy storm at this place, all the sick began to recover. Costansó, in his diary, date of October 22, says: "The day dawned overcast and gloomy. The men were wet. What excited our wonder was that all the sick, for whom we greatly feared that the wetting might prove harmful, suddenly found their pains very much relieved. This was the reason for giving the canyon the name of *La Salud.*"

*Los Gatos* (the cats) is the rather unpoetic name of a very pretty town in Santa Clara County, ten miles southwest of San José. From its location at the mouth of a canyon in the

127

Santa Cruz Mountains, the inference may be drawn that it was named in reference to the wild-cats which even at this day infest that region. John Charles Frémont, in his *Memoirs,* says: "The valley is openly wooded with groves of oak, free from under-brush, and after the spring rains covered with grass. On the west it is protected from the chilling influence of the northwest winds by the *Cuesta de los Gatos* (wild-cat ridge), which separates it from the coast."

## SUPPLEMENTARY LIST

*Almadén* (mine, mineral), a word of Moorish origin. New Almadén, in Santa Clara County, where there is a quicksilver mine, is named after the famous *Almadén* quicksilver mines of Spain.

*Alviso* (a surname). Alviso is in Santa Clara County, eight miles northwest of San José, and received its name from Ignacio Alviso, a native of Sonora, born in 1772, who was a member of Anza's party of colonists in 1775-76. He was the original Alviso of California, and was the grantee of *Rincón de los Esteros Rancho.*

*Arroyo Hondo* (deep creek).

*Coyote,* the native wolf of California. Coyote is an Aztec word, originally *coyotl.* The town of this name is situated thirteen miles southeast of San José.

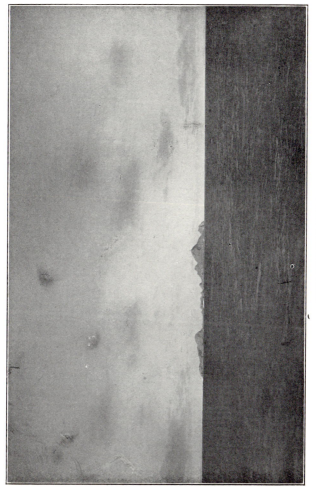

THE FARALLONES

" * * * standing like watch-dogs at our outer gate."

*Cupertino,* a town in Santa Clara County, named for Saint Joseph of Cupertino, who was born in 1603 in the village of Cupertino in the kingdom of Naples, This saint had very lowly beginnings, for, like Him of whom he was a devoted follower, he first saw the light in a stable. In his youth he was subject to ecstasies, and the children ridiculed him, calling him "open mouth." Although he had but little education and was scarcely able to read, by means of supernatural light he was enabled to solve the most intricate questions. His life was one long succession of visions and ecstasies, which were sometimes so profound that he could not be awakened from them by beating, or piercing his flesh with needles, or burning it with candles. He was once brought before the Inquisition on account of these ecstasies, being regarded as one possessed of the devil, but he retained his calm and joyous spirit.

*Las Llagas* (the wounds or stigmata of St. Francis),—in reference to the legend that St. Francis was supposed to have received, after a fast of fifty days, the miraculous imprint of the wounds of the Savior in his hands, feet and side. *Las Llagas* was the name of a place near Gilroy, and was also given by the padres to Alameda Creek.

*Madroño,* often misspelled *madrone,* is the

name given by the Spaniards to a very beautiful tree indigenous to California, which is thus described by Fremont in his *Memoirs:* "Another remarkable tree of these woods is called in the language of the country *Madroña.* It is a beautiful evergreen, with large, thick and glossy digitated leaves; the trunk and branches reddish-colored, and having a smooth and singularly naked appearance, as if the bark had been stripped off. In its green state the wood is brittle, very heavy, hard and close-grained; it is said to assume a red color when dry, sometimes variegated, and susceptible of a high polish. Some measured nearly four feet in diameter, and were about sixty feet high."

*Milpitas.* This word is one of the puzzles among California names. One definition given for it is "little gardens," from "milpa," meaning a corn patch. In that case the word must have been brought from Mexico by the missionaries, for the California Indians had no form of agriculture. These gardens were usually placed at a considerable distance from the missions, for, as fences were unknown in those days, it was necessary to plant the crops beyond the range of the cattle. For instance, the gardens of San Antonio Mission were located miles away, at what is still called the Milpitas Reservation, at the foot of the Santa Lucía Range. This did not

prevent damage by wild beasts, however, and to save the grapes when they were ripe from the bears it was the custom to build fires around the vineyards at night. Even so, it often happened that some hungry old grizzly, bolder than the rest, would be so sorely tempted that he would break through the circle of fire and feast to his heart's content.

Following the analogy of the Milipitas Reservation at San Antonio, it seems probable that the Milpitas of Santa Clara was so called because the mission gardens were located there.

Milpitas is the name of a village in Santa Clara County, which, for some unexplained reason, has come to be used as a term of derision, "the jumping-off place of creation."

*San Felipe* (St. Philip) is the name of a village in Santa Clara County. There were four saints of this name, perhaps the most distinguished being St. Philip Neri, a Florentine, born in 1515. He was the intimate friend of St. Charles Borroméo, patron of the mission at Monterey, and was the founder of the order of the Oratorians, "who were bound by no vows, and were not secluded from the world, but went about reading and praying with the sick and needy, founding and visiting hospitals and doing various charities." Then there was St. Philip of Bethsaida, who, going to Hieropolis, "found the people wor-

131

shiping a huge serpent, or dragon, which they thought to be a personification of Mars. Then Philip took pity on their ignorance. He held up the cross and commanded the serpent to disappear. Immediately it glided from beneath the altar, and as it moved it sent forth so dreadful an odor that many died, and among them the son of the King; but Philip restored him to life. Then the priests of the serpent were so wroth with the apostle that they crucified him, and when he was fastened to the cross they stoned him."—*(Stories of the Saints.)*

*San Martin* (St. Martin) is a town in Santa Clara County, six miles north of Gilroy. St. Martin has many legends connected with his history. Before he became a Christian, he was a soldier and was noted for his kindness and charity to his comrades. "The winter of 332 was so severely cold that large numbers perished in the streets of Amiens, where the regiment of St. Martin was quartered. One day he met at the gate a naked man, and taking pity on him, he divided his cloak, for it was all he had, and gave half to the beggar. That night in a dream Jesus stood before him, and on his shoulders he wore the half of the cloak that Martin had given the beggar. And he said to the angels who attended him, 'Know ye who hath thus arrayed me? My servant Martin, though yet unbaptized, hath

TAMALPAIS

" * * * like one great amethyst hanging against the sunset."

done this.' Then Martin was immediately baptized." Again it is told of him that being invited to sup with the emperor, "the cup was passed to Martin, before his Majesty drank, with the expectation that he would touch it to his lips, as was the custom. But a poor priest stood behind Martin, and to the surprise and admiration of all, the saint presented the full goblet to him, thus signifying that a servant of God deserved more honor, however humble his station, than any merely earthly potentate; from this legend he has been chosen the patron of all innocent conviviality."—*(Stories of the Saints.)*

# AROUND
## SAN FRANCISCO BAY

## IX

*San Francisco.* Many persons, misled by an incorrect translation of a certain passage in Palou's *Life of Serra,* have ascribed the naming of the bay of San Francisco (St. Francis), to the Portolá expedition of 1769, but, as a matter of fact, the outer bay, the great indentation in the coast outside of the Golden Gate, between Point Reyes and Mussel Point, had received this name many years before. In remonstrating with the *Visitador General* because no mission had been provided for St. Francis in Upper California, Serra remarked, "And is there no mission for our Father St. Francis?" Señor Gálvez replied, *"Si San Francisco quiere misión, que haga se halla su puerto y se le pondrá* (If St. Francis wants a mission, let him cause his port to be found and one will be placed there for him)." By "his port" Gálvez referred to a port already discovered and named, but which had been lost

sight of during the intervening years, and which he wished to have re-discovered. This is further carried out by the succeeding statements of Palou, in which he says that after failing to recognize the port of Monterey, "they came to the port of St. Francis, our father, and they all knew it immediately by the agreement of the descriptions which they carried," referring to descriptions obtained from the papers of the first discoverers. Father Crespi, who accompanied the expedition, says: "All the descriptions which we found here we read in the log-book of the pilot Cabrera Bueno, in order to form a judgment that this is the port of San Francisco. To make it all clear, the *Señor Commandante* ordered that during the day Sergeant Ortega should go out with a party of soldiers to explore." Further on in the same diary we read: "From the top of a hill we made out the great estuary, or arm of the sea, which probably has a width of four or five leagues." This is undoubtedly the first occasion when the eye of a white man rested upon "the great arm of the sea," that is, the inner harbor of San Francisco as we now know it.

It must be remembered that until the arrival of Portolá, the Spaniards only knew this part of the coast from the sea side, having no knowledge of that great inland sea known to us as the

135

bay of San Francisco. When the Portolá party
came up by land on their futile search for Monterey, they stopped to camp at a point near San
Pedro. Two parties were sent out, one under
Sergeant Ortega going up the peninsula till they
reached the Golden Gate, at which they looked.
The other was a deer hunting party sent over the
mountains lying between San Pedro and the bay,
who climbed Sweeny Ridge and from there saw
the inner bay. Portolá did not accompany either
of these parties and hence was not the first to
see the bay. In fact, he was awakened in the
night to be told by his men that they had found
a great arm of the sea. But afterwards Portolá
himself made two trips up and down the shore,
going as far as San José, and at that time he
saw the bay. He was, therefore, an actual eye-
witness of the discovery, and though he was not
the very first to see it, as the leader of the expedition he is fully entitled to be called its discoverer.

Palou ascribed the failure of the party to recognize the port of Monterey, and the consequent
continuance of their journey as far as San Francisco, to a direct interposition of the divine hand,
so that Gálvez's promise of a mission for St.
Francis might be carried out.

The honor of the christening of our world-
famous bay probably belongs to Sebastián Rod-

ríguez Cermeñón, a Portuguese navigator, who was commissioned in the year 1595 by Philip II to search for safe harbors along the coast for vessels in the Philippine trade. These ships usually shaped their return course so as to touch first at about the latitude of Cape Mendocino, making a knowledge of the harbors south of that point a matter of great importance, especially in stormy weather. Cermeñón had the misfortune to lose his vessel, the San Agustín, on Point Reyes, and was compelled to make his way home, with great peril and suffering, in a small boat. In his *Derrotero y Relación* (Itinerary and Narrative), under date of April 24, 1596, he says: "We sighted New Spain at Cape Mendocino on November 4, 1595 . . . . . We left the bay and port of San Francisco, which is called by another name, a large bay, in 38⅔ degrees, and the islets [Farallones] in the mouth are in 38½ degrees, the distance between the two points of the bay being twenty-five leagues." It is clear from this description that he referred to that great indentation in the coast between Point Reyes and one of the points to the south, possibly Mussel Point, and that he gave the name of San Francisco to it, displacing some other name by which it had been previously known. At any rate, if this is not the origin, it is likely to remain lost in the mists of the Pacific. Ban-

croft says: "There can be little doubt that Cermeñón named the port of his disaster *San Francisco*."

An absurd theory advanced by certain persons that the name was derived from that of Sir Francis Drake is wholly unworthy of consideration. The resemblance between the two names must be regarded as purely a coincidence, and any connection between *"El Pirata"* (the pirate) Drake, as the Spaniards usually called him, and the name of the gentle St. Francis must be taken in the light of a jest.

Portolá, then, although he was indubitably the discoverer of the bay as we know it — the inner harbor,—found the name already applied to the outer *ensenada* by his predecessor, Cermeñón.

It is held by quibblers that Portolá cannot in all fairness be considered the actual discoverer of the bay, since it is most probable that Lieutenant Ortega or perhaps some member of a hunting party which was sent out actually laid physical eyes upon it first.

A parallel might be drawn between the case of Portolá and that of Columbus. When the famous expedition of 1492 drew near to the shores of the new world, it was not the great admiral, but a common sailor, Rodrigo de Triana, by name, who first raised the thrilling

138

cry of "land! land!"; yet, nevertheless, the world justly awards the honor and glory of the discovery to Christopher Columbus, the leader and the soul of the party, whose splendid imagination and unconquerable resolution made it possible.

Although the Portolá party made a partial examination at this time of the shores of what they called the "great arm of the sea," and Captain Fages returned for further explorations in 1770, and again in 1772, when he stood on the present site of Berkeley and looked out through the Golden Gate, the mission was not established until 1776. Father Palou was its founder, and he states in his *Life of Serra* that the presidio was established with solemn religious services, September 17, 1776, on the day of the "impressions of the stigmata of St. Francis," but on account of a delay in receiving orders, the founding of the mission did not take place until October 8. On that day a procession was held with the image of St. Francis, and mass was celebrated by Father Palou himself.

So they prayed and sang their hymns, in the year of '76, while their hearts beat high with the zeal of the missionary, and, happily, no echo of the roll of drums and boom of minute guns came to them across the untrodden miles of mountain and plain, of forest and prairie, that

separated them from the alien race on the other rim of the continent, for whom they were all unconsciously preparing the way to the possession of a great principality.

No natives were present at this mass, for the reason that in the month of August they had been driven on their tule rafts to the islands of the bay and the opposite shores, by their enemies, the Salsonas, who lived about seven leagues to the southeast, and who had set fire to their *rancherías* and killed and wounded many of their people, the Spaniards not being able to prevent it.

The first settlement was three-fold, including the mission of *San Francisco de Asís,* on the *Laguna de los Dolores* (the lagoon of sorrows), the presidio, and the pueblo, separated from one another by about a league. The Pueblo was at first known as *Yerba Buena,* in reference to the profuse growth of that vine about the locality. The change of the name is ascribed by General Sherman, in his *Memoirs,* to jealousy of the town of Benicia, which was at first called *Francisca,* in honor of General Vallejo's wife, and was thought to bear too marked a resemblance to the name of the great patron, San Francisco. General Vallejo himself states that the change was made as a matter of convenience, to bring the three points of the triangle, church, town,

THE MISSION OF SAN RAFAEL, FOUNDED IN 1817

" * * * where the lily and the rose bloom from year's end to year's end."

and presidio, all under one name. Whatever the reason for the change, it is a matter of congratulation that it occurred, for the name of the venerable saint carries a dignity more commensurate to a noble city than the poetic, but less impressive *Yerba Buena.*

The church of *San Francisco de Asís,* popularly known as *Mission Dolores,* still stands in a good state of preservation, having almost miraculously withstood the earthquake and fire of 1906, which laid low all its proud modern neighbors. Of its patron, the gentle St. Francis, it may be said that he was the son of a rich merchant, but that he abandoned his riches, adopted vows of poverty, and founded the order of Franciscans. "While in a trance, or vision, after having fasted for fifty days, he received the miraculous imprint of the wounds of the Savior on his hands, feet, and side." His chief attributes were humility, poverty, and love for animals. In pictures he is always represented as accompanied by a pet lamb.

## THE GOLDEN GATE

Although this name, not being of Spanish or Indian origin, is not properly included in these pages, its close relationship to San Francisco, and its position as the gate-way to the entire state, will not permit it to be passed by.

In view of the comparatively recent origin of the name, 1844, and the accessibility of the story, it seems strange indeed that any writer should have advanced the theory that the Golden Gate received its name from Sir Francis Drake, yet this wholly unfounded explanation has found its way into print. In the first place, it has been pretty thoroughly established by historians that Drake never saw the inner harbor, and knew nothing of the narrow strait leading to it. In the report of his voyage, written by one of his companions, we read: "At 38 degrees toward the line, it pleased God to send us into a faire and good harborow, with a good wind to enter the same. Our General called this country *Nova Albion,* and that for two causes;—the one in respect of the white bankes and cliffes, which ly toward the sea; and the other that it might have some affinity with our country in name, which sometimes was so called." The white cliffs under Point Reyes answer so well to this description that there can be little doubt that Drake's anchorage was in the small outer bay under that point, now known as Drake's Bay; to say nothing of the fact that the account of the voyage has no word concerning the great land-locked harbor, with a narrow strait as its only entrance, a circumstance so novel that, as Bancroft justly observes, Drake could not have

failed to mention it had he known aught of it.

All discussion of the name *Golden Gate* is, moreover, brought to an end by the fact that its real author, John Charles Frémont, gives a circumstantial account of it in his *Memoirs*. After an elaborate description of the bay, and its surroundings, he says: "Between these points is the strait—about one mile broad in its narrowest part, and five miles long from the sea to the bay. To this gate I gave the name of *Chrysopylae,* or Golden Gate; for the same reasons that the harbor of Byzantium (Constantinople afterwards) was called *Chrysoceras,* or Golden Horn. The form of the harbor and its advantages for commerce, and that before it became an *entrepot* of eastern commerce, suggested the name to the Greek founders of Byzantium. The form of the entrance into the bay of San Francisco, and its advantages for commerce, Asiatic inclusive, suggested to me the name which I gave to this entrance, and which I put upon the map that accompanied a geographical memoir addressed to the senate of the United States, in June, 1848."

Here we have, told in the somewhat pedantic language of its author, the true story of the first appearance of the famous name *Golden Gate* upon the map of the world, and instead of its having been "named by Colonel Frémont because of the brilliant effect of the setting sun on

143

the cliffs and hills," as one writer has fondly
imagined, or from an idea connected with the
shining metal, which still lay buried deep from
the sight of man beneath the mountains of the
land, it was born in a sordid dream of commerce. Yet, for so wonderfully apt a name,
whatever may have been Frémont's motive in
selecting it, we owe him a debt of gratitude.

There is some disposition to doubt this explanation of the name *Golden Gate,* partly on
the ground of a distrust of Frémont's trust-
worthiness, and partly because of its far-fetched
nature. As to the latter objection it should
be remembered that he was that kind of man.
He was possessed of a certain amount of erudi-
tion which he was fond of showing off, and this
labored method of seeking for a name in the
old Greek was quite in keeping with his character. As to his reliability, although it is quite
possible that he colored events of a political
character to suit his own purposes, in ordinary
matters there seems to be no reason to doubt
his statements. At all events, the name Golden
Gate does in fact appear upon his map of 1848
as he says.

The first entrance through the Golden Gate
by a white man's craft of which history has any
record was made by Captain Juan Manuel de
Ayala, on August 5, 1775, in the ship *San Carlos,*

NAPA VALLEY

" * * * said to have been the cradle of the Suisun race."

alias *Toison de Oro*. It is a romantic circumstance that the second name of this vessel means Golden Fleece. (For a detailed story of this highly interesting voyage and entrance into the harbor of San Francisco, see the *Overland Monthly* for December, 1916.)

## ALCATRAZ

*Alcatraz* (pelican), the fortress-like island in the bay, just inside the channel, performs the triple duty of a fortified military post, prison, and light-house. Although but 1650 feet in length, it rises to a height of 130 feet above the water, and in the shadowy light just after sunset, its high, rocky walls, topped by the buildings of the fortification and prison, make a silhouette against the sky strikingly like a great dreadnaught, standing guard at the harbor's entrance.

The diary and chart of Captain Ayala, the first to enter San Francisco Bay from the sea, show that in reality he gave this name, in 1775, to the island now called Yerba Buena, "because of the great abundance of those birds." In some way not now known it was later applied to its present location. Alcatraz properly means albatross, but is used in Spanish-America to designate the pelican. One of the main thoroughfares in the city of Oakland also bears the name of *Alcatraz*.

145

## ANGEL ISLAND

*Angel Island,* the Americanization of *La Isla de los Angeles* (the isle of the angels), belies its name, since it has been devoted to the quite un-angelic business of quarantine station of San Francisco.

Palou, in speaking of the expedition of 1775, says: "They moved to the island which is in front of the mouth, which they called *Nuestra Señora de los Angeles* [Our Lady of the Angels], on which they found good anchorage, and going on land, they found plenty of wood and water."

The island was in fact discovered and named in August, 1775, by Captain Juan Manuel de Ayala, the first navigator to enter San Francisco Bay through the Gate. On August 27th a thanksgiving mass was celebrated on the beach of the island of Our Lady of the Angels, and, while the flag of Spain was waved, nine cheers were given for the King, no doubt to the intense surprise of the Indians looking on from the shore of the mainland.

## YERBA BUENA ISLAND

*Yerba Buena* (the good herb) is the name of a dainty little vine native to the California woods, which has an agreeable aromatic odor, and was

much in use among the Spanish as a medicinal herb, and to add a pleasant aroma to their tea. Frémont, who, whatever else may be said of him, had enough poetry in his soul to feel an expansive joy over the plant life of this flowery land, describes it as follows: "A vine with a small white flower, called here *la yerba buena,* which, from its abundance, gives its name to an island and town in the bay, was today very frequent on our road, sometimes running on the ground, or climbing the trees." It is said that the Hupa Indians were in the habit of weaving the tendrils of this vine in their hair for the sake of the perfume.

Some talk has arisen of late that this poetic and historic name is to be taken away from our island. Commuters, when you pass it on your daily journey, let your minds carry you back to the day when the delicate tendrils of the little vine waved on the island's steep slopes, and its sweet scent was wafted on the breeze from the Golden Gate, and do not, I pray you, consent to call it *Goat!*

## MARE ISLAND

*Mare Island,* in San Pablo Bay, separated from Vallejo by a strait one-half mile wide, a charming spot with an unpoetic name,—is another example of writers attempting to make diffi-

culties where none exist, and so they would have us believe that the name of this isle arose, like Venus, from *mare,* the sea. Apart from the fact that this labored method of naming places, by seeking in the Latin, was quite foreign to the custom of the Spaniards, it happens that the true story in this case is at hand, and can scarcely be doubted, since it occurred in the immediate family of Dr. Vallejo, who tells it thus: "In the early days, the only ferry-boat on the waters near Vallejo and Benicia was a rude one, made chiefly of oil barrels obtained from whaling ships, and propelled by sails. These barrels were secured together by beams and planking, and it was divided into compartments for the accommodation of cattle, to the transportation of which it was chiefly devoted. One day, while this boat was coming from Martinez to Benicia, a sudden squall overtook it, and the craft pitched fearfully; the animals, chiefly horses, became restive, and some of them broke through it. The boat was upset, and the living cargo thrown into the bay. Some of the livestock were drowned, and some managed to reach either shore by swimming. One of the horses, an old white mare, owned and much prized by General Vallejo, succeeded in effecting a landing on the island, and was rescued there a few days after by the General, who thereupon called the place

148

*La Isla de la Yegua* (the island of the mare)."

An interesting corroboration of this story is found on page 574 of Frémont's *Memoirs,* where he refers to the island as *La Isla de la Yegua.*

A statue of a white horse would perpetuate the history of this isle in a manner both appropriate and beautiful, in the same way that upon the heights of Angel Island a colossal figure of an angel, or of the Virgin, and upon Alcatraz a great pelican with outspread wings, might be placed to tell their stories. In the old world, many legends of the past are perpetuated in this way, and there is no reason why the equally romantic episodes in California's history should not be so commemorated, at least in those cases that lend themselves readily to purposes of art.

This island was discovered by Captain Ayala, who explored the bay in 1775, and was called by him Isla Plana (flat island).

## ALAMEDA

It has been thought that this name may have been derived from the resemblance between Alameda creek, at one time thickly shaded along its banks by willows and silver-barked sycamores, and an *alameda* (an avenue shaded by trees), but since the primary meaning of the word is "a place where poplar trees grow," from

149

*alamo* (poplar or cottonwood), it requires less stretching of the imagination to believe that some such grove of cottonwoods near the creek gave it the name. Fray Dantí, in his diary of the exploration of "the Alameda" in 1795, says: "We came to the river of the Alameda, which has many large boulders, brought down by floods, and is well populated with willows, alders, and here and there a laurel. At a little distance from where the river runs, the tides of the Estuary come."

Bancroft says, in his *History of California,* Vol. I: "In 1795 Sergeant Pedro Amador explored the eastern shore of San Francisco Bay, and in his report used the name of Alameda. It is probable that he applied the name, as it had been applied before, to a grove on the stream, since it is so used a little later."

From the name of an insignificant little stream, *Alameda* has come to be the designation of one of the most important counties in the state, and of the flourishing city on the east side of San Francisco Bay, nine miles east-southeast of San Francisco. The name as applied to the city did not originate with the Spanish discoverers, but was given by its first American founders. After a warm contest over the selection of the name, during which Leandro City, Peralta, and Elizabethtown were all considered, the

name of Alameda was finally chosen and formally adopted on June 11, 1853. The inference is obvious that the name was suggested to the founders from their familiarity with it as applied to the creek, and certainly all persons of taste will agree that their choice was a wise one, for there is no more charming place name in the state.

This city was once known as *Encinal* (place of oaks), on account of the groves of beautiful live-oaks there, nearly all of which have, most unfortunately, been sacrificed to so-called "improvements." Yet, some fine specimens still remain in the county, perhaps the best being those on the campus of the University of California, at Berkeley, Alameda County. The *encino* (live-oak) is thus described by Professor Jepson: "It is a low, broad-headed tree, commonly twenty to forty feet, but sometimes seventy feet high. The trunk is from one to four feet in diameter, usually short, and parting into wide-spread limbs, which often touch or trail along the ground." This tree has little commercial value, but is highly regarded for its hardy nature, which permits it to flourish in exposed localities along the coast, where no other tree thrives, and for the perennial green with which it adorns an otherwise often bleak landscape.—(Notes taken from *The Trees of California,* by Professor Willis

Linn Jepson, of the University of California.)

About the year 1800, Fathers Catalá and Viader, in charge of the mission of Santa Clara, in order to make it easier for the people in the pueblo of San José to attend church services at the mission, which was about three miles distant, made a road between the two places. With the help of the Indians, they planted trees, mostly willows, along this road, thus making a pleasant shady path for travelers in hot weather. This road was named the *Alameda*.

## LOS FARALLONES

*Los Farallones,* the three small islands standing like watch-dogs at our outer gate, about thirty-two miles due west of the entrance to the bay, derive their name from *farallon,* a word meaning "a small pointed island in the sea." Although this word is commonly employed by the Spanish to designate such islands, and its use in this case is perfectly obvious, the statement has been made that our isles were named for a certain Ferolla, one of the early navigators, a theory entirely without value.

The Farallones are frequented by multitudes of sea-fowl, which breed there and at one time supplied great quantities of eggs for the San Francisco market. For some twenty years or

more the United States Government, owing to the contentions of rival egg companies, has prohibited the gathering and sale of these eggs.

## MOUNT TAMALPAIS

"To see the sun set over Tamalpais,
Whose tented peak, suffused with rosy mist,
Blended the colors of the sea and sky
And made the mountain one great amethyst
  Hanging against the sunset."
                    —*Edward Rowland Sill.*

*Tamalpais* (bay mountain) is in Marin County, five miles southwest of San Rafael; it rises to a height of 2606 feet above sea level, and dominates San Francisco Bay and the surrounding country, offering one of the most magnificent panoramas of sea and land to be seen anywhere on the earth's surface. Its name is a compound of two Indian words, *tam-mal* ("bay" or "our country") and *pi-is* (mountain). The resemblance of the latter word to the Spanish *pais* (country) is thought by ethnologists to be purely accidental.

The story often told by guides and other persons that Tamalpais, because of a fancied resemblance in the mountain's outline to a woman lying down, means "the sleeping maiden," is purely the product of a vivid imagination.

A very remarkable circumstance in the history

153

of this mountain is the fact that it underwent a change of position at the time of the great earthquake of 1906, of course in conjunction with the entire sheet of the earth's surface upon which it stands. On that occasion, the northeast and southwest sides of the rift slipped upon each other, first carrying the sheet of land upon which Tamalpais rests to the north, then the "springback" carried it back toward the south again. According to the report of the State Earthquake Investigation Commission, "As a consequence of the movement, it is probable that the latitudes and longitudes of all points in the Coast Ranges have been permanently changed a few feet."

So the old mountain, sitting in Indian stoicism, indifferent to the storms that sometimes lash its sturdy sides, the fogs that roll in a white billowy sea around its foot, and earthquakes that shift its latitude and longitude some feet, has very appropriately received its name from the language of the aborigines who once dwelt at its base.

## MOUNT DIABLO

*Mount Diablo* (devil mountain) is an isolated, conical peak of the Coast Range, in Contra Costa County, about thirty-eight miles northeast of San Francisco. It rises 3849 feet above the level of the sea, and is the most conspicuous land-

mark in the central part of the state. General M. G. Vallejo tells the following story to account for the name: "In 1806, a military expedition from San Francisco marched against a tribe called the Bolgones, who were encamped at the foot of the mountain. There was a hot fight, which was won by the Indians. Near the end of the fight, a person, decorated with remarkable plumage, and making strange movements, suddenly appeared. After the victory, the person, called *Puy* (evil spirit) in the Indian tongue, departed toward the mountain. The soldiers heard that this spirit often appeared thus, and they named the mountain *Diablo* (devil). These appearances continued until the tribe was subdued by Lieutenant Moraga, in the same year."

If this be the true story of the naming of Mount Diablo, and there seems to be no good reason to doubt it, it is quite likely that the *Puy,* or devil, was one of the "medicine men" who played upon the superstitions of the Indians by pretending to be the "spirit of the mountain."

There is perhaps no other name in the state about which so many legends have clustered. One of these stories, related in a history of Contra Costa County published about twenty years ago, runs as follows: "There is a legend that the Bolbones Indians brought to the Spanish padres gold which they had found in the rocky

recesses of the mountain. The good fathers, foreseeing in the abundance of the 'root of all evil' the ruin of their pastoral plans of settlement, took all the gold thus gathered and placed it in a tub of water, after having secretly poisoned the water. They then asked the Indians to make their dogs drink from the tub. As a natural consequence, the animals died. The Indians thereupon declared the mountain to be the hiding place of the evil one, or *Puy,* which the padres translated into the Spanish name *Diablo.*" A bald fact that is calculated to throw discredit on this ingenious story is that Diablo is not a gold producing mountain.

Another account says that a party of troops were sent there to chastise troublesome Indians. In the night they saw moving lights in the thicket which they believed to be made by Indians, but in the morning, when they charged the thicket, no Indians were to be found, so the troops judged that the lights were caused by *el diablo.*

The fanciful legend of Bret Harte, which he says was partially substantiated in the report of Señor Julio Serro, the sub-prefect of San Pablo, relates that Father Haro, a priest living at the San Pablo Mission, met the devil on the summit of this mountain and received from his Satanic Majesty the prophecy that the Spaniards would be ousted from the land by the Anglo-Saxons. In this encounter the father suffered some in-

jury, and his muleteer insisted that he had in reality met a bear, but the prefect thought the enemy of souls might have very easily taken on the aspect of a bear.

Still another story has it that the mountain is two-horned, like the devil, and that this gave rise to the name.

Another has it that some vaqueros, who happened to be on the mountainside, saw sparks of fire issuing from what they supposed to be solid rock, whereupon they fled in terror, being convinced that it was the home of the devil.

The common belief among California Indians that peaks were the abodes of spirits favors the theory that the name had its origin in some Indian tradition, and makes the explanation offered by General Vallejo the most plausible among all those thus far presented.

One of the most amusing stories connected with this place is that about some Americans, who, observing the prevalence of *San* among California place names tacked it onto the mountain, calling it *San Diablo* (Saint Devil).

## SAUSALITO

*Sausalito* (little willow grove) is on the west shore of San Francisco Bay, in Marin County, six miles northwest of San Francisco. The name

in its present form is incorrectly spelled, the proper spelling being Sauzalito, diminutive of sauzal (willow grove). On some of the early maps it appeared as Saucelito, a form which has no existence in Spanish grammar and is entirely incorrect, the diminutive of sauce (willow) being saucito.

It is the name of one of the most delightful of the rose-embowered towns around the bay where many of the business men of San Francisco have their homes.

## MARIN COUNTY

Of Marin County, separated from San Francisco by The Golden Gate, and noted for the beauty of its scenery, we get the story from General M. G. Vallejo. It appears that in 1815 or '16, an exploring party from San Francisco had a fight with the Lacatiut tribe, so called from a certain root used by them as food, especially in the Petaluma Valley. During this fight the chief was captured and carried to San Francisco, but afterwards escaped, and kept up constant hostilities in Petaluma Valley. He was finally converted to Christianity, and did good service for the whites as ferryman on the bay, and on account of his skill in navigating these waters, they called him *El Marinero* (the sailor); it is

158

thought that the name of Marin County is a corruption of this word. *El Marinero* died at the mission of San Rafael in 1834.

## TIBURON

*Tiburón* (shark) is on the Marin County shore, opposite San Francisco. It has been facetiously suggested that this name may have been derived from "sharks" of the land variety, but it probably came from some story connected with those of the sea.

## SAN RAFAEL

Even in this land, so prodigal with its flowers from its northern to its southern borders, San Rafael, the county-seat of Marin County, fifteen miles north of San Francisco, is notable for the exceeding beauty of its gardens, where the lily and the rose bloom from year's end to year's end.

Raphael (God heals) is the angel of the spirits of men, and it is his business to gather the souls of the dead into the place where they are reserved for the day of judgment. He it was who taught men the use of simples to cure them of plagues and sickness after the flood. The "healer" seems peculiarly fitting as the patron saint of a place where nature has done so much for the "joy of living."

The mission of *San Rafael Arcángel* (St. Raphael the Archangel), founded in 1817, has now disappeared, not a vestige remaining of it. It was first established as an *asistencia,* or auxiliary, to the mission of San Francisco, for the purpose of moving some of the people there, in the hope that there would be less sickness and fewer deaths in its milder climate.

A spur of the Coast Range in Southern California bears the name of *San Rafael Mountains.*


## BENICIA

*Benicia* (a surname) is the name of a town in Solano County, on the north side of Carquínez Strait, twenty-eight miles northeast of San Francisco. Its story may best be told in the words of General Sherman, in the following quotation from his *Memoirs:* "We found a solitary adobe house, occupied by Mr. Hastings and his family, embracing Dr. Semple, the proprietor of the ferry. The ferry was a ship's boat, with a lateen sail, which could carry six or eight horses. It took us several days to cross over, and during that time we got well acquainted with the doctor, who was quite a character. He was about seven feet high. Foreseeing, as he thought, a great city on the bay somewhere, he selected Carquínez Straits as its location, and obtained

MOUNT SHASTA

" * * * its summit glistening with snow and visible at a distance of 140 miles down the valley."

from General Vallejo title to a league of land, on condition of building a city to bear the name of General Vallejo's wife, Francisca Benicia. Accordingly, the city was first called *Francisca.* At this time, where San Francisco now is was known as *Yerba Buena;* now some of the chief men of that place, knowing the importance of a name, saw their danger, and so changed the name to *San Francisco.* Dr. Semple was so outraged at their changing the name to one so nearly like his town that he, in turn, changed his town's name to the other name of Mrs. Vallejo, and *Benicia* it has been to this day."

## LAS PULGAS RANCHO

*Las Pulgas Rancho* (the fleas ranch), is near Redwood City. The story of this place, with its unpleasantly suggestive name, although of little importance in itself, is told here for the light it throws upon the manners and customs of the original dwellers in the land. Father Engelhardt, in his *History of the California Missions,* describes their way of living thus: "Their habitations were primitive, in summer often but a shady spot, or mere shelter of brush. Their winter quarters consisted of a flimsy structure of poles fixed in the ground, and drawn together at the top, at a height of ten or twelve feet. The

poles were interwoven with small twigs, and the structure then covered with tules, or tufts of dried grass. In some places these dwellings were conical in shape, in others oblong, and their size ranged according to the number of people. At a distance they resembled large bee-hives, or small hay-stacks. On one side there was an opening for a door, at the top another for smoke. Here the family, including relatives and friends, huddled around the fire, without privacy, beds or other furniture. A few baskets, a stone mortar or two, weapons, some scanty rags of clothing, food obtained from the hunt, or seeds, were kept here. All refuse food and bones were left where they were dropped, giving the earth floor the appearance of a dog-kennel. Fleas and other vermin abounded in this mass of filth, which soon became too offensive even for savages, and they adopted the very simple method of setting fire to the hut and erecting another."

After reading this description, we are not surprised when Father Crespi tells us that, having arrived at a deserted Indian village, and some of the soldiers having rashly taken refuge in the huts for the night, they soon rushed out with the cries of *"las pulgas! las pulgas!"* (the fleas! the fleas!). He goes on to say, "for this reason, the soldiers called it the *Rancheria de las Pulgas"*

162

(the village of the fleas), a name borne by the ranch to this day.

La Pérouse, in his *Voyage Autour du Monde,* says the padres were never able to change this form of architecture common to the two Californias. The Indians said they liked open air, and that it was convenient, when the fleas became too numerous, to burn the house and construct a new one, an argument not without merit.

## POINT LOBOS

*Point Lobos* (seal point, from *lobo marino,* sea-wolf) is just outside the Golden Gate, on the south side, near the spot where the seals crawling about on the rocks have long been one of the chief attractions of the famous Cliff House.

## SUPPLEMENTARY LIST

*Alamo* (cottonwood tree) is the name of a place in Contra Costa County, twenty-four miles northeast of San Francisco.

*Alvarado,* a surname, that of one of the first governors of the state. Alvarado is a village in Alameda County, on Alameda Creek, twenty-four miles southeast of San Francisco. Juan Bautista Alvarado was a central figure in California history. He was born at Monterey, Feb-

163

ruary 14, 1809, and from '27 on occupied various official positions, including that of governor of the state. Bancroft says of his character and appearance: "In physique Don Juan Bautista was of medium stature, stout build, fair complexion, and light hair; of genial temperament, courteous manners, and rare powers of winning friends. There was much in his character to praise, much to condemn. He was a man of dissipated habits, and engaged in intrigues, but in his favor it may be said that he had more brains, energy and executive ability than any three of his contemporaries combined; he was patriotic and with good intentions toward his country, honorable in private dealings, and never enriched himself by his intrigues. He was not personally guilty of having plundered the missions, only responsible through being governor at that time. The accusations made against him of an unjust policy towards foreigners were entirely false." The name of the principal street in Monterey also recalls the memory of this famous political "spell-binder" and "silver-tongued orator" of the Mexican Period.

*Bolinas,* the name of a town in Marin County, delightfully situated on Bolinas Bay, eighteen miles northwest of San Francisco. Bolinas is probably a corruption of *Baulines,* an Indian word of unknown meaning. A land grant called

*Los Baulines* was located at the same place, and was probably the name of an Indian village. Bolinas Bay appears on a map of 1859 as Ballenas, giving rise to another theory that the name may have been corrupted from *ballenas* (whales). The fact that this name was in very common use among the Spaniards for bays frequented by these sea mammals gives some color of plausibility to this theory.

Another suggestion is that it comes from *bolina,* a light wind, but no historical support has been adduced for this theory.

Until further evidence is unearthed, this name must be placed among the doubtful, with the odds in favor of its being a corruption of the Indian name of the land grant, Baulines.

*Point Bonito* (pretty point) is the southern extremity of Marin County, on the north side of the Golden Gate. This name has been corrupted from *Punto de Bonetes* (hat point), which was given to it in 1776. It was originally named *Bonete* in reference to its resemblance to a sort of hat worn by some of the clergy, and it is so called in the old Spanish documents. When a vessel approached the north point she would see three heads, each resembling a *bonete*. The south head has since been cut down to give a more advantageous position for the light-house.

*Carquinez* is the name of the strait flowing

165

between the counties of Contra Costa and Solano, and connects San Pablo Bay with Suisún Bay. The strait is eight miles long, and at its narrowest part nearly a mile wide. All the waters flowing through the great central valley of the state from the Sierra Nevada pass through this strait. According to the scientists the name *Carquínez* is derived from Karkin, the name of an Indian village in that region. Fray José Viader, diarist of the Moraga expedition of 1810, says: "We went on to explore the plain and ridge of Los Carquinez, an estuary on which they say is the village of the Carquines." Other diarists speak of this Indian village and tribe under the name of the Carquines, making it fairly certain that the origin of the name is Indian.

The name has been immortalized by Bret Harte in his sketch called *In the Carquinez Woods,* in which there is a fine description of a redwood forest.

*Contra Costa* (opposite coast), so called on account of its original position directly opposite San Francisco. It should be explained that the name Contra Costa, which scarcely seems appropriate in its present application, was originally applied to the whole of the coast opposite San Francisco. Afterwards the part directly facing San Francisco was cut off to form Alameda

County, thus destroying the significance of the name Contra Costa.

*Corte Madera* (wood-cutting place) was so called because Luís Antonio Argüello once cut timbers there to use in repairing the presidio at San Francisco.

*Martínez* (a surname) is the name of the county-seat of Contra Costa County, and is on the south shore of Suisún Bay, thirty-six miles northeast of San Francisco. Ignacio Martínez was a native of the city of Mexico, born in 1774. He was a military officer under the Mexican government in California, and was *comandante* at San Francisco from 1822 to '27. Bancroft says of him: "He was not popular as an officer, being haughty and despotic, but as a rancher he is spoken of as a very courteous and hospitable man. The town of Martínez takes its name from him or his family."

*Merced Lake* (Mercy Lake) is near San Francisco. This lake was discovered and named by a land party under Captain Bruno Heceta in September, 1775. Its full name is *Nuestra Señora de la Merced* (Our Lady of Mercy).

*Montara Point* and Montara Mountains are in the western part of San Matéo County. Montara is a surname.

*Olema,* said to be an Indian word meaning "coyote valley," is the name of a town in Marin

County, one mile from the head of Tomales Bay, and thirty-five miles northwest of San Francisco.

*Otay,* in San Diego County, is named from an Indian word meaning "brushy."

*Pacheco,* a surname, that of a pioneer family of California. The town of Pacheco is in Contra Costa County, thirty miles northeast of San Francisco. Although Governor Romualdo Pacheco, of whom Bancroft says that "his record as a citizen, in respect of character, attainments and social standing was a good one," was the most prominent member of the family, the town was not named in his honor, but for Salvio Pacheco, a man who served in many military and civil offices. "He spent his life on Mount Diablo Rancho, on which is the town bearing his name." Pacheco is also the name of a street in San Francisco.

*Pescadero* (fishing place) is in a fertile valley of San Matéo County, on the coast about forty-four miles south of San Francisco. There are a number of *Pescaderos* in the state.

*Pinole* is said to be an Aztec word, applied to any kind of grain or seeds, parched and ground. Of this flour a very appetizing sort of gruel was made. The town of Pinole is in Contra Costa County, twelve miles west of Martínez. It is the site of extensive powder works. See Index.

*Portolá* (a surname), is the name of a town in

168

San Matéo County, and of another in Plumas County, which were named in honor of the celebrated discoverer of San Francisco Bay. It is unfortunate that this name is often mispronounced as Portóla. Many original signatures of this famous explorer are extant, showing conclusively that the accent was on the last syllable—Portolá.

*Potrero* (pasture ground) is one of the districts of San Francisco. This is only one of the many *Potreros* in the state.

*Presidio* is a word used by the Spaniards in the double meaning of prison or military post. It may be that the custom of using convicts as soldiers, prevalent with the Spanish, had something to do with this double usage of the word. The Presidio of San Francisco, now a regular military post of the United States, although still retaining its Castilian name, is picturesquely and delightfully situated on the north end of the peninsula. There is also a government presidio at Monterey.

*Point Reyes* (kings point) was named by Vizcaíno in honor of the "three wise men," or "holy kings," because it was discovered on the day of their devotion. The date of the discovery and naming was December 6, 1603. This point is in Marin County and is the outer point of Drake's Bay, where the noted adventurer is supposed to

have made his anchorage, and where Cermeñón was wrecked.

*Rodéo* (round-up of cattle.) Rodéos were held, and in some parts of the state still take place, for the purpose of separating and branding the cattle belonging to individual owners, an operation decidedly necessary when pastures were unfenced, and in early days one of the most picturesque features of California life. The village of Rodéo is in Contra Costa County.

*San Anselmo* (St. Anselm) is in Marin County.

*San Bruno,* a village near San Francisco, was named for St. Bruno, the founder and first abbot of the Carthusian Order. This order of monks is among the most severe in its rules, requiring almost perpetual silence of its members. Its devotees are only permitted to speak together once a week. They never eat flesh, and are compelled to labor constantly.

*San Gerónimo* (St. Jerome) is the saint usually pictured as accompanied by a lion, in commemoration of the well-known story of the removal of a thorn from the foot of one of those beasts by Jerome, and the devotion of the lion to him afterwards. San Gerónimo is the name of a small stream in Marin County, noted for its salmon fisheries.

*San Gregorio* (St. Gregory) is in San Matéo County, twenty-four miles southwest of Redwood

City. St. Gregory was a noble Roman who devoted his wealth to charity, and turned his home into a hospital and monastery. He was elected to the high office of Pope, and became the composer of what is called from him the "Gregorian Chant."

*San Leandro* (St. Leander) is in Alameda County, on San Leandro Creek, sixteen miles southeast of San Francisco. St. Leander was at one time Bishop of Seville, and is one of the patron saints of that city.

*San Lorenzo* (St. Lawrence) was a saint who suffered martyrdom by being roasted on a gridiron. The legend relates that he said to his tormentors, "I am now sufficiently cooked on this side, turn me over and roast me on the other." San Lorenzo is in Alameda County, twenty miles southeast of San Francisco.

*San Matéo* (St. Matthew) is the name of a county bordering on San Francisco Bay, and of a town on the west shore of the bay, twenty-one miles south of San Francisco. St. Matthew was a Hebrew by birth, and the author of the book of the Scriptures that bears his name.

*San Pablo* (St. Paul) is in Contra Costa County, on San Pablo Bay, fifteen miles northeast of San Francisco. One of the legends concerning St. Paul is that "the church called 'San Paolo delle Tre Fontane,' near Rome, is built

171

over three fountains which are said to have sprung up at the three places where the head of St. Paul fell and bounded, after being cut off by the executioner. It is said that the fountains vary in the warmth of the water,—the first, or the one where the head fell, being the hottest; the next, or that of the first bound, cooler; and the third still cooler." One of the leading streets in the city of Oakland also bears the name of *San Pablo*.

*San Quentin* (properly San Quintín) is a village in Marin County, on the west shore of San Francisco Bay, eleven miles north of San Francisco. This place, where the forbidding walls of the State's Prison shut out the light of California's glorious sun from the unfortunates enclosed there, very fittingly bears the name of a saint whose gloomy story runs thus: "San Quintín was the son of Zeno. He became converted and gave up a high command which he held in the Roman army, in order to preach. He labored especially in Belgium, and suffered death by being impaled on an iron spit." It is probable, however, that the town was not directly named for this saint, but received the name indirectly from Point Quintín, on the Marin Coast, which was so called from an Indian chief of that region who had been thus christened by the Spaniards,

the *San* being afterwards most inappropriately added by the Americans.

*San Ramón* (St. Raymond) is in Contra Costa County, nine miles east of Hayward. "St. Raymond belonged to the Order of Mercy, and labored for the captives among the Moors. By the Mahometans, among whom he was long a captive, for the ransom of his Christian brethren, his lips were bored through with a red-hot iron, and fastened with a padlock," an effective, if cruel method of preventing him from preaching the Christian faith.

*Suñol* (a surname). Suñol is a town in Alameda County, thirty-six miles southeast of San Francisco. In Fremont's *Memoirs* he refers to Don Antonio Suñol, probably a member of the same family for whom this town is named.

*Tocaloma* is a delightful secluded glen and creek in Marin County, not far north of San Francisco, where a hunting and fishing preserve is maintained. The word is Indian, but its meaning has not been ascertained.

*Tomales Bay* is an inlet of the Pacific Ocean, extending southeastward into Marin County. It is fourteen miles long. The village of Tomales is on the bay of the same name, fifty-five miles northwest of San Francisco. The name *Tomales* is a Spanish corruption of the Indian *tam'-mal* ("bay" or "our country") a word which came to

173

be applied to the natives in the neighborhood of San Francisco Bay.

*Vallejo* (a surname) is the name of a place in Solano County. The Vallejos were among the most prominent of the California pioneer families. "The founder of the family was Ignacio Vicente Ferrer Vallejo, born at Jalisco, Mexico, in 1748. He came of a family of pure Spanish blood, and of superior education. The most distinguished of his large family was Mariano Guadalupe, born at Monterey in 1808. Don Mariano served with great ability in various capacities under the Mexican government, and was at one time *Comandante General* of California. He was the founder of Sonoma, and it was to his untiring efforts that the development of the north was largely due. He foresaw the fate of his country, and finally cast in his lot with the United States, for which he seems to have been ill repaid. I have found none among the Californians whose public record in respect of honorable conduct, patriotic zeal, executive ability, and freedom from petty prejudices of race or religion or sectional politics is more evenly favorable than his."—(Bancroft.)

NORTH OF
SAN FRANCISCO

X

*Sonoma,* the name of the northern county, and of the town in the beautiful Sonoma Valley, forty-five miles north of San Francisco, is of doubtful origin. It is probable that it comes from Indian, rather than Spanish sources. In the native dialect of that region there is the constantly recurring ending *tso-noma,* from *tso* (the earth), and *noma* (village),—hence, *tsonoma* (earth village or earth place). The name was given by missionaries to a chief of the Indians there, and later applied to all the Indians at the mission. From Indian sources it seems there was a captain among them who was commonly called *Sonoma,* but who was known by a different name among his own people.—(University of California Publications in American Archaeology and Ethnology.)

Fray José Altimira, diarist of an exploring expedition to that region in 1823, says, "We came to the plain called Sonoma from the Indians who formerly lived there," The one thing that is quite clear about this name is that its origin is undoubtedly Indian.

It has been said that Sonoma means "valley of the moon," in reference to the shape of the valley, but there is probably more of poetry than of truth in this story. The California Indians lacked the imagination to have thought of such a name.

At this place, *San Francisco de Solano,* the last of the great chain of missions, was founded July 4, 1823. The mission buildings have been put in a fair state of preservation and the church has been restored by the state.

## NAPA

*Napa* is the name of a county, river and city, the county adjacent to San Pablo Bay, into which the river falls. The town is the county-seat of Napa County, and is on the river of the same name, about thirty-nine miles northeast of San Francisco. The Napa Soda Springs are an interesting natural feature of this place.

*Napa,* accented in some of the old documents as *Napá,* was the name of an Indian tribe who

176

EL RIO DE LOS SANTOS REYES (THE RIVER OF
THE HOLY KINGS)

" * * * named in honor of the three wise men."

occupied that valley, said to have been one of the bravest of the California tribes, and who constantly harassed the frontier posts. Kroeber, however, says no village of that name was ever located in that region, so the origin seems to be obscure. The entire tribe was practically wiped out by smallpox in 1838.

According to S. A. Barrett, in the University of California Publications in American Archaeology and Ethnology, there is a Pomo Indian word, *napa,* meaning "harpoon point," between which and the name of the town of Napa there may be some connection.

## CARNE HUMANA

Among the names of the old Spanish land grants are many that hold a suggestion of interesting and sometimes tragic tales, now lost in the dim shadows of the past. Of such is *Carne Humana* (human flesh), the name of a grant in Napa County, near St. Helena. This spot may have been the scene of one of those horrible acts of cannibalism to which the Indians of the entire Southwest were quite generally addicted. Captain Fages, in his diary of one of the expeditions to San Francisco Bay, mentions that this practice prevailed among the Indians of that region to a certain extent, but seems to have been con-

177

fined to the eating of the bodies of enemies slain in battle, and only the relatives of the slayer were permitted to take part in the abhorrent feast.

## SANTA ROSA

*Santa Rosa* (St. Rose), the county-seat of Sonoma County, is fifty-seven miles northwest of San Francisco.

An interesting story is told of Santa Rosa de Lima, said to be the only canonized female saint of the New World. She was born at Lima, in Peru, and was distinguished for her hatred of vanity, and her great austerity, carrying these characteristics to such an extreme that she destroyed her beautiful complexion with a compound of pepper and quicklime. When her mother commanded her to wear a wreath of roses, she so arranged it that it was in truth a crown of thorns. Her food consisted principally of bitter herbs, and she maintained her parents by her labor, working all day in her garden and all night with her needle. The legend relates that when Pope Clement X was asked to canonize her, he refused, exclaiming: *"India y Santa! Asi como llueven rosas!"* (An Indian woman a saint! That may happen when it rains roses!) Instantly a shower of roses began to fall in the Vatican, and did not cease until the Pope was

convinced of his error. This saint is the patroness of America, and is represented as wearing a thorny crown, and holding in her hand the figure of the infant Jesus, which rests on full-blown roses.

## MENDOCINO COUNTY

*Mendocino County,* in the northwestern part of the state, is distinguished for its extensive forests of redwoods. The main belt of these trees extends through this county, and they may here be seen in their highest development. They vary in height from 100 to 340 feet, and reach a diameter of from two to sixteen feet, having a red, fibrous bark sometimes a foot in thickness. Notwithstanding their great size, the delicacy of their foliage, which takes the form of flat sprays, gives them a graceful, fern-like appearance. The age of mature redwoods is said to range from 500 to 1300 years. The special characteristics of the wood of these trees are, its durability when buried in the soil, and its resistance to fire. Commercially it is valuable for many purposes, being preferred to steel for water supply conduits, and, in the form of saw-dust, found to be better than cork for packing fresh grapes.—(Notes from *The Trees of California,* by Professor Willis Linn Jepson, of the University of California.)

Probably the first written mention of these

179

trees occurs in the diary of Gaspar de Portolá, the discoverer of San Francisco Bay, whose attention was attracted to them while on his way up the coast, and from whom they received the name of *palo colorado* (redwood). Altogether, the credit of their discovery seems to belong to Portolá, although it has been given by some persons to Archibald Menzies, who wrote a description of the trees in 1795.

The village of Mendocino is on the coast, about 130 miles northwest of San Francisco. The name was first applied to the cape, which was discovered and named in honor of Don Antonio de Mendoza, first Viceroy of New Spain, by certain ships returning from the Philippines.

## KLAMATH

*Klamath* is the name of a village in Humboldt County, but is particularly known as applied to the Klamath River, which flows in a deep and narrow canyon through the counties of Siskiyou and Humboldt.

The word, in its different forms of *Klamath, Tlametl,* and *Clamet,* is the name by which these Indians were known to the Chinooks, and through them to the whites, their proper designation in their own language being *Lutuami.*— (Bancroft's *Native Races,* Vol. I, page 444.)

The meaning of the word has not been positively ascertained, although it is thought by ethnologists to be a possible corruption of *Maklaks* (people, community,—literally, the encamped). The Klamaths were a hardy people, who had many slaves captured from other tribes. The slave trade seems to have been carried on quite extensively among California Indians.

## MODOC COUNTY

*Modoc,* the county in the northeastern corner of the state, is notable as having been the home of the only California tribe that ever caused serious trouble to the United States Government. The Modoc wars are a matter of history.

The Modocs were a fierce tribe of Indians who lived at the head-waters of Pit River, and the name is thought by some persons to mean "head of the river," or "people, community," but ethnologists are of the opinion that it means "south people," probably used by tribes living north of the Modocs. Bancroft, quoting from Steele, in Indian Affairs Report of 1864, page 121, says: "The word *Modoc* is a Shasta Indian word, and means all distant, stranger, or hostile Indians, and became applied to this tribe by white men in early days from hearing the Shastas refer to them by this term." It does not appear that

Bancroft had any genuine scientific authority for this statement.

Powers, in his *Tribes of California,* states that some persons derive this name from *Mo-dok-us,* the name of a former chief of the tribe under whose leadership they seceded from the Klamath Lake Indians and became an independent tribe. As it was common for seceding bands to assume the name of their leader, Powers is inclined to accept this explanation of the name.

Professor Kroeber says: "Modoc means 'south,' nothing more or less, and these people were so called by the Klamath, their kinsmen on the north."

## SHASTA

Under the various forms of Shaste, Saste, and Sastika, this name was applied by other neighboring tribes to the Indians usually called Shastas, but it is *not* their name for themselves. The name was applied to a group of small tribes in Northern California, extending into Oregon, who were soon extinguished by the development of mining operations.

Bancroft, in his *Native Races,* says, "Shasta was apparently the name of a tribe living about 1840 near Yreka, a tribe made up of several groups. They were a sedentary people, living in small houses, similar to those in use by the

Indians on the coast immediately to the west. Their food was made up of acorns, seeds, roots, and fish, particularly salmon. The salmon was caught by net, weir, trap, and spear. Their arts were few. They had dug-out canoes of a rather broad, clumsy type. The bow was their chief weapon, and their carving was limited to rude spoons of wood and bone. Painting was little used, and basketry was limited to basket caps for the women, and small food baskets of simple form. The tribe soon succumbed to the unfavorable environment of the mining camp, and is now almost extinct . . . . . The Shasta Indians were known in their own language as *Weohow,* a word meaning 'stone house,' from the large cave in their country."

Whatever may be the derivation of its name, there is no question that Mount Shasta, with its snow-capped summit, has but few rivals for scenic beauty among its mountain sisterhood. It is an extinct volcano, with a double peak, and rises to a height of 14,380 feet. There are minor glaciers on the northern slope. Fremont says of it: "The Shastl peak stands at the head of the lower valley, rising from a base of about one thousand feet, out of a forest of heavy timber. It ascends like an immense column upwards of 14,000 feet (nearly the height of Mont Blanc), the summit glistening with snow, and visible

from favorable points of view, at a distance of 140 miles down the valley."

On a United States map of date of 1848, drawn by Charles Preuss from surveys made by Fremont and other persons, the name appears spelled as *Tshastl.*

Mount Shasta is in Siskiyou County, and is the most conspicuous natural feature in that part of the state.

## SISKIYOU COUNTY

Except that it is of Indian origin, nothing authentic has been obtained concerning *Siskiyou,* the name of the county in the extreme north of the state. Several popular theories have been advanced, one to the effect that Siskiyou means "lame horse." If that be true the word must have been introduced into the Indian language after the coming of the Spaniards, since horses were unknown to the Indians before that period. Another story, perhaps more pleasing than true, runs as follows: "On the summit of a mountain in Oregon, just over the divide, there is a beautiful, level spot, watered by cool springs, which overlooks the country for miles around. Here the powerful Shasta, Rogue River, and Klamath tribes used to meet to smoke and indulge in dancing and games. They called the place *Siski-you,* the 'council ground.'"

Siskiyou County is notable for its mountain scenery, and includes within its borders the famous Mount Shasta.

## TRINITY COUNTY

*Trinity County* received its name from Trinidad Bay, which was discovered and named by Captain Bruno Ezeta, on Trinity Sunday, in the year 1775. Trinidad is the Spanish word meaning Trinity.

Trinity River was so named through the mistaken belief that it emptied into Trinidad Bay.

Trinidad is also the name of a village in Humboldt County, on the ocean shore, twenty miles north of Eureka.

## YREKA

*Yreka,* (pronounced Wy-reé-kah), the name of the county-seat of Siskiyou County, is an Indian word, of which the spelling has probably been corrupted, perhaps in a spirit of facetiousness, from the original *Wai-ri-ka* to its present eccentric form. Various theories have been offered in explanation of the word, but the only one apparently based on scientific data seems to be that it means "north place."

*Yreka* is said by Powers, in his *Tribes of California,* to be the Indian word for "mountain,"

185

especially applied to Mt. Shasta. Its former spelling was *Wai-ri-ka*. Here is a contradiction between scientists.

## SUPPLEMENTARY LIST

*Agua Caliente* (hot water, hot springs), a village in Sonoma County, forty-five miles north of San Francisco.

*Alturas* (heights), the county-seat of Modoc County, 110 miles north of Reno.

*Point Arena* (sandy point) is the name of the cape on the Mendocino coast, and of the village in that county, 110 miles northwest of San Francisco.

*Bodega,* a surname, that of its discoverer, Don Juan de la Bodega y Quadra, Captain of the schooner Sonora, who sailed into Bodega Bay October 3, 1775. This bay, and the town of Bodega Roads are in Sonoma County, about sixty-four miles northwest of San Francisco.

Governor Alvarado held the peculiar theory that this place was named in reference to the wine cellars (bodegas) which were common there during the period of the Russian occupation, but the resemblance between this word and the name of the discoverer is purely accidental. The origin of the name is thoroughly authenticated in the Spanish documents, including Pa-

186

lou's *Noticias,* and the bay is honored in bearing the name of one of the bravest navigators that ever sailed the Southern Sea—Juan Francisco de la Bodega.

*Point Cabrillo,* a surname, that of the celebrated Spanish explorer, Juan Rodríguez Cabrillo, discoverer of California.

*Calistoga,* one of those hybrid words of which California has too many. This word was the invention of Samuel Brannan, an early settler, and is compounded of the first syllable of California and the last of Saratoga. It is given here lest it be mistaken for Indian or Spanish.

*Cazadero* (hunting-place).

*Chileno* (Chilean, native of Chile).

*Punta Delgada* (thin or narrow point). See *Punta Gorda.*

*Cape Fortunas* (adventures) was so named by Ferrelo in 1543 on account of experiencing there a great gale of wind.

*Del Norte* (of the north) is the name of the county in the extreme northwestern corner of the state.

*García* (a surname), the name of a creek in Mendocino County.

*Punta Gorda* (thick or broad point). Punta Gorda and Punta Delgada are adjacent points on the northern coast whose contrast in shape is indicated by their names. See *Punta Delgada.*

*Gualala,* a village in Mendocino County, forty miles west of Cloverdale. This is an Indian word, "probably from *walali,* a generic term of the Pomo language, signifying the meeting-place of the waters of any in-flowing stream with those of the stream into which it flows, or with the ocean. The present spelling is probably influenced by the Spanish."—(S. A. Barrett, in California Publications of Archaeology and Ethnology. Other authorities give the original form of the word as *Wah-lah Wah-lah,* repeated.

*Honcut,* in Butte County, was named for a Maidu Indian village.

*Hoopa,* a village in Humboldt County, on the Trinity River, was named for the Hupa Indians, a tribe on the lower Trinity River, or rather for the valley in which they lived as it was known to Yurok Indians. Hoopa Mountain was named in the same way.

*Hueneme,* in Ventura County, is originally a Chumashan place name, *Wene'me* or *Wene-mu.*

*Hyampom,* in Trinity County, is a northern Wintun Indian name of location.

*Point Laguna* (lagoon point).

*Oro Fino* (fine gold) is the name of a village in Siskiyou County, twenty-five miles southwest of Yreka. This name is in contrast to the place called *Oro Grande* (coarse gold) in the southern part of the state.

*Petaluma,* the name of a town in Sonoma County, forty-two miles northwest of San Francisco. Petaluma was the name of an Indian village situated near the site of the present town on a low hill, and according to S. A. Barrett the word is compounded of *peta* (flat) and *luma* (back), making *Petaluma* (flat back) in reference to the shape of the hill or ridge.

Professor Kroeber says: "Petaluma is a Coast Miwok Indian name meaning 'flat back,' no doubt from the appearance of the elevation on which the village was situated."

*Pomo* is northeast of Ukiah. "Pomo was an Indian village on the east bank of the Russian River, in the southern end of Potter Valley, a short distance south of the post-office at Pomo. The word is an ending, meaning 'people of, village of.' "—(S. A. Barrett.)

*Tomales Bay* is just north of Drake's Bay, in Marin County. The word is a Spanish corruption of the Indian *tamal* (bay).

*Ukiah* is the county-seat of Mendocino County, and is on the Russian River, 110 miles northwest of San Francisco. "The word is said to be derived from the Indian *yokaia, yo* (south) and *ka-ia* (valley), the name of a village about six miles southeast of the present town of Ukiah."

189

# THE CENTRAL VALLEY

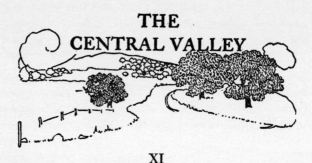

## XI

## TEHAMA COUNTY

*Tehama County* lies at the extreme northern end of the great Central Valley of the state. There is a village of the same name in the county, on the Sacramento River, twelve miles southeast of Red Bluff.

The name *Tehama* was derived from an Indian tribe, but the meaning of it has not been ascertained. Two definitions have been offered: "high water," in reference to the overflowing of the Sacramento River, and "low land," but these may be among those attempts to account for our names by making the name fit the circumstances, a method which has resulted in many errors. All that can be positively stated is that the word is of Indian origin.

## COLUSA

*Colusa* is a county in the northern part of the Central Valley, and has a county-seat of the same name, situated on the west bank of the

190

Sacramento River, sixty-five miles northwest of Sacramento. The city and county are named from the tribe and former village of *Kolu,* usually pronounced by the Indians as *Koroo.*

## YUBA

*Yuba* is the name of a county in the Central Valley, of Yuba City, the county-seat of Sutter County, and of the Yuba River, which is formed by the union of three branches rising in the Sierra Nevada.

The name *Yuba* was first applied to the river, the chief tributary of the Feather. The theory has been advanced that it received the name of *Uba,* or *Uva,* the Spanish word for grapes, from an exploring party in 1824, in reference to the immense quantities of vines loaded with wild grapes growing along its banks, *Uba* becoming corrupted into *Yuba,* but Powers, in his *Tribes of California,* says Yuba is derived from a tribe of Maidu Indians named *Yu-ba,* who lived on the Feather River. This is probably the true explanation of the name. It is to be noted that Frémont, in his *Memoirs,* speaks of it as Indian: "We traveled across the valley plain, and in about sixteen miles reached Feather River, at twenty miles from its junction with the Sacramento, near the mouth of the Yuba, so called from a

191

village of Indians who live on it. The Indians aided us across the river with canoes and small rafts. Extending along the bank in front of the village was a range of wicker cribs, about twelve feet high, partly filled with what is there the Indians' staff of life, acorns. A collection of huts, shaped like bee-hives, with naked Indians sunning themselves on the tops, and these acorn cribs, are the prominent objects in an Indian village."

## YOLO

*Yolo* is the name of a county in the northern part of the Central Valley, and of a village near Woodland.

*Yolo,* or *Yoloy,* was the name of a Patwin tribe, and the word is said by the Bureau of Ethnology to mean "a place abounding with rushes."

In 1884 there were still forty-five of the tribe living in Yolo County.

## SOLANO

This county, situated in the Central Valley, immediately northeast of San Francisco, was named, at the request of General Mariano Vallejo, in honor of an Indian chief of the Suisunes who had aided him in war against the

IN THE SIERRA NEVADAS
"East Vidette, the Alps of the King-Kern divide."

other natives. The name of this chief in his own tongue is said to have been *Sem Yeto,* "the Fierce one of the Brave Hand," or *Sum-yet-ho,* "the Mighty Arm," and, judging by the description given of him by Dr. Vallejo, he must have been a living refutation of the common belief that the California Indians were invariably squat and ill-formed, for he was a splendid figure of a man, six feet, seven inches in height and large in proportion. He was converted to Christianity and received the name of the celebrated missionary, Francisco Solano, as well as a grant of land containing 17,752 acres, known as the Suisún Grant.

## SUISUN

*Suisún Bay* is a body of navigable water connected with San Pablo Bay by the Carquinez Strait, and is the outlet of the San Joaquín and Sacramento Rivers. Suisún City is in Solano County, on a slough, about fifty miles northeast of San Francisco. Suisún was the name of an Indian village on that bay. The name was probably first given to the land grant.

This region was the home of an important tribe of Indians who had an interesting and tragic history. General Vallejo says that in 1817 a military expedition under command of

Lieutenant José Sánchez crossed the straits of Carquínez on rafts, for the double purpose of exploring the country and reducing it to Christianity. "On crossing the river they were attacked by the Suisún tribe, headed by their chief Malaca, and the Spaniards suffered considerable loss; the Indians fought bravely, but were forced to retire to their *ranchería,* where, being hotly pursued, and believing their fate sealed, these unfortunate people, incited by their chief, set fire to their own rush-built huts, and perished in the flames with their families. The soldiers endeavored to stay their desperate resolution, in order to save the women and children, but they preferred this doom to that which they believed to await them at the hands of their enemies." The Suisún tribe is now entirely extinct, a large number having been carried off by a frightful epidemic of smallpox. Dr. Vallejo states that this tribe, a people described by him as possessing many attractive qualities, was estimated by his father to number at least 40,000 persons in 1835. After the great epidemic, which was brought down by the Russians from the north, and which lasted during the three consecutive years of 1837-38-39, there were barely two hundred left. Thus the disappearance of the California Indians was occasioned, not only by the white man's bullets or

fire-water, the deteriorating influence of a changed mode of living and the loss of native sturdiness through an acquired dependence upon the church, but suddenly and fearfully by the introduction of the hideous diseases of civilization.

## SACRAMENTO

*Sacramento County* and the city of the same name, the state capital, situated near the center of the Great Valley, received their names from the river, which, following the usual custom of the Spaniards, was christened first, being named in honor of the Holy Sacrament.

In 1808 Lieutenant Gabriel Moraga led an expedition to what is now known as the Feather River, which he called the Sacramento, and as he called the great river which it joins farther down by the same name, it is evident that he regarded the two as composing the main stream. When he later came to what is now known as the Upper Sacramento he considered it to be a branch, which he called Jesús María, a name it long retained for that part of its course. For this conclusion he had some justification in the fact that at the point where the Sacramento and the Feather come together it is the latter which makes a straight course north and south with the lower Sacramento

whereas the upper Sacramento flows in at that point from the west.

## COSUMNE

*Cosumne* is the name of a village in Sacramento County, about twenty-two miles southeast of Sacramento. The Cosumne River rises in El Dorado County, near the Sierra Nevada, and enters the Mokelumne about twenty-five miles south of the city of Sacramento. The name is derived from a well known tribe who gave the early Padres much trouble and for whom the river was named.

The Bureau of Ethnology has an interesting paragraph on the manners and customs of these Indians: "They went almost naked; their houses were of bark, sometimes thatched with grass, and covered with earth; the bark was loosened from the trees by repeated blows with stone hatchets, the latter having the head fastened to the handle with deer sinews. Their ordinary weapons were bows and stone-tipped arrows. The women made finely-woven conical baskets of grass, the smaller ones of which held water. Their amusements were chiefly dancing and foot-ball; the dances, however, were in some degree ceremonial. Their principal deity was the sun, and the women had a ceremony which

196

resembled the 'sun dance' of the tribes of the upper Missouri. Their dead were buried in graves in the earth. The tribe is now practically extinct."—(Quoted from Rice, in *American Anthropology,* III, 259, 1890.)

## SAN JOAQUIN

*San Joaquin County,* famous for its vast fields of wheat, is a part of the great Central Valley, and the river of the same name rises in the Sierras, flows north-northwest through the valley and unites with the Sacramento River near its mouth.

The river was named in honor of St. Joachim, the father of the Virgin. Lieutenant Moraga first gave the name to a rivulet which springs from the Sierra Nevada, and empties into Lake Buena Vista. The river derived its name from this rivulet.

The rich valley of the San Joaquin, two hundred miles long and thirty miles wide, with its wide, treeless expanses where the wild grasses grew rankly, was once a paradise for game. Frémont says: "Descending the valley we traveled among multitudinous herds of elk, antelope, and wild horses. Several of the latter which we killed for food were found to be very fat." Herds of wild horses still range in California and Nevada, and are sometimes captured for sale, fine specimens bringing high prices.

197

## STANISLAUS

*Stanislaus* is the name of the county just south of San Joaquín, and of one of the tributaries of the San Joaquín River. The Stanislaus River, one of the most important of the streams which take their rise in the wild and picturesque region of the higher peaks of the Sierra, descends to the plains through rock-bound cañons and joins the San Joaquín in the central trough of the valley. It is the scene of Bret Harte's humorous poem, *The Society Upon the Stanislaus.*

The word *Stanislaus* is said to be derived from an Indian chief of that region, who became Christianized and was baptized under the Spanish name of *Estanislao.* He was educated at Mission San José, but became a renegade, and incited his tribe against the Spaniards. In 1826 he was defeated in a fierce battle on the banks of the river now bearing his name. Another, and more probable theory is that the river was first named by the Spaniards for Saint Stanislaus, and, following the usual course of procedure, the name was afterwards applied to the county. There were two saints bearing this name, both of Polish origin. Stanislaus Kostka was born in Poland in 1550, and is one of the favorite saints of that country. He was canon-

ized for his saintly character, and is invoked for palpitations of the heart and dangerous illnesses. Stanislaus of Cracow was born in 1030. He is the patron saint of Poland, and is invoked in battle. He suffered a violent death at the hands of King Boleslaw, whom he had reproved for his dissolute life.

Frémont thus describes the scenery along the Stanislaus: "Issuing from the woods, we rode about sixteen miles over open prairie partly covered with bunch grass, the timber reappearing on the rolling hills of the River Stanislaus, in the usual belt of evergreen oaks. The level valley was about forty feet below the upland, and the stream seventy yards broad, with the usual fertile bottom land which was covered with green grass among large oaks. We encamped in one of these bottoms, in a grove of the large white oaks previously mentioned."

## MERCED

*Merced* (mercy) is the name of the county south of Stanislaus, of its own principal stream, and of its county-seat. The river was named by the Spaniards, in honor of the Virgin, *El Río de Nuestra Señora de la Merced* (the river of our Lady of Mercy). This name was given to the stream by an exploring party under Sergeant

199

Gabriel Moraga in 1806, as an expression of their joy and gratitude at the sight of its sparkling waters, after an exhausting journey of forty miles through a waterless country.

According to Frémont, this stream was called *Auxumne* by the Indians: "In about seventeen miles we reached the Auxumne River, called by the Mexicans *Merced* . . . . . We encamped on the southern side of the river, where broken hills made a steep bluff, with a narrow bottom. On the northern side was a low undulating wood and prairie land, over which a band of about three hundred elk was slowly coming to water, feeding as they approached."

The Merced River is notable in that it flows along the floor of the Yosemite Valley. Like all the other streams that have their rise in the Sierra, its character in its upper and lower reaches is vastly dissimilar. In the days of its turbulent youth it is a wild and boisterous stream, and in the voice of its hissing, roaring waters the wayfarer hears no sound of "mercy," but after it makes its tremendous plunge down the western slope of the Sierra, and debouches upon the floor of the valley, it takes on a serene air of maturity, and widens into a placid river, its current flowing sluggishly between low, level banks.

## MADERA COUNTY

*Madera* (wood, timber) is the name of the county to the southwest of Stanislaus. It occupies a stretch of fertile land, and was called *Madera* by the Spaniards on account of its heavy growth of timber.

## FRESNO COUNTY

*Fresno* (ash-tree), so called in reference to the abundance of those trees in that region, is the name of a county in the San Joaquín Valley, in the heart of the grain and fruit country. Raisins and wine are its especial products. Its capital city and principal stream also bear the name of Fresno.

## KINGS COUNTY

This county, now appearing under its English form, originally received its name from the river, which was discovered by a Spanish exploring party in 1805, and called by them *El Río de los Santos Reyes* (the river of the Holy Kings), in honor of the "three wise men."

A considerable part of the area of this county was at one time covered by Tulare Lake, but the shrinkage of that body of water through the withdrawal of its sources of supply has added

nearly the whole of the territory occupied by its waters to the arable land of the county. This subject is further discussed under the head of Tulare.

The river seems to have been known at one time as the *Lake Fork,* by which name Frémont mentions it in the following paragraph: "We crossed an open plain still in a southeasterly direction, reaching in about twenty miles the Tulare Lake river. This is the Lake Fork, one of the largest and handsomest streams in the valley, being about one hundred yards broad, and having perhaps a larger body of fertile lands than any of the others. It is called by the Mexicans *El Río de los Reyes.* The broad alluvial bottoms were well wooded with several species of oaks. This is the principal affluent of the Tulare Lake, a strip of water which receives all the rivers in the upper or southern end of the valley."

## TULARE COUNTY

*Tulare* (place of tules, or rushes) is the name of a county in the south-central part of the state, of Tulare Lake in Kings County, and of a town in the San Joaquín Valley. The county is remarkable for the high mountain peaks of the Sierra Nevada, on its northeast border. Among these is Mount Whitney, about 14,500 feet in height.

*Tulare Lake,* in Kings County, at one time filled a shallow depression about thirty miles in length, and received through a number of small streams the drainage from the southern part of the Sierra Nevada, soon losing the greater part of this water by evaporation. It is now practically dry, as a result of the withdrawal for irrigation purposes of Kings and Kern rivers, and the territory formerly covered by it has been to a great extent placed under cultivation. The lake was discovered in 1773 by Comandante Fages, while hunting for deserters from the presidio at Monterey, and called by him *Los Tules* (the rushes), from the great number of those plants with which it was filled. In 1813 Captain Moraga passed through the valley of this lake, and named it *Valle de los Tules* (valley of the rushes).

The Tulare Indians exhibited both more courage and more ingenuity than was usual among the tribes of California, and the Spaniards had more than one lively fight with them. On one of these occasions, the Indians, seeing themselves worsted, retired into the tules on the river bank, where they remained hidden. The Spaniards, not wishing to expose themselves to unnecessary danger, surrounded the place and waited for hunger to drive the enemy out, but the Indians concocted a cunning scheme by

203

which they made good their escape. With un-expected skill, they constructed some manikins of the tules and then tossed them, unseen, into the current of the river. When these immitation men floated into the view of the Spaniards they took them for the Indians trying to swim down stream, and so followed after them along the bank, shooting as they ran. Meanwhile the Indians quietly decamped in the other direction.

The Ttulareños were in the habit of going across the mountains to the coast for abalones, and it was their custom when on these trips to mark their trails to those coming after by placing stones on the ground in the shape of a "v," the apex indicating the direction in which they were traveling. These sign-posts of the old Indian trails are still occasionally found in the mountains of that region, and no doubt many a wayfarer has wondered about their meaning.

## SUPPLEMENTARY LIST

*Acampo* (common pasture) is the name of a village in San Joaquín County. See Final Index.

*Arroyo Buenos Aires* (creek of the good airs) is in San Joaquín County.

*Caliente* (hot) is the name of a town in Kern County.

*Chico* (little) is the name of a town in Butte

County, ninety-six miles north of Sacramento. This place derives its name from the Rancho Chico (the little ranch), of which General John Bidwell was the original grantee. The Arroyo Chico and the town both took their names from the ranch.

*Chowchilla,* a large ranch in the San Joaquín Valley. The name, which was first given to the river, is of doubtful origin, being claimed by two widely different tribes. Fremont refers to this name under a somewhat different spelling: "The springs and streams hereabout were waters of the *Chauchiles* and *Mariposas* rivers, and the Indians of this village belonged to the *Chauchiles* tribe."

*Dos Palos* (two sticks, or trees) is in Merced County, twenty miles southwest of Merced.

*Esparto* (feather-grass) is a town in Yolo County.

*Esperanza* (hope) is in Kings County, west of Lake Tulare.

*Hornitos* (little ovens) is in Mariposa County, sixteen miles northwest of Mariposa. Two theories have been advanced for this name. One is that it was given by some Mexican settlers on account of the extreme heat there; the other, and the one most commonly accepted by the residents of the place, is that it was so called by the Mexicans in reference to a number of

bake ovens made of rock and mud which were built there in the early fifties by a company of German miners. *Hornos* (ovens), of brick and adobe, built out-of-doors, and used to bake the bread for several families, were in very common use among the first Spanish settlers of California. Ovens were also used by the Indians, for, instead of eating their food raw or imperfectly cooked, they used quite elaborate methods in its preparation. Their ovens are thus described in the *Handbook of American Indians,* by Dr. Pliny E. Goddard, of the American Museum of Natural History: "The pit oven, consisting of a hole excavated in the ground, heated with fire, and then filled with food, which was covered over and allowed to cook, was general in America, though as a rule it was employed only occasionally, and principally for cooking vegetal substances. This method of cooking was found necessary to render acrid or poisonous foods harmless, and starchy foods saccharine, and as a preliminary in drying and preserving food for winter use. Most of the acorn-consuming Indians of California cooked acorn mush in small sand-pits. The soap-root was made palatable by cooking it in an earth-covered heap. The Hupa cook the same plant for about two days in a large pit lined with stones, in which a hot fire is maintained until the stones

206

and surrounding earth are well heated; the fire is then drawn, the pit lined with leaves of wild grape and wood sorrel to improve the flavor of the bulbs, and a quantity of the bulbs thrown in; leaves are then placed on top, the whole is covered with earth, and a big fire built on top." Mr. Charles B. Turrill states that "the meal of the ground acorns was placed in shallow hollows in the sand and water poured on it, by which means the bitter principle was leached out. Then the meal was placed in baskets and cooked by putting hot stones therein. The cooking was done in the basket, not in the sand." Other Indians used pit ovens for baking clams, and the Panamints of California roasted cactus joints and mescal in pits. The Pueblo Indians used dome-shaped ovens of stone plastered with clay, a form that may have been imitated by the Spaniards, since their ovens were of that character.

*Modesto* (modest) is the county-seat of Stanislaus County, and is thirty miles south of Stockton. According to residents of this town, "The place was first named Ralston in the year 1870, in honor of Mr. Ralston, who was then a very prominent resident of San Francisco, and president of the Bank of California. He was so modest that he preferred that some other name be adopted, so the name was changed to *Modesto*."

If this be the true story, it was surely a unique reason for the naming of a town.

*Oroville* (goldtown) is a hybrid word made up of the Spanish *oro* (gold) and the French *ville* (town). Oroville is the county-seat of Butte County, and is on the Feather River, in the heart of a mining and fruit region.

*Río Vista* (river view) is in Solano County, on the Sacramento River. Modern. Incorrect construction. It should be *Vista del Río.*

*Tehachapi,* an Indian word of which the meaning has not been ascertained, is the name of the mountain pass in Kern County across the Sierra Nevada, of which it approximately marks the southern limit, and of a town in the same county, thirty-five miles southeast of Bakersfield.

"In the famous Tahichapah Pass was a tribe called by themselves *Ta-hi-cha-pa-han-na,* and by the Kern Indians *Ta-hich.* This tribe is now extinct."—(Powers' *Tribes of California.)*

*Vacaville* is situated in a beautiful and fertile valley in Solano County. It received its name from a family named *Vaca,* who were at one time prominent in that region. Manuel Vaca, the founder of the family, was a native of New Mexico, and came to California in 1841. "He was a hospitable man of good repute."

IN THE HIGH SIERRAS

"Above the snow line, south from Mount Brewer."

IN THE SIERRA

## XII

*The Sierra Nevada,* California's wonder-land, derives its name from *sierra,* saw, and *nevada,* snowy,—descriptive of the saw-toothed outlines of the summits of the range, and the mantle of perpetual snow that covers the highest tops.

The term *Sierra Madre,* absurdly translated by some persons as "Mother of Christ," means, of course, "Mother Sierra," that is, the largest mountain range personified as the mother of the smaller ranges.

"The Sierra Nevada is generally considered to extend from Tehachapi Pass in the south to Lassen Peak in the north, and constitutes the dividing ridge between the great basin on the east, to which it falls abruptly, and the San Joaquín and Sacramento Valleys on the west. It is characterized by deep and narrow valleys, with almost vertical walls of rock thousands of feet in height, and its scenery is of surpassing grandeur, much more imposing than that of the

Rockies. Many of its higher summits are covered with perpetual snow."—(Lippincott's *Gazetteer.*)

## PIT RIVER

Among the many tributary streams that carry the waters of the Sierra Nevada down the western slope into the Sacramento, the *Pit,* often incorrectly spelled *Pitt,* is one of the most important, and, although not properly belonging in these pages, is included for the sake of the information to be gained concerning Indian customs.

The natives along this river were in the habit of digging pits near the banks to catch bear and deer, and, on occasion, even their human enemies. The pits were dug in the regular trails of animals, twelve to fourteen feet deep, conical in shape, with a small opening at the top, covered with brush and earth. Signs, such as broken twigs, were placed as a warning to their own people, and sharp stakes were placed in the bottom to impale any creature that might fall in. Another account of this custom is given in Miller's *Life Among the Modocs:* "Pits from ten to fifteen feet deep were dug, in which natives caught man and beast. These man-traps, for such was their primary use, were small at the mouth, widening toward the bottom, so that exit was impossible, even were the victim to

210

escape impalement upon sharpened elk and deer horns, which were favorably placed for his reception. The opening was craftily concealed by means of light sticks, over which earth was scattered, and the better to deceive the unwary, travelers' footprints were frequently stamped with a moccasin in the loose soil." It was from these Indian pits that the river received its name.

## PLUMAS

*Plumas* (feathers) is the name of a county in the northeastern part of the state. It is drained by the Feather River, which flows through one of the deepest and most picturesque canyons in California. The county is characterized by its wild and rugged scenery, its deep canyons and extensive forests of evergreen trees. In the northwest corner Lassen Peak, now an active volcano, rises to a height of 10,437 feet.

The county derives its name from its principal stream, which now appears under its English form of *The Feather,* but which was originally named *El Río de las Plumas* (the river of the Feathers), by Captain Luis A. Argüello, who led an exploring party up the valley in 1820, and whose attention was attracted by the great number of feathers of wild fowl floating on the surface of the river. Even to this day the valley of

the Feather has remained a favorite haunt of the wild ducks and geese, as will be attested by the many hunters who seek sport there during the season. By an inconsistency, the county has retained the original Spanish name, *Plumas,* while that of the river has been Americanized. An erroneous and extremely far-fetched explanation of the name has often appeared in print to the effect that it was derived from a fancied resemblance between the spray of the river and a feather.

## THE AMERICAN RIVER

The *American River,* another of the names which have been translated from the original Spanish, is formed by three forks rising in the Sierra Nevada, and empties into the Sacramento at the site of the city of that name. The three branches forming it run in deep canyons, sometimes two thousand feet in depth, and the scenery along its course is of rugged and striking character.

The river was originally called *El Río de los Americanos* (the river of the Americans), probably from the presence on its banks of a company of western trappers, who lived there from 1822 to 1830, and *not* "because it was the usual route of travel by which Americans entered the state," as is stated by Bancroft and others.

212

In Frémont's time it was still known by its Spanish name, by which he refers to it in the following paragraph: "Just then a well-dressed Indian came up, and made his salutations in very well-spoken Spanish. In answer to our inquiries he informed us that we were upon the *Río de los Americanos,* and that it joined the Sacramento River about ten miles below. Never did a name sound more sweetly! We felt ourselves among our countrymen, for the name of American, in these distant parts, is applied to the citizens of the United States."

## EL DORADO COUNTY

*El Dorado* (the gilded man). Although it is known to most people, in a vague, general way, that the name *El Dorado* was given to this county on account of the discovery of gold there, the romantic tales connected with the name are probably not so well known. The Indians of Peru, Venezuela, and New Granada, perhaps in the hope of inducing their oppressors to move on, were constantly pointing out to the Spaniards, first in one direction, then in another, a land of fabulous riches. This land was said to have a king, who caused his body to be covered every morning with gold dust, by means of an odorous resin. Each evening he washed it off,

213

as it incommoded his sleep, and each morning had the gilding process repeated. From this fable the white men were led to believe that the country must be rich in gold, and long, costly, and fruitless expeditions were undertaken in pursuit of this phantom of *El Dorado*. In time the phrase *El Dorado* came to be applied to regions where gold and other precious metals were thought to be plentiful. According to General Vallejo, one Francisco Orellana, a companion of the adventurer Pizarro, wrote a fictitious account of an *El Dorado* in South America, "a region of genial clime and never-fading verdure, abounding in gold and precious stones, where wine gushed forth from never-ceasing springs, wheat fields grew ready-baked loaves of bread, birds already roasted flew among the trees, and nature was filled with harmony and sweetness." Although old Mother Nature has not yet provided us with "bread ready-baked" or "birds ready-roasted" in California, her gifts to her children have been so bountiful that they may almost be compared to the fabulous tales of *El Dorado,* the gilded man.

## PLACER COUNTY

*Placer,* the county in the Sierra famous for its surface gold-mining, has a puzzling name for

which no satisfactory explanation has yet been found. Although it has been used in Spanish countries for centuries in the sense of surface mining, dictionaries remain silent upon the subject. The theory often advanced that the word is a contraction of *plaza de oro* (place of gold) bears none of the marks of probability, and another that it means "a river where gold is found" is not supported by adequate authority. One old Spanish dictionary gives the meaning of *placer* as "a sea bottom, level and of slight depth, of sand, mud, or stone," and states also that the word is sometimes used to designate places where pearl diving is carried on. It may be that the word was extended from this usage to include placer mining, since in that case the gold is found in shallow pockets near the surface. This theory is offered here as a mere suggestion.

Placer County has some of the most striking mountain scenery in the state, and has been the theatre of many remarkable events in its history, particularly those connected with the "days of '49." In the town of Placerville, the county-seat of El Dorado County, there is an instance of a change of name from English to Spanish for the better, for this place was originally called *Hangtown,* in commemoration of the hanging of certain "bad men" on a tree there.

215

## THE TRUCKEE RIVER

The *Truckee River* rises on the borders of El Dorado and Placer counties, and is the outlet of Lake Tahoe, discharging its waters into Pyramid Lake in Nevada. This mountain stream is justly celebrated for the wild charm of its scenery. There is a village bearing the same name, in Nevada County, well-known to travelers through being on the regular route to Tahoe. At this place winter sports, tobogganing, skiing, skating, etc., are provided for San Franciscans, who need to travel but a few hours to exchange their clime of eternal spring for the deep snows of the Sierra.

The explanation generally accepted for the name of *Truckee* is that it was so called for an Indian, definitely known to be a northern Paiute chief, who guided a party of explorers in 1844 to its lower crossing, where the town of Wadsworth now stands. The party, who were suffering from thirst, felt themselves to be under such obligations to the Indian for having guided them to this lovely mountain stream, with its crystal waters and abundance of fish, that they gave it his name. Of this Indian it is said that "he joined Frémont's battalion, and was afterwards known as Captain Truckee; he became a great favorite with Fremont, who gave him a Bible. When he

died he asked to be buried by white men in their style. The miners dug a grave near Como, in the croppings of the old Goliah ledge. Here he was laid to rest, with the Bible by his side."—*(History of Nevada County.)*

## LAKE TAHOE

*Tahoe* is another of the Indian names whose meaning can not be ascertained with any degree of certainty. The definition "Big Water," the one usually given, is considered doubtful by ethnologists. The statement has been made by intelligent Indians now living on the banks of the lake that the word, pronounced *Dá-o* by them, means "deep" and "blue." Yet it is much to know that this pearl among all lakes has at least been fortunate enough to receive an ni-digenous name, escaping by a narrow margin the ignominious fate of being called Lake Bigler, for a former governor of the state. It appears that Frémont was the first to give to this body of water a name, and it is shown upon his map under the rather indefinite title of Mountain Lake. Afterward it was known for a short time as Lake Bigler. The story goes that in 1859 Dr. Henry de Groot, while exploring the mountains, learned that *tah-oo-ee* meant "a great deal of water," and from this Tahoe was evolved as an

appropriate name, but did not become attached to the lake until the period of the Civil War. During that time the Reverend Thomas Starr King, the famous "war" clergyman of San Francisco, visited the lake, and inspired by indignation against the Democratic Governor Bigler, whom he regarded as a secessionist, he definitely christened it *Tahoe,* for which we may be grateful to his memory, regardless of the motives by which he was actuated.

Tahoe is partly in Placer, and partly in El Dorado, at the eastern base of the Sierra Nevada, a portion of its waters also extending into the state of Nevada. It is twenty-two miles long and ten wide, and has an elevation of 6,225 feet above sea level. It is especially remarkable for its great depth, being over 1,500 feet deep.

## AMADOR COUNTY

*Amador,* literally "lover," but in this case a surname. Amador is the long, narrow county lying between Calaveras and El Dorado, and was probably named in honor of the Amador family, either Don Pedro Amador, or his son, José María. Pedro Amador is said to have been a "soldier of fortune" in the Spanish army, who came to California in 1771. His son, José María, was also a soldier and a renowned Indian

218

fighter, and was known to be living as late as 1883.

## CALAVERAS

*Calaveras* (skulls) is the name of a county in the central part of the Sierra Nevada, on the eastern border. This county is famous for its gold and copper mines, and its Giant Sequoias. The river, to which the name of Calaveras was first given, rises in the foothills of the Sierra Nevada and flows southwest, emptying into the San Joaquin about fifteen miles below Stockton.

The river received its rather lugubrious name at the hands of Captain Moraga, who led the first expedition up the Sacramento and San Joaquin rivers. In his diary, Moraga says that the river tribes fought against those of the Sierra for possession of the salmon in the stream, and that in one battle as many as three thousand were said to have been killed and left on the field. A great number of skulls, relics of this bloody conflict, were found by Moraga scattered along the creek bed, and caused him to give it the name of *Las Calaveras*. We find in Fremont a corroborating reference to the salmon as a cause of dissension among the Indians of that region: "This fish had a large share in supporting the Indians, who raised nothing, but lived on what nature gave. A 'salmon water,' as they

named it, was a valuable possession to a tribe or village, and jealously preserved as an inheritance."

Particular interest was aroused in the Indian relics of this county some years ago by the finding of the celebrated "Calaveras skull," purporting to have been taken from the Tertiary deposit, a stratum in which no human remains had ever before been discovered. A close examination into the circumstances, however, caused scientists to look with great doubt upon the assertion that the skull had been taken from the Tertiary deposit. In the *Handbook of American Indians,* published by the Smithsonian Institute, the following reference appears: "Remains of aborigines are plentiful in this county, embedded in ancient river gravels, from which gold was washed. By some scientists these remains were thought to belong to the Tertiary Age, but their resemblance to the modern Indian makes this doubtful. The Calaveras skull, still preserved in the Peabody Museum of Archaeology and Ethnology, at Cambridge, Massachusetts, was said to have come from the gravels of Bald Mountain, at a depth of 130 feet, but there are good reasons for suspecting that it was derived from one of the limestone caves so numerous in that region."

## TUOLUMNE

*Tuólumne* is the name of the county in the Sierra just east of Calaveras, and of the river which rises at the base of the Sierra Nevada, and flows into the San Joaquín, twenty-five miles south of Stockton, a part of its course running through a deep canyon.

Here we have another of the river names ending in *umne,* already discussed under the heading of *Cosumne.* As stated before, *umne* probably means "people of," and it is held by some authorities that the meaning of *Tuólumne* is "people of the stone houses, or caves." Bancroft maintains this theory, holding that the name is a corruption of *talmalamne,* a group of stone huts or caves, or collection of wigwams." Objection has been raised to this theory on the ground that the Indians of California were not cave-dwellers, but universally lived in flimsy huts made of sticks and grass. This objection is cleared away in some measure by a very interesting paragraph in the diary of Padre Pedro Muñoz, who accompanied the Gabriel Moraga expedition of 1806 into that region. The passage in question relates: "On the morning of this day, the expedition went toward the east along the banks of the river, and having traveled about six leagues, we came upon a village called

*Tautamne.* This village is situated on some steep precipices, inaccessible on account of their rough rocks. The Indians live in their *sótanos* (cellars or caves); they go up and come down by means of a weak stick, held up by one of themselves while the one who descends slips down. They did not wish to come down from their hiding-places, and for me the ascent was too difficult. This village probably has about two hundred souls, judging by the considerable mass which we repeatedly made out among the rocks and corridors [or ledges] in the manner of balconies, which the precipice made." This meeting with the cave-dwellers occurred at a spot about six leagues from the Guadalupe River, after the expedition had left the Merced. It is not, of course, to be inferred from this circumstance that the California Indians were genuine "cliff dwellers," but rather that, at least in the mountainous parts of the state, they may have had the habit of taking refuge in natural caves from inclement weather or attacks of enemies.

As to the pronunciation of the word, it is said that the Indians called it *Tu-ah-lúm-ne,* rather than *Tuólumne,* which is the general usage.

## MARIPOSA

*Mariposa* (butterfly) is famous as the county that holds within its borders two of the wonders of the earth, the Yosemite Valley and the Giant Sequoias. Some of these trees are three hundred feet high, thirty feet in diameter, and 2,400 years old, having unfolded their feathery fronds before Christ came upon the earth. According to Professor Jepsen, "they are the direct descendants of the species dominant in the Tertiary Period," and thus are a living reminder of the plant life of that dim and distant past of which the animal life is pictured for us in the fossil remains of the mammoth and saber-tooth tiger of the La Brea asphalt beds.

Nearly every writer who has attempted to account for the name *Mariposa* has fallen into the error of ascribing it to the charming little flower called the Mariposa lily. Frémont, with his intense appreciation of the beauty of the wild flowers covering the whole country with a carpet of many hues at the time of his passage over the Sierra, says: "On some of the higher ridges were fields of a poppy which, fluttering and tremulous on its long thin stalk, suggests the idea of a butterfly settling on a flower, and gives to this flower its name of Mariposa (butterfly), and the flower extends its name to the stream."

223

It is almost a pity to demolish such a pretty story, yet it is unavoidable, for the true explanation is at hand in the diary of Padre Muñoz, who accompanied the Gabriel Moraga expedition of 1806 into the Sierra.  He says: "This spot [not far from the Merced River] was called *Las Mariposas* (the butterflies) on account of their great multitude, especially at night and in the morning, so much so that they became excessively annoying, carrying their desire to hide from the rays of the sun so far that they followed us everywhere, and one even entered into the ear of one of the leaders of the expedition, causing him a great deal of annoyance, and not a little trouble in getting it out."  This story is corroborated by the fact that at the present day equally great numbers of butterflies, equally annoying, swarm through the mountain forests during a certain part of the autumn.

## YOSEMITE

*Yosemite* (grizzly bear, not *large* grizzly bear, according to the scientists), said to have been called *Yohamite* by the natives, is one of the few Indian names whose meaning has been ascertained with a reasonable degree of certainty. It must be remembered that Yosemite, like most Indian words, has been greatly corrupted from

EL RIO DE LAS PLUMAS (FEATHER RIVER)
"To this day the valley of the Feather is a favorite haunt for
wild ducks and geese."

its original form, which was *u-zú-mai-li, o-só mai-ti* or *uh-zú-mai-ti,* according to the tribe using it, and the valley was never known by this name to the Indians, but always as *A-wa-ni,* from the name of their principal village. Considering the great alteration of the name from its native form, it does not seem to be a matter of vital importance whether it shall now be used as one word, Yosemite, or in two words, Yo Semite, although the latter form was at one time the more general usage, and is greatly preferred by some persons. It is probable that the first white men to look into the valley were members of the Joseph R. Walker expedition of 1833, but it is fairly certain that this party did not descend into the valley. There are vague reports of hunters having entered as early as 1844, but the first recorded entrance was made in 1851, by a party in pursuit of fleeing Indians. The name was chosen by Dr. L. H. Bunnell, surgeon of the expedition, who tells the story in his *Discovery of the Yosemite.* He gave it the name of an Indian tribe living there and to whom this name had been given by other tribes, they calling themselves *Ah-wah-nee.* Their chief, Tenei-ya, said that when he was a young man the name *Yosemite,* or *Yohamite,* had been chosen because the tribe lived in the mountains and valleys which were the favorite resorts of the

bears, and because his people were expert in killing them. He also said, perhaps in a spirit of boasting, that the name was bestowed upon his tribe to express the idea that they were held in as much fear as the bears.

Indian names, few of which can be scientifically defined, have been given to many peaks and waterfalls in the valley. In the folder printed by the Southern Pacific Railroad Company more or less fanciful definitions are given for these names, for which there is no foundation in fact except in the case of Yosemite itself and *Hunto,* which really does mean "eye," though not *"watching* eye." Tenaya Peak was probably named for the Yosemite chief, Ten-ei-ya. The definition of *Pi-wa-ack* as "cataract of diamonds" is absurd on its face, for a moment's thought will remind any one that diamonds were wholly unknown to the Indians of that time and place.

*"Ma-ta* (the canyon), a generic word, in explaining which the Indians held up both hands to denote perpendicular walls."—(Powers' *Tribes of California.)*

*"Tis-se-yak* is the name of an Indian woman who figured in a legend. The Indian woman cuts her hair straight across the forehead and allows the sides to drop along her cheeks, presenting a square face, which the Indians account the acme

of female beauty, and they think they discover this square face in the vast front of South Dome."—(Powers' *Tribes of California.)*

*Cho-ko-nip-o-deh,* translated as "baby basket" in the Southern Pacific folder, means literally "dog-place" or "dog-house."—(Powers' *Tribes of California.)*

## MONO

*Mono* is the name of a county on the eastern border of the state, and of the lake near the eastern base of the Sierra Nevada. This lake is fourteen miles long and nine miles wide, and is peculiar in having no outlet, its waters being strongly saline and alkaline. It lies 6,730 feet above sea level and is almost completely destitute of animal life.

This name, corrupted from *Monache,* the name of the Indians of this region, through its resemblance to the Spanish word *mono* (monkey), has been the cause of considerable confusion, and of a number of extravagant theories, such as the supposed existence of monkeys in that country, or the resemblance of the natives to those animals, but the similarity between the two words is regarded by ethnologists as purely accidental. The meaning is obscure, but it is said that the name was applied to some Sho-

shonean tribes of southeastern California by
their neighbors on the west.

## INYO

*Inyo,* a word of unknown meaning, was the
name of a tribe of Indians in the Sierra. Inyo
County is on the eastern border of the state,
adjacent to Nevada. Its largest stream is the
Owens River, which flows into Owens Lake, another body of saline water having no outlet.
This county has the unenviable distinction of
containing within its borders the terrible "Death
Valley," where the bones of so many unfortunates have been left to whiten under the desert
sun, and which still claims a victim now and
then. This desolate valley is forty miles long,
lying far below the level of the sea, is destitute
of all vegetation, totally without water, subject
to terrific heat, and in all respects well deserves
its funereal name. Inyo is unique in containing
the highest and lowest points in the United
States, Mount Whitney and Death Valley, within
sight of each other. In other parts of the county
the mountain scenery is of remarkable grandeur,
and the gold mines in which it is unusually rich
are still worked with profit.

## AMARGOSA RIVER

*Amargosa* (bitter) is the very appropriate name of a river of Nevada and southeastern California which flows into Death Valley, sometimes known also as the Amargosa Desert. The mountains lying northeast of the river's upper course are sometimes called the Amargosa Mountains. Fremont gives a characteristic picture of this dreary country in the following paragraph: "We traveled through a barren district, where a heavy gale was blowing about the loose sand, and, after a ride of eight miles, reached a large creek of salt and bitter water, running in a westerly direction, to meet the stream bed we had left. It is called by the Spaniards *Amargosa,* the bitter water of the desert."

## SUPPLEMENTARY LIST

*Alta* (high) is a village in Placer County, sixty-eight miles northeast of Sacramento, two miles from the great American Canyon. The altitude of this place is 3,607 feet above sea level. The name is modern and was only given to the place after the building of the Central Pacific Railroad.

*Cerro Gordo* (large, thick hill) is the name of a famous mining camp in Inyo County.

*Cisco* is a town in Placer County, situated at an altitude of 5,934 feet above sea level. Cisco is a word of disputed origin. It has been said to be derived from the Algonquin word *cisco,* meaning a fish, a sort of oily herring found in the Great Lakes, but it seems unlikely that such a name should be transported all the way from the Great Lakes to the Sierra, especially as no fish of that kind is to be found there. Other persons believe the word to be derived from the Spanish *cisco* (broken pieces of coal), but for this there appears to be no legitimate reason. In the *History of Placer County* the statement is made that the town was named for John J. Cisco, at one time connected with the United States Government, an explanation which is possibly the true one.

*Esmeralda* (emerald), a village in Calaveras County.

*Hetch Hetchy* is the Indian name of a deep valley in the Sierra, lying north of the Yosemite, which will some day cease to be a valley and become a lake, as the people of San Francisco have succeeded in obtaining the permission of the United States Government to turn it into a reservoir for the city's water supply. An explanation of the meaning of the word Hetch Hetchy has been obtained through the kindness of John Muir, who says: "I have been informed

by mountaineers who know something of the Indian language that Hetch Hetchy is the name of a species of grass that the Tuólumne Indians used for food, and which grows on the meadow at the lower end of the valley. The grain, when ripe, was gathered and beaten out and pounded into meal in mortars." The word was originally spelled *Hatchatchie.*

*Lancha Plana* (flat-boat) is in Amador County, and its story is thus told by Mr. Junius Farnsworth, an old resident of Stockton: "This town is located across the Mokelumne River from Poverty Bar, a name given to a gravel bar in the river which was exceedingly rich in placer gold, and to which thousands of early day miners were attracted. Those who came from the north side of the Mokelumne centered in Lancha Plana and reached Poverty Bar by means of a flat-boat, or flat ferry. The Spanish soon designated the settlement on the north bank of the river as Lancha Plana, as it was the point at which the flat-boat tied up."

*Moquelumne* is the name of a river which rises in the high Sierra in Alpine County, flows southwesterly and empties into the San Joaquín. The word is a corruption of the Miwok *Wakalumitoh,* the Indian name of the river. The Moquelumne family was made up of an aggregation of tribes which occupied three sections,

one lying between the Cosumnes and Fresno rivers, another in Marin, Sonoma, and Napa counties, and a third occupying a small area in the south end of Lake County.—(A. L. Kroeber, in American *Anthrop.* VIII, No. 4, 1906.) The Miwoks constituted the great body of this family, the different branches of which were connected by a similarity of languages. The Miwoks are described as being quite low in the scale of civilization, and "it has been asserted that this tribe of Indians ate every variety of living creature indigenous to their territory except the skunk. The skins of jack-rabbits were rudely woven into robes, and they bought bows and arrows from the mountain Indians for shell money. Cremation of the dead was usual, and all possessions of the departed were burned with them. Their names were never afterward mentioned and those who bore the same names changed them for others. Widows covered their faces with pitch, and the younger women singed their hair short as a sign of widowhood."— *(Handbook of American Indians.) Muk-kel* was the name of the principal village of this tribe, and if umne does in fact mean "people of," Moquelumne may be "people of the village of Muk-kel."

*Panamint Range* of mountains was named for the Panamint tribe, who belonged to the Sho-

shonean family, and lived around the Panamint Valley, in Inyo County, southeastern California. Many unfortunate seekers after gold have lost their lives in this desolate mountain range.

*Pinto Range* (painted or spotted range), so called because of the variegated colors of the rocks. This range is in Inyo County.

*San Andreas* (St. Andrew) is the county-seat of Calaveras County, and is situated near the Calaveras River, fifty-six miles southeast of Sacramento. Placer gold mining was at one time extensively carried on here. St. Andrew, the patron saint of this place, was the brother of Simon Peter, and was the first called to be an apostle. He suffered martyrdom by being crucified, supposedly on a cross shaped like the one that bears his name. He is the patron of the Order of the Golden Fleece, and of the great Order of the Cross of St. Andrew.—*(Stories of the Saints.)* San Andreas is anomalous in being almost the only Spanish name in the mining district. The circumstances of its naming have not been ascertained. San Andrés Valley was named in 1774 by an exploring expedition to San Francisco Bay.

*Sonora,* named for the province of Sonora in Mexico, is the capital of Tuolumne County, and is situated ninety miles southeast of Sacramento. It received its name from the large num-

ber of Sonorans from the Mexican province who mined there in the very early days. This is a mining period name and has no real connection with Spanish names.

*Tenaya Peak* in Yosemite Valley is named for Ten-ei-ya, chief of the Yosemite Indians.

*Vallecito* (little valley) is in Calaveras County, fifty-five miles northeast of Stockton.

*Wawona,* in Mariposa County, is said by some authorities to be a Moquelumnan word meaning "big tree," but this definition is regarded by ethnologists with doubt.

## CAMINO REAL

*Camino Real* (royal road, or the King's highway). The Camino Real was the road connecting the missions, and was the chief means of intercourse between the different settlements during the early years of the state's history. After American occupation the road fell into disuse, but at present is being reconstructed along the old route, with many extensions and branches, and will, when finished, be one of the finest in the United States.

234

## PRONUNCIATION OF SPANISH NAMES

While it scarcely falls within the province of this book to enter into an elaborate discussion of the matter of pronunciation of Spanish names, it is thought desirable to present a few of the simplest rules, with some examples, so that persons unacquainted with the language may avoid at least the worst of those pit-falls set for their inexperienced feet by our nomenclature. It should be mentioned that in California the Spanish-American usage, rather than the Castilian, is followed in the pronunciation of the *c* and *z* and *ll*. The rules of pronunciation quoted here are those given in Ramsey's text books, generally regarded as excellent authority.

### VOWELS

*A* sounds like *a* in *ah*, midway between the English *a* in *father* and that in *fat*. Example, *Pala*, pronounced *Pah'lah*.

*E* sounds like *a* in *hay*, its sound being slightly varied according to situation. Example, *Rode'o*, pronounced *Ro-day'o*.

*I* sounds like *ee* in *bee*. Example, *Vista*, pronounced *Vees'tah*.

*O* sounds like *o* in *hope*. Example, *Contra Costa*, pronounced *Cone'trah Coast'ah*. This name is frequently mispronounced by using the short sound of *o*, as in *not*.

*U* sounds like *u* in *rule*. Example, *La Punta*, pronounced *La Poon'tah*.

*Y*, when a vowel, is equivalent to *i*. *Y* is considered a vowel only when standing alone, as in *y* (the conjunction *and*), or at the end of a word, as in *ley* (law),

but is sometimes used interchangeably with *I* at the beginning of a word, as in *San Ysidro*, pronounced *San Ee-see'dro*, and sometimes spelled *Isidro*. In other cases it is a consonant and is pronounced like the *y* in the English *yard*.

## CONSONANTS

Only those consonant sounds differing from English usage need be mentioned here.

*C* has two sounds. Before *e* and *i* it is pronounced like *s* in *seat*, that is, in Spanish-American usage; examples, *Cerro*, pronounced *Ser'ro*, and *Cima*, pronounced *See'mah*. In all other cases *c* has the sound of *k*; examples, *Carlos*, pronounced *Kar'loce*, *Colorado*, pronounced *Ko-lo-rah'do* (each *o* long, as in *hope*), *Cuesta*, pronounced *Kwes'tah*, and *Cruz*, pronounced *Kroos*.

*Ch* has the sound of *ch* in church. Example, *Chico*, pronounced *Chee'ko*.

*D* is slightly softened, and when occurring between vowels and at the end of words it is almost like *th* in *then*. Examples, *Andrade*, pronounced *Ahn-drah'-dthay*, and *Soledad*, pronounced *Sole-ay-dadth*.

*G* has two sounds. Before *e* and *i* it has the sound of strongly aspirated *h*. Examples, *German'*, pronounced *Hare-mahn'* and *giro*, pronounced *hee'ro...* In all other cases it sounds like *g* in *go*. Examples, *Gaviota*, *Goleta*, *Guadalupe*, *Granada*. In *gue* and *gui* the *u* is regularly silent; exceptions to this rule are marked by the diæresis, as in *Argüello*, pronounced *Ar-gwayl'yo*, or in Spanish-American, *Ar-gway'yo*.

*H* is silent except in the combined character *ch*. Example, *La Honda*, pronounced *La On'dah*, with long *o*, as in *hope*.

*J* has the sound of strongly aspirated *h*. Examples, *Pájaro*, pronounced *Pah'hah-ro*, and *San José*, pronounced *San Ho-say'* This letter is one of the worst stumbling blocks in the pronunciation of Spanish names.

*Ll* has the sound of the letters *lli* in the English *million*, but in many parts of Spanish - America it is pronounced like *y* in *beyond*. The latter is not considered an elegant pronunciation. Example, *Vallejo*, properly pronounced *Val-yah'ho*, but in Spanish-American, *Va-yay'ho*.

*N* with the tilde, *ñ*, has the sound of the letters *ni* in the English *pinion*. Example, *Cañada*, pronounced *Cahn-yah'dthah*.

*Q* only occurs before *ue* and *ui*, and sounds like *k*, the following *u* being always silent. Example, *San Quintin*, pronounced *San Keen-teen'*.

*S* has the hissing sound of *s* in *say, base,* and is never pronounced like *sh* as in *mansion*, or *z* as in *rose*. Thus in *Santa Rosa* the *s* is sharply hissed and is not pronounced as *Santa Roza*.

*Z* is sounded in Spanish-America like sharply hissed *s*, as in *say* or *base*. Example, *Zamora*, pronounced *Sah-mo'rah*. In Castilian *Z* is like *th—Thamora*.

A peculiarity of pronunciation common to almost all Spaniards is the confusion of the *b* and the *v* so that one can hardly be distinguished from the other. Vowel sounds are pronounced shortly and crisply, never with the drawling circumflex sound sometimes heard in English. Without going into the complications of the divisions of syllables, it may be stated that the fundamental principle is to make syllables end in a vowel as far as possible; examples, *Do-lo-res* (not *Do-lor-es*), *Sa-li-nas* (not *Sal-in-as*).

## ACCENT

All words ending in *n* or *s* or a vowel are regularly accented on the next to the last syllable; examples, *Sausalíto, Altúras, cómen.* All others are accented on the last syllable; examples, *San Rafael', Avenal'.* In words following the above rules no mark is used, but in the exceptions, which are many, the stress must be indicated by the written accent. Examples, *Portolá, Jolón, álamo, àngeles.*

## ARTICLES

In the Spanish language articles agree with their nouns in gender and number. The forms of the definite article are *el* (singular) and *los* (plural) for the masculine, *la* singular) and *las* (plural) for the feminine. Examples, *El Portal* (the portal, or gate), *Los Gatos* (the cats), *La Paz* (the peace), *Las Vírgenes* (the virgins).

## LIST OF NAMES MOST LIKELY TO BE MISPRO-
## NOUNCED, WITH THEIR PHONETIC
## PRONUNCIATION

*Agua*.....................pronounced *Ah'gwah.* Spanish Americans often mispronounce
this word by leaving out
the *g,* calling it *ah'wa.*

*Aguajito*................ " *Ah-gwah-hee'to.*

*Alameda*............... " *Ah-lah-may'dthah.*

*Los Angeles*......... " *Loce Ahng'hell-ess.*

*Asunción*.............. " *Ah-soon-see-on',* with the
*o* long, as in *hope.*

*El Cajon'*............... " *El Kah-hon',* with the *o*
long, as in *hope.*

*Camino Real*....... " *Kah-mee'no Ray-ahl'.*

*Cañada*................. " *Kahn-yah'dtha,* with the
*d* slightly softened like
*th* in *then.*

*Carpinteria*......... " *Kar-peen-tay-ree'ah.*

*Carquinez*............ " *Kar-kee'ness.*

*Conejo*................... " *Ko-nay'ho.*

*Corral*................... " *Kore-rahl'.*

*Dolores*................. " *Do-lo'ress.*

*Farallones*............ " *Fah-rahl-yo'ness,* in
Spanish-American, *Fa-
rah-yo'ness.*

*Los Gatos*............. " *Loce Gah'tos,* the *o* long
as in *hope.*

*Guadalupe*............ " *Gwa-dah-loo'pay.*

*La Jolla*................. " *La Hole'yah,* or in Spanish-American, *Ho'yah.*

*La Joya*................. " *La Ho'yah.*

*La Junta*............... " *La Hoon'tah.*

239

| | | |
|---|---|---|
| *Laguna Seca*........ | " | *Lah-goo'nah Say'cah.* |
| *Lagunitas*.......... | " | *Lah-goo-nee'tas.* |
| *Matilija*.............. | " | *Mah-tee-lee'hah.* |
| *Merced*............... | " | *Mare-sedth'*, with the *d* slightly softened like *th* in *then.* |
| *Mesa*.................... | " | *May'sah.* |
| *Ojo*..................... | " | *O'ho*, with the *j* strongly aspirated. |
| *Pájaro*................ | " | *Pah'hah-ro.* |
| *Paso Robles*........ | " | *Pah'so Ro'blace.* |
| *Portolá*.............. | " | *Por-to-lah'.* |
| *Punta Arenas*..... | " | *Poon tah Ah-ray'nas.* |
| *Rodéo*................. | " | *Ro-day'o*, not *ro-dee-o.* |
| *Salinas*.............. | " | *Sah-lee'nas.* |
| *San Gerónimo*.... | " | *Sahn Hay-ró-nee-mo.* |
| *San Jacinto*........ | " | *Sahn Hah-seen'to.* |
| *San Joaquín*....... | " | *Sahn Ho-ah-keen'.* |
| *San José*............. | " | *Sahn Ho-say'.* |
| *San Juan Bautista* | " | *Sahn Whan Bau-tees'ta.* |
| *San Julián*.......... | " | *Sahn Hoo-lee-ahn'.* |
| *San Luis Obispo.* | " | *Sahn Loo-ees' O-bees'po.* |
| *San Martín*......... | " | *Sahn Mar-teen'.* |
| *San Quintín*....... | " | *Sahn Keen-teen'*, colloquially spelled *Quentin.* |
| *Santa Fé*............ | " | *Sahnta Fay'.* |
| *Santa Inez*.......... | " | *Sahnta Ee-ness'.* |
| *San Ysidro*......... | " | *Sahn Ee-see'dro*, also spelled *Isidro.* |
| *Suñol*................. | " | *Soon-yole'.* |
| *Vallejo*.............. | " | *Val-yay'ho*, in Spanish American *Vah-yay'ho.* |
| *Las Virgenes*...... | " | *Las Veer'hen-ess.* |

EL RIO DE LOS AMERICANOS (AMERICAN RIVER)

"It runs in deep canyons and the scenery along its course is rugged and striking."

# FINAL LIST AND INDEX

*Abalone,* the great sea-snail of the Pacific Coast. See page 58.

*Acalanes,* a land grant in Contra Costa County, probably named for an Indian village—Akalan, or something similar.

*Acampo* (common pasture). See page 204. This name is used here in the sense of "camp," and was given by the Southern Pacific Railroad years ago, in reference to a camp of wood choppers and Chinese which was located there.

*Acolito* (acolyte) is in Imperial County.

*Adelaida* (a feminine Christian name), a village in San Luís Obispo County.

*Adelante* (onward, forward), now changed to Napa Junction, is in Napa County. This place was called *Adelante* in the hope that its location on Napa River would cause it to become the principal city of the valley.

*Adiós,* goodbye, is in Kern County. Its application has not been ascertained.

*Adobe* (sun-dried brick).

*Agua* (water) is in very common use in refer-ring to springs, usually accompanied by a qual-ifying adjective.  See page 239.  This word is usually mispronounced by Spanish Americans.

*Agua Amargosa* (bitter water).  See page 114.

*Agua Caliente* (hot water, hot springs).  See pages 59 and 186.

*Agua Cayendo* (falling water).

*Agua Dulce* (sweet water, fresh water).

*Agua Fria*, cold water, cold springs.

*Agua Hedionda*, stinking water, sulphur spring.

*Aguaje del Centinela*, water hole, or watering place of the sentinel, the title of a land grant.

*Agua del Medio* (middle springs).

*Aguajito*, little water hole.  Near Monterey, in a delightful little glen, there were a number of these springs, or water holes, where the women were in the habit of doing the town washing, kneeling upon the ground and wash-ing the clothing directly in the springs.  This place was called *Los Aguajitos* (the water holes), by the Spanish residents, and "washer-woman's canyon" by the Americans. In the pas-toral days of California, entire families climbed into their ox-carts, made with solid wooden wheels, and, provided with a liberal lunch bas-ket, made a picnic of "blue Monday" under the

green trees of *Los Aguajitos* canyon. See page 239.

*Agua Mala,* bad water, Creek. In Monterey County.

*Agua Mansa,* still water, smooth-running current. One writer, for what reason does not appear, defines this as "house water." This place is in Southern California, near Colton. The term was applied to the Santa Ana River, on account of its silently flowing current.

*Aguanga,* in Riverside County, has no connection with the Spanish *agua,* water, but is a place or village name of the Shoshonean Luiseño Indians. The meaning is not known. (Kroeber, *California Place Names of Indian Origin,* page 33.)

*Agua Puerca* (dirty or muddy water).

*Agua Puerca y las Trancas* (muddy water and the bars, or stiles). This was the peculiar title of a land grant, based, no doubt, upon some trivial circumstance now forgotten. One writer has translated it as "water fit for pigs and Frenchmen," a gratuitous insult to the French people of which the Spaniards were not guilty. This writer evidently mistook the word *puerca* (muddy or dirty) for *puerca* (sow), and by some strange twist of the imagination, seems to have taken *trancas* to mean Frenchmen!

*Aguas Frias* (cold waters) is in Butte County.

*Agua Tibia* (tepid or warm water, warm spring). See page 29.

*Agua de Vida* (water of life).

*Aguilar* (the place of eagles).

*Las Aguilas* (the eagles). *Real de las Aguilas* means the "camp of the eagles."

*Ahwanee* (an Indian place name), popularly but not authentically translated as "a deep or grassy valley," is the name of a place in Madera County. It was the name by which Yosemite Valley was known to the Indians, from the name of this principal village, A-wa-ni, which stood directly at the foot of Yosemite Fall.

*Alameda* (an avenue shaded by trees, or a cottonwood grove). This word is derived from *álamo,* a poplar tree known in the West as cottonwood. See pages 149 and 239.

*Los Alamitos* (the little cottonwoods). See page 59.

*Alamo* (cottonwood). See page 163.

*Los Alamos y Agua Caliente* (the cottonwoods and hot spring), the title of a land grant.

*Alcalde* (mayor, justice of the peace). This place is in the southern part of Fresno County.

*Alcatraz* (pelican), see page 145.

*Alessandro* (Alexander). This place is in Riverside County. This form of the name, used by Helen Hunt Jackson in her famous book,

*Ramona,* is Italian. The Spanish form is *Alejandro.*

*Alhambra,* near Los Angeles, is said to have been named for the famous Alhambra of Spain. The Alhambra was an ancient palace and fortress of the Moorish monarchs of Granada in Southern Spain, probably built between 1248 and 1354. The word signifies in Arabic "the red," and was perhaps given to this building in allusion to the color of the bricks of which the outer walls are constructed. "The marvelous beauty of the architecture of this structure has been greatly injured by alterations, earthquakes, etc., yet it still remains the most perfect example of Moorish art in its final European development." A curious example of corruption is found in the name of Alhambra Creek, situated near the town of Martinez, Contra Costa County. The question naturally arises as to what possible connection there could be between an obscure little stream in California and the famous old Moorish palace of the Alhambra in Spain. Investigation shows that there is, as a matter of fact, no connection at all, and that the true story of the name runs as follows: In 1772 Captain Fages passed that way at the head of an exploring party and named this stream Arroyo del Hambre (hunger creek), in reference to the destitution observed among the Indians in the neighborhood. From

245

*del hambre* to *al hambre,* then to alhambra is
not a very long or difficult road for careless
people to travel. Unless the name of the place
in Los Angeles County is modern the same corruption may have occurred in its name, and its
origin may have no connection with the famous
Moorish palace in Spain.

*El Alisal* (alder grove).

*Aliso* (alder), see page 59.

*Los Alisos* (the alders), but used in California
to mean sycamores.

*Almadén* (mine, mineral). See page 128.

*Alta* (high). See page 229.

*Alta Loma* (high hill), in San Bernardino
County, is an example of improper arrangement
of Spanish words. It should be *Loma Alta,* in
accordance with the usage of the Spanish language in placing the adjective after the noun.

*Alta Mesa,* high table-land, in Santa Clara
County.

*Altaville* (high town), in Calaveras, is one
more of the unfortunate examples of combining
the two languages — the Spanish *alta* and the
French *ville.*

*Alto* (high) is near San Francisco.

*Los Altos* (the heights) is about fifteen miles
from Los Gatos.

*Alturas* (heights). See page 186.

*Alvarado* (a surname). See page 163.

*Alviso* (a surname). See page 128.

*Amador* (a surname). See page 218.

*Amargosa* (bitter). See page 229.

*American River.* See page 212.

*Anacapa Island.* This name is Indian, but the popular story that it means "vanishing island, disappearing island," is probably not authentic. "*Anacapa* is a corruption of Vancouver's Indian name of the island, *Enneeapah;* the engraver spelled it *Enecapah* on the chart, and subsequent compilers have endeavored to give it a Spanish form."—(Geo. Davidson in *United States Coast and Geodetic Survey.*)

*Anahuac* was the name of an Indian village in San Diego County.

*Andrade* (a surname). This place is near Calexico.

*Los Angeles* (the angels). See pages 38 and 239.

*Angel Island.* See page 146.

*Las Animas* (the souls). See page 50.

*Año Nuevo* (new year). See page 114.

*Aptos* is said to be an Indian name, meaning "the meeting of two streams," in reference to Valencia and Aptos Creeks. As this was a method of naming very much in vogue among the Indians, it is likely that this is the true explanation of Aptos.

*Arena* (sand). See page 186.

*Las Arenas* (the sands).

*Punta de Arenas* (sandy point), a cape on the coast of Mendocino County.

*Argüello* (a surname). See page 82.

*Armada* (fleet, squadron). The Armada was the name of the great fleet sent against England by Philip II in 1588. Whether the name of this town, situated in Riverside County, has this origin has not been ascertained.

*Las Aromitas y Agua Caliente* (the little perfumes and hot spring), title of a land grant.

*Aromas* (the odors, perfumes) is in San Benito County. This name may refer to some aromatic shrub growing there.

*Arroyo* (a creek or small stream). The designation *arroyo* is sometimes applied to the dry bed of a former stream. It does not, as is sometimes thought, refer only to a bed with steep sides, but is applied as well to shallow streams flowing through level country.

*Arroyo de la Alameda* (creek of the cottonwood grove).

*Arroyo Buenos Aires* (creek of the good airs). See page 204.

*Arroyo del Burro* (jackass creek).

*Arroyo Chico* (little creek). See page 204.

*Arroyo del los Dolores* (creek of the sorrows). Dolores Creek in San Francisco was so named "because this was the Friday of Sorrows."

*Arroyo de los Gatos* (creek of the cats—wildcats).

*Arroyo Grande* (big creek). See page 97.

*Arroyo Hondo* (deep creek). See page 128.

*Arroyo de la Laguna* (creek of the lagoon).

*Arroyo Medio* (middle creek).

*Arroyo de las Nueces y Bolbones* (creek of the walnuts and Bolbones). This name, which has been retained up to the present time in the English guise of Walnut Creek, was bestowed by Sergeant Gabriel Moraga, who led a party on an exploring expedition into the interior in August, 1810. Bolbones, or Bolgones, was the name of a tribe of Indians living in that vicinity.

*Arroyo del Norte* (creek of the north).

*Arroyo Pasajero* (creek roadway or passage). It is in Fresno.

*Arroyo Pinoso* (piny creek). It is in Fresno County.

*Arroyo Real de las Aguilas* (creek of the camp of the eagles).

*Arroyo del Rodéo* (creek of the cattle roundup).

*Arroyo Seco* (dry creek). See page 114.

*Arroyo del Toro* (creek of the bull) is in Riverside County.

*Asfalto* (asphalt), incorrectly spelled *asphalto,* is in southwestern Kern County.

*Asunción* (ascension). See pages 74 and 239.

*Atascadero* (bog-mire). See page 97. The

Atascadero is one of the largest ranches in the state, comprising of 22,000 acres.

*Avena* (oats) is in Inyo County.

*Avenal* (a field sown with oats). See page 97.

*Avenales* (fields of oats).

*Avila* ( a surname), eight miles from San Luís Obispo, was probably named for a pioneer family of Los Angeles. There is a city of the same name in Spain, a place noted for its romantic history and its ancient fortifications, which still remain one of the mural wonders of the world.

*Azul* (blue). In the foothills of the Santa Cruz Mountains in Santa Clara County there are some springs of water bearing the name of Azul, and the blueness of the water, rivaling the sky as it runs away from the springs, makes the name seem appropriate. On some old maps the Santa Cruz Mountains are marked as Azul (blue) Mountains.

*Azusa.* See page 59. This is the name of a place in Los Angeles County. According to a correspondent, Azusa is said to mean "Skunk Hill."—(Kroeber, p. 33.)

*El Bailarín* (the dancer). See page 76.

*Balboa,* in Orange County, is presumably named in honor of the famous discoverer of the Pacific Ocean, Vasco Nuñez de Balboa, who first set eyes on the glorious expanse of waters to the west of the great American continents on

September 26, 1513. When he descended the mountains and finally stood on the shore of the new sea he took possession of it in the name of the King of Spain, calling it "The South Sea," in contradistinction to the North Sea, as the Atlantic was then called by the Spaniards. It was left for Magellan, seven years later, to give it its permanent appellation—El Mar Pacifico (the peaceful sea).

*Ballena* (whale). See page 30.

*Bally,* or *Bully* Mountains, in Shasta County near the Trinity line, is from the Wintun Indian boli (pronounced "bawli"), and means "spirit." Bully Choop, Yallo Bally and Bully Hill in Shasta County have the same origin.— (Kroeber, p. 35).

*Bandini* (a surname). See page 59.

*Los Baños* (the baths), is in Merced County, thirty-five miles southwest of Merced. This place was so called from the creek, which has large, deep pools of clear water that were used by the early inhabitants as a bathing place.

*Barranca* (ravine).

*La Barranca Colorada* (the red ravine).

*Barril* (barrel).

*Barro* (clay).

*Batata* (sweet potato) is in Merced County, and is so called because it lies in the best sweet potato growing district in California.

*Baulines,* see page 164.

*Bella Vista* (beautiful view).

*Bellota* (acorn) is in San Joaquín County.

*Benicia* (a surname). See page 160.

*Berenda,* probably a mispelling of berrenda (female antelope), is in Madera County.

*Berrendo* (antelope). See page 30.

*Berrendos* (antelopes). See page 30.

*Berros* (water-cresses) is in San Luís Obispo County.

*Berryessa* (a surname). This name has been corrupted in the spelling, which was originally Berrelleza. The names of Nicolás Antonio Berrelleza and Maria Isabel Berrelleza are given among the first settlers of San Francisco in the Anza expedition of 1776. (Diary of Father Font, p. 447).

*Blanco* (white). See page 114.

*Boca* (mouth) in this case refers to the mouth of the Truckee River, in Nevada County.

*La Boca de la Cañada del Pinole* (the mouth of the valley of the cereal meal). This was a land grant, which received its peculiar name from the fact of the Spaniards having been compelled to live on pinole while they awaited the return of a party with supplies from Monterey. See *Pinole,* page 168.

*Boca de la Playa* (mouth of the beach).

*Boca de Santa Mónica* (mouth of Santa Mónica).

*Bodega* (a surname). See page 186.

*Bolinas,* probably a corruption of *Baulines,* an Indian word. See page 164.

*Bolsa* (pocket), often used to mean a "shut-in place," or a pocket of land. See page 60.

*La Bolsa* (the pocket) is near Newport Beach.

*Las Bolsas* (the pockets). Land grant in Orange County.

*Bolsa de Chamisal,* land grant, (pocket of the wild cane, or reeds). The chamisal, sometimes incorrectly spelled chemisal, is defined in the dictionaries as wild cane, or reed, but in California, at least, it is applied to a "shrub attaining a height of six or eight feet. Its thickets are almost impassable except by bears or similar animals, as the branches are low and very stiff and tough. In some places men are only able to penetrate it by crawling."—(Mr. Charles B. Turrill.)

*Bolsa Chica* (little pocket).

*Bolsa de las Escorpinas* (pocket of the perch) land grant.

*Bolsa Nueva y Moro Cojo* (new pocket and lame Moor). The word *Moro* was often used to mean anything black, as, for instance, a lame black horse, for which the Moro Cojo Rancho,

near Monterey, is said to have been named. Name of land grant.

*Bolsa del Pájaro* (pocket of the bird) name of land grant.

*Bolsa del Potrero, y Moro Cojo ó la Sagrada Familia* (pocket of the pasture, and the lame Moor or the Holy Family). This is the combined name of several land grants.

*Bolsa de San Felipe* (pocket of St. Philip) name of land grant.

*Bonita* (pretty) is in San Diego County.

*Bonito* (pretty). See page 165.

*Boronda Creek* is in Monterey County. Boronda is the name of a pioneer family.

*Borregas* (sheep) creek. It is in Santa Cruz County.

*La Brea* (the asphalt). See page 40.

*Bronco* (wild, rough) Flat. Bronco was the name usually applied to the small, wiry horses formerly in use in California, especially on the cattle ranges. These horses were valued for their endurance and speed, but were inclined to be unruly.

*El Buchón* (the big craw). See page 97.

*Buena Park* (good park), rather unsatisfactory mixture of Spanish and English, is in Orange County. Park is commonly used in Mexico; e.g., Popo Park at Popocatapetyl.

*Buena Vista* (good view).

*Buenos Aires* (good airs) is in Los Angeles County.

*Bueyes* (oxen).

*Los Burros* (the donkeys, or jackasses), is in San Luís Obispo County.

*Caballada Creek* (creek of the horse drove). It is in San Luís Obispo County.

*Cabeza* (head).

*Dos Cabezas* (two heads).

*Cabeza de Santa Rosa* (head of St. Rose).

*Cabezón* (big head). See page 60.

*Cabrillo* (a surname), the name of a cape on the coast of Mendocino County. See page 187. The name of Juan Rodriguez Cabrillo is one of the most eminent in the annals of California, for he was the first white man to set eyes on her shores. See page 20.

*Cádiz,* between Needles and Barstow, was probably named for the well-known Spanish city of the same name. "In naming the stations on the Southern Pacific Railroad from Mojave to Needles going east, an alphabetical order was used, Barstow, Cádiz, Daggett, etc., until Needles was reached."

*Cahto,* Mendocino County, Indian, probable meaning "lake," preferably spelled *Kahto.*

*Cahuenga,* near Los Angeles, is an Indian name, that of a former village. See page 61.

*Cahuilla* is said to be a corruption of the Indian word Ka-wia. See page 61.

*El Cajón* (the box, or canyon). The name of *El Cajón* was first given to a valley lying about fifteen miles east of San Diego. The valley comprises about 16,000 acres of level land entirely surrounded by hills several hundred feet high, thus presenting a box-like appearance that gave rise to its name. See pages 31 and 239.

*Cajón Pass* is in San Bernardino County.

*Calabazas* (pumpkins). See page 61.

*Calaveras* (skulls). See page 219.

*Calera Valley* (lime kiln valley) is on the ocean shore of San Mateo County.

*Calexico*, on the border of Lower California, is a hybrid word made up of the first part of California and the last of Mexico. Its counterpart on the Mexican side is Mexicali, in which the process is reversed.

*Caliente* (hot). See page 204.

*Caliente Creek*. See page 31. This creek was so named because its water is warm.

*California*. See page 9.

*Calistoga*. See page 187.

*Calneva* and *Calvada* are two more hybrids, made up of syllables from California and Nevada.

*Calor,* near the Oregon line, is likely to cause confusion by its resemblance to the Spanish

SHORE OF LAKE TAHOE

" * * * pearl among all lakes."

word *calor* (heat); this Calor is one of those composite words to which Californians are so regrettably addicted, and is made up of the first syllables of California and Oregon.

*Calpella* was named for the chief of a village situated just south of the present town, near Pomo, in Mendocino County. The chief's name was Kalpela.

*Calvada,* Sierra County, hybrid of California and Nevada.

*Calzona* is another trap for the unwary, through its resemblance to the Spanish word *calzones* (breeches); it is one more of those border towns bearing names made up of the syllables of two state names, in this case, California and Arizona.

*Camanche,* a post town in Calaveras County, was so named in honor of the great Camanche, or Comanche tribe, whose remarkable qualities are thus described by Father Morfi in his *Memorias de Texas,* a document written about the year 1778: "The Comanche nation is composed of five thousand fighting men, divided into five tribes, each with a different name. They are very superior to all the others in number of people, extent of the territory that they occupy, modesty of their dress, hospitality to all who visit them, humanity toward all captives except Apaches, and in their bravery, which is remark-

able even in the women. They live by hunting
and war, and this wandering disposition is the
worst obstacle to their reduction, for it induces
them to steal. Nevertheless, they are very generous with what they have, and so proud that
one alone is capable of facing a whole camp of
enemies if he cannot escape without witnesses
to his flight." Both spellings are used in the
original records.

*Camarillo,* in Ventura County, was no doubt
named for Juan Camarillo, who probably came
to California in 1834 with the Hijar colony. He
was owner of the Calleguas rancho at San Buenaventura.

*Camaritas* (small cabins or rooms). The application of this name has not been ascertained.
It may refer to Indian huts seen by the Spaniards, or may have a totally different meaning.

*Camino* (road) is in Eldorado County.

*Camino Real* (royal road, or the King's highway). See pages 234 and 239.

*Campo* (a level field, a camp, the country).
See page 32.

*El Campo* (the field or camp), places in Marin
and San Diego Counties.

*Campo de los Franceses* (field or camp of the
Frenchmen).

*Campo seco* (dry field or camp), in Calaveras
County.

*Camulos,* or *Kamulas.* See page 81.

*Cantua Creek* is in Fresno County. Cantua is a family name.

*Cañada* (valley or dale between mountains). In California Cañada is commonly used in the sense of canyon. See page 239.

*Cañada de los Alisos* (valley of the alders).

*Cañada del Bautismo* (valley of the baptism). See page 32.

*Cañada de los Capitancillos* (valley of the little captains), possibly a reference to Indian leaders, who were sometimes so called.

*Cañada de la Carpintería* (valley of the carpenter-shop). See page 77.

*Cañada de los Coches* (valley of the pigs). *Coche,* used in the sense of "pig," is a Mexicanism, said to have originated in the state of Sonora.

*Cañada del Corte de Madera* (valley of the wood-cutting place).

*Cañada Gobernadora* (valley of the gobernadora, a certain plant native to California). It is in Orange County.

*Cañada del Hambre y las Bolsas* (valley of hunger and the pockets), a name said to have been given to this canyon because some Spanish soldiers nearly perished of starvation there. A *bolsa* is a pocket, or shut-in place.

259

*Cañada de los Ladrones* (valley of the thieves) is in Santa Bárbara County.

*Cañada Larga* (long valley).

*Cañada de los Muertos* (valley of the dead).

*Cañada de los Nogales* (valley of the walnut-trees).

*Cañada de los Noques* (valley of the tan-pits).

*Cañada del Osito* (valley of the little bear). See page 97.

*Cañada de los Osos y Pecho y Islay,* valley of the bears and breast (perhaps referring to Pecho Mountain in San Luís Obispo County), and wild cherry, combined name of land grant. *Islay* is said to be a California Indian word meaning wild cherry. Islais Creek, San Francisco, may take its name from the wild cherry.

*Cañada de los Pinos* (valley of the pines).

*Cañada de Raymundo* (valley of Raymond).

*Cañada del Rincón en el Rio San Lorenzo de Santa Cruz* (valley of the corner section on the river San Lorenzo of Santa Cruz). Land grant.

*Cañada del Rodéo* (valley of the rodéo) is in Santa Bárbara County.

*Cañada Salada* (salt valley).

*Cañada de Sal si Puedes* (valley of "get out if you can"). See page 89.

*Cañada de San Felipe y las Animas* (valley of St. Philip and the souls).

*Cañada Segunda* (second valley).

260

*Cañada Tortuga* (valley of the turtle) is in Santa Bárbara County.

*Cañada de los Vaqueros* (valley of the cowboys).

*Cañada Verde, y Arroyo de la Purísima Concepción* (green valley and creek of the immaculate conception).

*Cantil* (a steep rock), in Kern County.

*Capay,* in Yolo County, is from the Indian *kapai,* meaning "stream."—(Kroeber, p. 37.)

*Capistrano.* See page 28.

*El Capitán* (the captain), the name of a precipice in the Yosemite Valley.

*Capitán* (captain), the name of a flag station in Santa Bárbara County. It was named for a ranch owned by Captain Ortega, which was called *Capitan,* in reference to his title.

*Capitancillos* (little captains). Canada de los Capitancillos is the name of a canyon in Santa Clara County and the creek which flows through it. The origin of this name has not yet been unearthed, but it may possibly have some reference to Indian leaders met at that place by the Spaniards, who had a habit of referring to such chiefs or leaders in the documents as *capitancillos,* "little captains." This, however, is merely conjecture.

*Capitan Grande* (big captain). The origin of this name has not been ascertained, but it prob-

ably referred to an Indian chief. It is the name of an Indian reservation in San Diego County.

*La Carbonera* (the charcoal pit).

*Carmelo* (garden, or garden-land). See page 115.

*Carmenita* (the diminutive of the feminine name Carmen). The name of a station on the Southern Pacific Railroad in Los Angeles County. The usual form is Carmencita.

*Carnadero,* a corrupt word used to mean "butchering-place."

*Carne Humana* (human flesh). See page 174.

*Carne Humana* (human flesh). See page 177. Applied to sheep used for mutton, rather than wool.

*Carpintería* (carpenter-shop). See pages 77 and 239.

*Carquínez.* See pages 165 and 239.

*Carriso* (large water bunch grass or reed-grass). See page 32.

*Casa Blanca* (white house). See page 61.

*Casa Desierta* (deserted house) is in Los Angeles County.

*Casa Grande* (big house). This place was so called by the Spanish explorers on account of an unusually large Indian house they saw here. They speak of finding a "large village of many houses, and among them one extremely large." This place is not to be confused with the famous *Casa Grande* in Arizona.

262

*Casa Loma* (house hill). Improper combination; it should be *Casa de la Loma*. It is in Riverside County.

*Casa Verde* (green house). Gun club in Monterey County.

*El Casco* (the skull, or outside shell of anything). See page 61. As *casco* also has the meaning of potsherd, or fragment of a broken vessel, a theory has been deduced that it was so called because of a resemblance between the hollow in the hills where the place is located and a potsherd. This is one of those extremely farfetched theories which are not likely to have any basis in fact.

*Castac,* an Indian word. The name of an Indian village in Tejón Pass. Castake Lake in the Tejón Pass region derives its name from this village. According to Professor A. L. Kroeber, *castac* means "my eyes."

*Castroville.* Castro was the name of an important and numerous Spanish - Californian family, the most noted member of which was General José Castro. The town of Castroville, however, was not named for General Castro, but for the heirs of Simeón Castro, his uncle, who was the grantee of the Bolsa Nueva y Moro Cojo Rancho, and owned the land where Castroville now stands. The town was laid out by his son and daughter, Juan Bautista Castro, and Maria

Antonia Castro de Sanchez. They gave the right of way to the Southern Pacific Railroad, for which they received a life pass on the trains. They named the station Castroville. When the name was changed to Del Monte Junction descendants of the family protested, but it did no good. The town of Castroville, now known as Del Monte Junction, is near Monterey.

*Catalina.* See page 48.

*Cayeguas* was named for a former Indian village near San Buenaventura. This village was among those mentioned in the mission archives. This name is sometimes spelled on the maps "Calleguas."

The meaning of the word *Cayeguas* is "my head."—(A. L. Kroeber.)

*Cayucos.* See page 97.

*Cazadero* (hunting-place). See page 187.

*Centinela* (sentinel).

*El Centro* (the center), three miles from Imperial and so named because it is practically the center of the valley. This name is recent.

*El Cerrito* (the little hill) is in Contra Costa County. The name refers to a small hill or eminence which commands a fine view of San Francisco Bay. There is also an El Cerrito in San Matéo County.

*Cerro* (hill), near Sacramento.

*Cerro Chico* (little hill).

*Cerro Gordo* (fat, thick hill). See page 229.

*Los Cerritos* (the little hills), in Los Angeles County.

*Los Cerros* (the hills).

*Cerro de las Posas* (hill of the pools or wells). The translation "hill of the seat" has been given to this by one writer, apparently without any justification. *Posa,* or *poso,* was in constant use among the Spaniards in the sense of "pool" or "well."

*Cerro del Venado* (hill of the deer).

*El Chamisal* (thicket of wild cane or reed).

*Chico* (little). See page 204.

*Chico Vecino* (Chico neighbor) is the name of a suburb of the town of Chico in Butte County.

*Chileno* (Chilean, native of Chile). See page 187.

*Las Chimeneas* (the chimneys), old volcanic rock shaped like chimneys. This place is in San Luís Obispo County.

*Chino,* a word which may mean a Chinese, or a person with curly hair. The town of Chino, in San Bernardino County, took its name from the land grant called *Santa Ana del Chino,* but why the grant was so called has not been ascertained. As the word also means a half-breed Indian, it is possible that the grant may have been made to a person of this mixed blood, hence the name; but this is only conjecture.

*Chiquita* (little).

*Chiquito Peak* (little peak) is in Fresno County.

*Cholame* was the name of an Indian village in San Luís Obispo County near Mission San Miguel. See page 98.

*El Chorro* (a gushing stream of water). This place is in San Luís Obispo County. It is the name of a creek, and was so named for a waterfall on its course.

*Chowchilla* was the name of an Indian tribe of the Central Valley. See page 205.

*Chualar.* See page 115.

*Chula Vista* (pretty view). See page 32.

*Ciénaga* (swamp) is in Los Angeles County.

*Las Ciénagas* (the swamps).

*Las Ciénagitas* (the little swamps).

*Ciénaga del Gabilán* (the swamp of the hawk).

*Ciénaga Larga* (long swamp) is in San Bernardino County.

*Ciénaga de los Paicines,* swamp of the Paicines (Indian tribe).

*Ciénaga Redondo* (round swamp) is in San Bernardino County.

*El Cierbo* (the deer), properly spelled *ciervo*, is the name of a town in Contra Costa County.

*Cima* (summit), between San Bernardino and Las Vegas.

*Cimarrón* (wild, unruly). The Spaniards applied this word to plants or animals indiscrim-

inately, sometimes using it in reference to the wild grapes which they found growing in such profusion in California, sometimes in reference to wild Indians. The writer who translated it as "lost river" must have drawn upon his imagination for that definition.

*Cisco.* See page 230.

*Los Coches* (the pigs).

*Codornices Creek* (quail creek).

*Cojo* (lame). See page 82.

*Rancheria del Cojo* (village of the lame one), so called from a lame Indian seen there.

*Coloma,* a town in El Dorado County, so named from the Koloma tribe, a division of the Nishinam group. It was at this place that Sutter's Mill, where gold was discovered in 1848, was situated, and it is also there that the Native Sons erected a monument to James W. Marshall.

*Colorado* (red). Name of the great river dividing California from Arizona, so called because of the reddish color of its waters.

*Colusa,* an Indian word, meaning not ascertained. See page 190.

*Concepción.* See page 82.

*Conejo* (rabbit) is the name of several places. See pages 62 and 239.

*Conejo Peak* (rabbit peak) is in Ventura County.

*Contra Costa* (opposite coast). See page 166.

267

*Cordero* (literally "lamb"), but probably a surname here.

*Córdova,* near Sacramento. Córdova or Córdoba is the name of a province of the Argentine Republic, in South America. Cattle raising is its chief industry. The California town may have been directly named for the city of Córdova in Mexico.

*Corona* (crown).

*Coronado Beach.* See page 25.

*Corral* (yard, enclosed piece of ground). See pages 116 and 239.

*Corralillos Canyon* (canyon of the little corrals, or yards). It is in Santa Bárbara County.

*Los Corralitos* (the little yards).

*Corral de Piedra* (yard enclosed by a stone fence). See page 116.

*Corral de Tierra* (earth corral). See page 116.

*Corral Viejo* (old corral), in Monterey County.

*Corte Madera* (wood-cutting place) is in Marin County. When the Spaniards prepared to build their houses or church buildings they sent carpenters to the woods to cut the timbers, and it is probably in reference to some such matter that this place was named. See page 167.

*Cortina,* a town in Colusa County. *Cortina,* the Spanish word for "curtain," is a corruption of *Kotina,* the name of the chief of a former village near the east bank of Cortina Creek.

*Coso Mountains,* in Inyo County, were named for the Coso or Cosho Indians.

*La Costa* (the coast). See page 33.

*Cosumne,* a word of Indian derivation, said to mean "fish, salmon." See page 196.

*Cotate,* in Sonoma County, derived its name from a former Indian village. Mr. George Page, whose family have been in possession of the Cotate ranch since 1849, states that he has never been able to ascertain the meaning of the word.

*Coyote* (western wolf). See pages 33 and 128.

*Los Coyotes* (the wolves).

*Cresta* (crest of a mountain), in Butte County.

*Cristianitos* (little Christians) Canyon. It is in San Diego County.

*Crucero* means here "cross-roads," in reference to a railroad crossing.

*Las Cruces* (the crosses) is in Santa Bárbara County.

*Cruz* (cross). *Santa Cruz* (holy cross). See page 112.

*Cucamonga,* in San Bernardino County, derived its name from an Indian village. See page 62.

*Cueros de Venado* (hides of deer), the name of a land grant.

*Cuesta* (hill, ridge, slope of a hill). Cuesta is the name of the old stage road leading from Santa Margarita to San Luís Obispo. It was so

named because the road came over the crest of the Santa Lucia range. See page 98.

*Cupertino.* See page 129.

*Cypress Point.* See page 107.

*Dehesa* (pasture ground) is in San Diego County.

*Delgada Point* (thin, or narrow point). See page 187.

*De Luz* (literally "of light"), but in this case a surname.

*Del Mar* (of the sea). Modern. See page 35.

*Del Monte* (of the wood or hill). The Hotel del Monte, near Monterey, was so called from the grove of magnificent live-oaks in which it stands. Modern.

*Del Norte* (of the north) is the name of the county in the extreme northwestern corner of the state. The second part of this name is frequently mispronounced as one syllable—*nort.* It should be in two syllables, pronounced *nór-tay.*

*Del Paso* (of the pass).

*Del Rey* (of the king).

*Del Rio* (of the river).

*Del Rosa* (of the rose). Unless this is a surname, the construction is incorrect, and should be *De la Rosa.*

*Del Sur* (of the south) is in Los Angeles County.

*Descanso* (rest). See page 33.

*Diablo* (devil). See page 154.

*Diaz Canyon* is in Fresno County. Diaz is a family name.

*Divisadero* (lookout or observation point), name of a street in San Francisco. It seems to be a coined word, made up from *divisar,* to spy out, to observe.

*Dolores* (sorrows, pains). For Mission Dolores see pages 140 and 239.

*Domínguez* (Dominic) is a Christian name. It is in Los Angeles County.

*El Dorado* (the gilded man). See page 213.

*Dos* (two).

*Dos Cabezas* (two heads).

*Dos Palmas* (two palms).

*Dos Palos* (two sticks, or trees). See page 205.

*Dos Pueblos* (two towns). See page 83.

*Dos Ríos* (two rivers) is in Mendocino County, at the junction of the south and middle forks of the Eel River. It appears on some maps in its English form of Two Rivers.

*Dos Valles* (two valleys).

*Duarte* (a surname). See page 62.

*Dulzura* (sweetness). See page 33.

*Point Duma,* on the coast north of San Pedro, was named by Vancouver for "the reverend friar Father Francisco Duma, priest at Buena Ventura," as an expression of his gratitude for the father's courtesy in furnishing the explorers

with abundant supplies of vegetables from the mission gardens.

*Eliseo* (Elisha).

*Embarcadero* (landing-place). There were a number of *embarcaderos* in the state, in Sonoma, Santa Clara and other places. The street skirting the San Francisco water front is now called the *Embarcadero,* having been recently changed from East Street.

*Encanto* (enchantment, charm), is in San Diego County. Encanto "was so named on account of its especially pleasant climate, being frostless, and always cool in the summer, with beautiful views of the ocean and bay and the city of San Diego. It was named by Miss Alice Klauber."

*Encinal* (live-oak woods) is in Santa Clara County. *Encina* refers to the live-oak, *roble* to the common oak.

*Encinal y Buena Esperanza* (oak woods and good hope), the combined name of two land grants.

*Las Encinitas* (the little live oaks). See page 34.

*El Encino* (the live-oak). See page 151.

*Ensenada* (bay), used often by the Spaniards in referring to a large, wide-open bay.

*Entre Napa* (between Napa), the name of a land grant referring to the land between Napa Creek and Napa River.

MARIPOSA SEQUOIAS

" * * * some of these unfolded their feathery fronds before Christ came upon the earth."

*Entre Napa ó Rincón de los Carneros,* combined name of two land grants (between Napa or corner of the sheep).

*Escalón* (step) is the name of a place twenty miles from Stockton, on the Santa Fé Road. According to Mr. Romane Moll, a resident of Escalón, the word is used in the sense of "stepping-stone," and was taken from a city in Mexico, where an important battle was fought during the recent revolution. This explanation has not been verified.

*Escondido* (hidden). See page 34.

*El Escorpión* (the scorpion).

*Esmeralda* (emerald). See page 230.

*Espada* (sword). See page 79.

*Esparto* (a sort of tough feather grass). See page 205.

*Esperanza* (hope). See page 205.

*Espinosa* (a surname). This place is in Monterey County.

*Espíritu Santo* (holy ghost).

*Esquón* (a surname).

*Estanislao.* See page 198.

*Estero* (an estuary or creek into which the tide flows at flood time).

*Los Esteros* (the estuaries). See page 98.

*Estero Americano* (American Estuary).

*Estrada* (a surname). This place is in Monterey County.

*Estrella* (star). See page 98.

*Estudillo* (a surname). Near San Leandro.

*Etiwanda,* in San Bernardino County, is a transplanted Indian name, given in honor of an Indian chief of Michigan, by Mr. George Chaffey, founder of the California colony.

*Falda* (skirt, slope of a hill). In San Diego County.

*Famoso* (famous) is in Kern County. The origin of this name has not been ascertained.

*Fandango Peak* is in Modoc County. The *fandango* is a Spanish dance. Its application in this case has not been ascertained.

*Farallones* (small pointed islands in the sea). See pages 152 and 239.

*Feather River.* See page 211.

*Felipe* (Philip).

*Feliz* (happy, fortunate), also a surname.

*Fernández* (a surname).

*Fernando* (Ferdinand).

*Figueroa,* a street in Los Angeles, named for José Figueroa, regarded as the best of the Mexican governors of California.

*Point Fermín,* north of San Pedro, was named by Vancouver for the father president of the Franciscan Missions, Fermín Francisco Lasuén.

*Las Flores* (the flowers). See page 62.

*Fortunas* (fortunes). Cape Fortunas is on the

coast of Humboldt County, north of Cape Mendocino. See page 187.

*Fresno* (ash tree). See page 201.

*Gabilán,* or *Gavilán* (hawk). See page 116.

*Gamboa Point,* on the coast of Monterey County. *Gamboa* is a surname.

*Garapato Creek* is possibly a corrupted spelling of *Garapito* (wood-tick) *Creek.*

*García* (a surname). See page 187.

*Garvanza* (chick-pea). See page 62.

*Gato* (cat) is in Santa Bárbara County.

*Los Gatos* (the cats). See pages 127 and 239.

*Gaviota* (sea gull). See page 83.

*Germán* (a surname of a pioneer family).

*Golden Gate.* See page 141.

*La Goleta* (the schooner). This place is said to have been so called because a schooner was stranded there in the early days. See page 84.

*Gonzales* (a surname). See page 117.

*Gorda* (fat). See pages 117 and 187.

*Graciosa* (graceful, beautiful).

*Granada* is twenty-seven miles from San Francisco, on the Ocean Shore Line, and was probably named for the province in Spain of the same name. Granada also means pomegranate.

*Las Grullas* (the cranes). See page 117.

*Guadalupe* (much used as a Christian name). See pages 84 and 239.

*Guadalupe y Llanitos de los Corréos* (Guadalupe and the plains of the mails, or the mail carriers), combined name of two land grants. *Corréos* may have been used in reference to mails brought by messenger to the Spaniards while they were encamped on these plains. In March, 1776, Captain Anza, founder of San Francisco, Sergeant Moraga, and Father Font passed through the Santa Clara Valley on their way to the port of San Francisco. On their return trip they found a little river pouring into the head of the bay of San Francisco, and they named the river Nuestra Señora de Guadalupe.

*Gualala,* an Indian word. See page 188.

*Guatay,* a San Diego County Reservation, named from the Diegueño Indian word *kwatai* (large).

*Guenoc,* from *Wennok,* the Indian name of a little valley and lake in Lake County.

*Guerrero,* name of a street in San Francisco, in honor of Francisco Guerrero, former military comandante of that place.

*Guijarral* (pebblestones) Hills are in Fresno County.

*Los Guilicos,* in Sonoma County, named from an Indian village called *Willikos.*

*Guinda* (fruit of the wild cherry) in Yolo County near Woodland.

*La Habra* (the opening, or pass), here refers

276

to an opening in the hills, and is situated a short distance southeast of Whittier, in Orange County.

*Hacienda.* This word has several significations, one of them being reduction works in a mine. It was in this sense that it was used at New Almaden quicksilver mine, about twelve miles south of San José. A village has grown up at this point and has inherited the name of Hacienda from the reduction works at the mine.

*Hermosa* (beautiful). See page 62.

*Hermosillo,* probably named for the town of Hermosillo in Mexico.

*Hernández* (a surname) is in San Benito County.

*Hetch Hetchy.* A deep valley in the Sierra. See page 230.

*Honcut,* a place south of Oroville, in Butte County, named from a tribe of Maidu Indians who formerly lived near the mouth of Honkut creek.

*Honda* (deep). Honda is in Santa Bárbara County, and there is also *La Honda,* referring to a deep canyon, in San Matéo County. The name is incomplete in this form, and probably in its original form was *La Cañada Honda.*

*Hoopa.* See page 188.

*Hornitos* (little ovens). See page 205.

*Hoya* (hole or hollow), name given by the

Portolá party to a deep ravine in the Santa Lucía Mountains where they camped.

*Huasna,* in San Luís Obispo County, received its name from a former Indian village near Purísima Mission in Santa Bárbara County. The signification of the word has not been ascertained.

*Hueneme,* the name of a former Chumash Indian village on the coast, a few miles south of Saticoy, in Ventura County. See page 188.

*Los Huecos* (the hollows).

*Huerhuero Creek.* Huerhuero is said to be a corruption of *güergüero,* a stream of water which makes a gurgling noise. An attempt is made to imitate the sound by the word. Huerhuero Creek is in San Luís Obispo County, near Paso de Robles.

*Huerta de Romualdo ó el Chorro* (orchard of Romualdo, a Christian name, or the gushing stream). This is the combined name of two land grants.

*Huichica,* the name of a land grant derived from an Indian village called *Hutchi,* formerly situated near the plaza in the town of Sonoma.

*Huililic,* the name of a former Indian ranchería near Santa Bárbara. Mentioned in the mission archives.

*Hunto* (eye) is the Indian name of a mountain in the Yosemite.

278

*Hyampom,* in Trinity County, is an Indian name, meaning not ascertained. See page 188.

*Iaquá,* the name of a place in Humboldt County, was a sort of familiar salutation, something like our "hello," with which the Indians of Humboldt and adjacent counties greeted each other when they met. From hearing the word so often the whites finally adopted it as the name of this place.

*Ignacio* (Ignatius), a town in Marin County, named for Ignacio Pacheco, Spanish pioneer.

*Inaja,* or *Inoje,* was the name of a former Indian village near San Diego. Mentioned in the mission archives. The meaning of the word *Inaja* is "my water."

*Indio* (Indian). See page 62.

*Inyo.* See page 228.

*Islais Creek* may have been named for the wild cherry trees (*islay*) growing along its banks.

*Isleta* (small island).

*Ivanpah,* in San Bernardino County, is probably a southern Paiute Indian word.

*Jacinto* (hyacinth), also used as a Christian name.

*Jamacha* was a former Indian village near San Diego. It is the name of a wild squash plant.

*Jamón* (ham). The application of this peculiar name has not been ascertained, but there is always the possibility that it is a corrupted

279

word and has no such meaning. In Palou's *Noticias* reference is made to a ham which was divided among the officers and men. This name may be a reference to this trivial episode.

*Jamul,* in San Diego County, is a place name of the Diegueño Indians. It means "foam" or "lather," but what the application may be has not been ascertained.

*Jarame,* the name of a tribe thought to have been natives of the region around San Antonio, Texas.

*Jesús María* (Jesus Mary).

*Jimeno,* a surname of a pioneer family.

*La Jolla.* See pages 34 and 239.

*Jolón.* See page 117.

*La Joya* (the jewel). This name is comparatively modern, and has its origin in the fact that the residents, like those of every other California town, thought their place the bright particular "jewel" of the locality. La Joya Peak is in Los Angeles County. See pages 62 and 239.

*Juan* (John). *Juana* (Jane).

*Joaquín* (Joachim) Rocks and Ridge are in Fresno County.

*Juárez* (a surname). The name of Benito Juárez, the Mexican patriot who led the national armies to victory against Maximilian, is one of which every native of that country must be proud. This man was a brilliant example of the

triumph of natural genius over tremendous obstacles. He was of pure native blood, and had so few advantages in his youth that at the age of twelve he was still unable to read or write, or even to speak the Spanish language. Yet, his ambition once aroused, he succeeded in acquiring a collegiate education, graduating with the degree of Bachiller (bachelor in science or art), and later became President of the Mexican Republic. Among the early settlers of California is the name of Cayetano Juárez, who was at one time an official at Solano, and who took part in many Indian expeditions.

*La Junta* (union, junction, meeting of persons for consultation or of rivers). See page 239.

*Las Juntas* (the junctions, or meetings).

*Kawia,* the name of an Indian tribe near Fresno. It has no connection with *Cahuilla,* although the pronunciation is the same, *Kah-weé-ah.*

*Kings County and River.* See page 201.

*Klamath.* See page 180.

*Laguna* (lake or lagoon), in Sonoma and Orange Counties. There were many *lagunas* in the state. See page 62.

*Laguna del Corral* (lake or lagoon of the yard). See page 35.

*Point Laguna* (lake or lagoon point). See page 188.

*Laguna de las Calabasas* (lagoon of the pumpkins). The name refers to the wild gourds that grow in that locality. See page 61.

*Laguna de la Merced* (lagoon or lake of mercy). Lake Merced. See page 167.

*Laguna de los Palos Colorados* (lagoon of the redwoods).

*Laguna Puerca* (muddy lagoon), in the San Francisco district. This name does not mean "Hog Lake," as has been stated.

*Laguna del Rey* (lagoon of the king).

*Laguna de San Antonio* (lagoon of St. Anthony).

*Laguna Seca* (dry lagoon). See page 240.

*Lagunitas* (little lagoons or lakes), one in Inyo County and one in Marin County. See page 240.

*Lancha Plana* (flat-boat). See page 231.

*Largo* (long). This place is in Mendocino County. The word is explained as the translation into Spanish of the name of a man called Long, a pioneer of Mendocino County, but the explanation bears the familiar marks of invention.

*Laureles* (laurels). See page 117.

*Lechuza* (barn-yard owl) Canyon. It is in Los Angeles County.

*Lerdo* (a surname) is in Kern County.

*La Liebre* (the hare, or jack-rabbit).

*Linda Rosa* (lovely rose) is forty-eight miles from San Bernardino.

*Linda Vista* (lovely view). See page 35.

*Lindo Lake* (beautiful lake). It is in San Diego County.

*Llagas* (wounds, or stigmata). See page 129.

*Llanada* (a wide, level plain). See page 117.

*Llanitos de los Corréos* (plains of the mails). *Corréos* was used to mean a King's messenger, mail or bag of letters, and it is possible that at this point a messenger or mail carrier caught up with the exploring party.

*Llano* (a flat, level field). There are places bearing this name in Los Angeles and Sonoma Counties.

*Llano de Buena Vista* (plain of the good view).

*Llano de Santa Rosa* (plain of St. Rose).

*Llano Seco* (dry plain).

*Llano de Tequisquite* (plain of saltpetre). *Tequisquite* is an Aztec word.

*Llorones* (the weepers), a name given to a place in the vicinity of San Francisco Bay, for the reason given in Palou's account of the expedition to that region in 1775, as follows: "The launch went out again with the pilot Bautista Aguiray to examine the arm of the sea that runs to the southeast; they saw nothing more than two or three Indians who made no other demonstration than to weep, for which reason the

283

place was called *La Ensenada de los Llorones* (the bay of the weepers)." This was Mission Bay.

*Lobitos* (little seals) is on the Ocean Shore Line, near San Francisco.

*Lobos* (wolves, also sea-wolves, or seals). See pages 117 and 163.

*Loconoma Valley.* The name of this valley, in which Middletown, Lake County, is situated, is an Indian word meaning "wild goose village."— (Kroeber.)

*Loma* (hill).

*Point Loma* (hill point). See page 35.

*Loma Linda* (beautiful hill) is in San Bernardino County.

*Loma Pelona* (bald hill) is near Santa Bárbara.

*Loma Portal* (hill gate). Exactly what meaning is intended to be conveyed by this very evidently American-given name it is difficult to say. Certainly no Spaniard would have used such a combination. It is in San Diego County.

*Loma Prieta* (dark hill). See page 117.

*Lomas de la Purificación* (hills of the purification).

*Lomas de Santa Ana* (hills of Santa Ana), land grant in Orange County.

*Lomas de Santiago* (hills of St. James).

*Loma Vista* (hill view), near Los Angeles.

Modern and improper in construction. It should be *Vista de la Loma*.

*Lomerías Muertas* (dead hills), possibly should be Lomerías de los Muertos (hills of the dead).

*Lomitas* (little hills), north of San Francisco.

*Lompoc,* an Indian name. See page 86. It has been stated that this word means "little lake," but there seems to be small authority for such a definition.

*López* (a surname). See page 98.

*Lorenzo* (Lawrence).

*Lucas Canyon,* in Orange County. This is probably an abbreviation of San Lucas, whose story is told under the proper heading.

*Lugo* (a surname), that of a family of early settlers. This place is thirty miles from San Bernardino.

*Luís* (Louis) range. It is in San Luís Obispo County.

*Luna* (moon) Mountain. It is in San Bernardino County.

*De Luz* (a surname). *Corral de Luz* was the name given to a place in San Bernardino County by the Spaniards in reference to a large horse corral built by an Englishman named Luce, which they Spanicized into *Luz*. See page 35.

*Madera* (wood). See page 201.

*Madrone,* properly spelled Madroño, a native tree of California. See page 129.

285

*Málaga,* the name of a province in Southern Spain celebrated for its exports of grapes, raisins, oranges, lemons, figs and almonds. As raisins are among the chief products of this part of Fresno County, the town of Málaga was so named from the Spanish province.

*Manca,* or *Manka.* To prevent the unwary from falling into the erroneous belief that this name is Spanish or Indian, the rather humorous story of Manka is told here. The story goes that it was named for a German who came there in '67, built a little sixteen by twenty-four foot shanty and sold whisky. It was his proud boast that in the fifteen years he ran this business he never renewed his stock. The inference may be drawn.

*Manteca* (lard, butter) is near Modesto. This place was so called by the railroad company in reference to a creamery existing there. In Spanish America butter is called *mantequilla.*

*Manana* (apple) is in Los Angeles County.

*Manzanar* (an orchard of apple trees, or possibly a thicket of the wild manzanita). This place is in Inyo County.

*Manzanita* (little apple), a native shrub that is one of the most striking objects in the California woods. Frémont says of it: "A new and singular shrub was very frequent to-day. It branched out near the ground, forming a clump eight to ten feet high, with pale green leaves of

286

an oval form, and the body and branches had a naked appearance as if stripped of the bark, which is very smooth and thin, of a chocolate color, contrasting well with the pale green of the leaves." Towns in Marin, San Diego, and Tehama Counties bear the name of *Manzanita.*

Powers, in his *Tribes of California,* describes the method of making manzanita cider practiced by the Indians, as follows: "After reducing the berries to flour by pounding, they carefully remove all the seeds and skins, then soak the flour in water for a considerable length of time. A squaw then heaps it up in a little mound, with a crater in the center, into which she pours a minute stream of water, allowing it to percolate through. In this way she gets about a gallon an hour of a really delicious beverage, clear, cool, clean, and richer than most California apple cider. As the Indians always drink it up before it has time to ferment, it is never intoxicating." Frémont also mentions this as a very delicious drink that he had tasted when among the Indians.

*Manzanita Knob,* in Tulare County, is near the summit of the Sierra.

*Mapache Peak* (raccoon peak).

*Mar* (the sea).

*Del Mar* (of the sea). See page 35.

*El Mar Pacifico* (the peaceful sea). See page 16.

*Mar Vista* (sea view). Improper construction; should be *Vista del Mar*.

*Mare Island.* See page 147.

*Maricopa* is the name of an Arizona tribe. The word is said to mean "bean people," which is probably the correct definition.—(A. L. Kroeber.)

*Marin.* See page 158.

*Marina* (shore, seacoast) is in Monterey County. A portion of the sea-beach in San Francisco is also called The Marina.

*Mariposa* (butterfly). See page 223.

*Martínez* (a surname). See page 167.

*Matilija.* See pages 80 and 240.

*Médanos,* also spelled *Méganos* (sand-banks, or dunes). This place is in Contra Costa County. These dunes, between Antioch and Black Diamond, were named in May, 1817, by Lieutenant Luís Argüello, who led an exploring party into that region. The place still retains the name.

*Media* (middle) is in Madera County.

*Mendocino.* See page 179.

*Mendota* (a surname) is in Fresno County.

*Merced* (mercy). See pages 167, 199 and 240.

*Mesa* (table, table-land). See pages 36 and 240.

*La Mesa* (the table or table-land) is in San Diego County. See page 36.

VERNAL FALLS IN THE YOSEMITE VALLEY

"The valley was called by the Indians 'Awani,' from the name
of their principal village."

*Mesa de Burro* (table-land of the donkey) is in Riverside County.

*Mesa Coyote* (coyote table-land). It is in Monterey County.

*Mesa Grande* (big table-land). See page 36.

*Mesa de Ojo de Agua* (table-land of the spring).

*Mesquite* (a native shrub of the locust variety).

*Milagro Valley* (miracle valley) is on the ocean shore of San Matéo County.

*Milpitas.* See page 130.

*La Mirada* (the view). See page 63.

*El Mirage* (mirage) is in San Bernardino County. It is more properly spelled Miraje.

*Miramar* (sea-view) is the name of a post town in San Diego County and of a summer resort near Santa Bárbara. Miramar is the name of the king's chalet at the famous resort in Spain, San Sebastian. The chalet stands on an eminence overlooking the Bay of Biscay.

*Miramontes* (a surname). Candelario Miramontes, a native of Mexico, was the grantee of the Pilarcitos Rancho in '41.

*Misión Vieja,* or *La Paz* (old mission or the peace). Land grant.

*Misión Vieja de la Purísima* (old mission of the most pure), that is, of the Immaculate Conception.

*Mocho Peak,* in Santa Clara County. *Mocho* means "cropped, cut off."

*Modesto* (modest). See page 207.

*Modoc* (people of the south). See page 181.

*Mohave* is an Indian tribal name of disputed meaning. It has been stated that it comes from *hamucklihabi* (three hills), but this view is positively contradicted by scientists. In the documents of the Spanish explorers the Mohaves are referred to as Amajabas. The Mohave River is remarkable in that it has no true outlet, but sinks into the alkaline soil of the desert near the middle of San Bernardino County.

*Mokelumne.* See Moquelumne.

*Molino* (mill, or mill-stone). See page 63.

*Los Molinos* (the mills, or mill-stones). See page 63.

*El Río de los Molinos* (the river of the mill-stones), now called Mill Creek, in Tehama County). See page 63.

*Mono.* See page 227.

*Montalvo* (a surname), in Ventura County. See page 63.

*Montara.* See page 167.

*Monte* (hill or wood). *Monte* was generally used in the sense of "wood" or "forest" by the Spanish-Americans of the eighteenth century.

*Monte de Oro* (mountain of gold). It is in Butte County.

*El Monte* (the hill or the wood).

*Del Monte* (of the wood or hill). In the case of

the Hotel del Monte, near Monterey, the name refers to the grove of fine live-oaks in the center of which the hotel stands.

*Montecito* (little hill or wood). See page 78.

*Monterey* (hill or wood of the king). See page 101.

*Monte Vista* (mountain view). Modern and improper in construction. It should be *Vista del Monte*.

*Montezuma* Island, Slough, and Hills, in Solano County on the shore of Suisun Bay. This name has a curious history, for it was given, not by Spaniards, but by an advance agent of the Mormons, Lansing W. Hastings, who came in 1846 to select a site for a colony of that peculiar sect in this territory, then under Mexican rule. The story goes that the Mormons hoped to gain the sympathy of the Mexicans through their common hatred of the United States, and to further this plan by flattering the Mexicans they called the place Montezuma City. Bayard Taylor, in his book *Eldorado,* speaks of the city of Montezuma as a solitary adobe house on a sort of headland projecting into Suisun Bay, and fronting its rival three-house city of New York, on the Contra Costa shore. Unfortunately for the Mormons, their plan to establish an independent colony in this fertile and sightly spot was ruined by the raising of the American flag at Monterey,

and after a stay of three years the lone colonist abandoned his one-house city and followed the excited rush to the gold mines. Nothing but the name remains to commemorate this abortive attempt to set up a Mormon commonwealth in California.

*Moraga* (a surname). Lieutenant Gabriel Moraga is one of the outstanding figures in the history of California. He took part in forty-six expeditions against the Indians, in all of which he displayed courage and ability of no mean order. He was the son of José Joaquín Moraga, the first comandante at San Francisco, and is described by a contemporary as "a tall, well-built man of dark complexion, brave, gentlemanly, and the best Californian soldier of his time." He died in 1823 and was buried in the graveyard at the Santa Bárbara Mission. Moraga village and Valley and Moraga Road, in the east bay region inadequately recall the name of this intrepid exploror.—(*History of California,* Charles E. Chapman.)

*Moquelumne,* or *Mokelumne.* See page 231.

*Moreno* (a surname). One of the leading members of this numerous family was Antonio Moreno, a native of Lower California.

*Moro Cojo* (lame Moor). See page 118.

*Morón* (hillock, mound). This place is near Bakersfield.

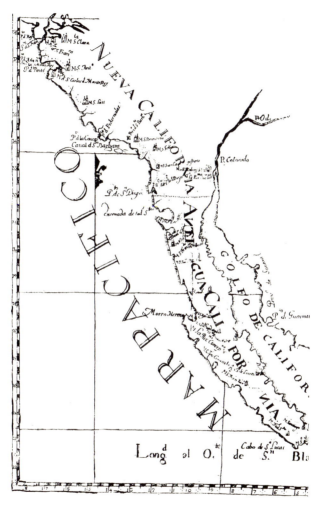

MAP OF THE MISSIONS

Used by the courtesy of Father Engelhardt.

*Morro* (a round headland, bluff). This place, in San Luís Obispo County, receives its name from Morro Rock, a remarkable round rock with nearly perpendicular sides, 600 feet high, situated at the entrance to the bay. The name has no reference to its grey color, as some people imagine, but refers to its shape—round like a head. It is upon such a rock that the well-known Morro Castle at Havana is situated. See page 98.

*Mugu Point,* on the coast of Ventura County. The Mugus were a tribe of Indians. The word *mugu* means "beach."

*Muñiz* (a surname).

*Murietta* (a surname). See page 63.

*Nacimiento* (birth). See page 98.

*La Nación* (the nation). See Del Rey.

*Napa,* formerly pronounced Napá. See page 176.

*Naranjo* (orange-tree), in Tulare County.

*La Natividad* (the nativity). See page 118.

*Natoma* is a name about which the romanticists have concocted some pleasing theories upon very slender foundation. According to scientists it is a tribal name, indicating direction, a favorite method of naming among the Indians. It may mean "north people," or "up-stream," or "downstream," or some such term of direction. By a severe wrench of the imagination, as has been suggested, it may be considered that "up-stream"

would eventually lead to the mountains, and that in the mountains there were people, among whom there were undoubtedly girls, and in this "long-distance" manner Mr. Joseph Redding's definition of Natoma as the "girl from the mountains" might be evolved, but the imagination is likely to suffer from such a violent strain. In the same way, the persons who believe it to mean "clear water" may have acquired this idea from the simple fact that the word contains an indirect reference to the stream in pointing out the direction of its current. It is disappointing perhaps, but nevertheless true, that California Indian nomenclature has little of romance behind it. The Indians usually chose names based upon practical ideas, most often ideas of direction, such as "north people," "south people," etc.

*Navajo,* also spelled *lavajo* (a pool where cattle go to drink). This word is said by the Bureau of Ethnology, however, to be not Spanish but Indian.

*Navarro* (a surname). In Mendocino County, west of Ukiah.

*Nevada* (snowy). See page 209.

*El Nido* (the nest). See page 36. It is thought that this place was so named because of its location in the hills and mountains suggesting the idea of a nest in the landscape, but there is no definite information about it. It is far more

probable that the name originated in some definite story about a bird's nest, just as the name Río Nido is said to have come from an eagle's nest, once seen in a tree on the bank of the river.

*Los Nietos* (literally "the grandchildren," but in this case a surname). See page 63.

*Nimshew,* in Butte County. This is an Indian word, from *Nimsewi* (big river), a division of Maidu Indians living on upper Butte Creek, in Butte County, near the edge of the timber.

*Nipomo,* in San Luís Obispo County, was named from a Chumash village.

*Los Nogales* (the walnut-trees).

*Noriega,* the name of a street in San Francisco, honors José de la Guerra y Noriega, noted pioneer of Santa Bárbara.

*Del Norte* (of the north). See page 187.

*Novato* (new, beginning anything, but possibly in this case a surname). The exact origin of the name of this California town has not been ascertained. The place is in Marin County and as there was a land grant there called *El Rancho de Novato,* the probabilities are that it is a surname of some family of early settlers.

*Noyo* is in Mendocino County. It was the Indian name of a creek, not the one now bearing the name of Noyo, but of another one in the vicinity.

*Nuestra Señora del Refugio* (our lady of refuge).

*Nuevo* (new). In Riverside County.

*Oakland* was originally called *Las Encinas* (the live-oaks), having been named by the comandante at Monterey as the result of the report of Lieutenant Vallejo of the great number of those trees growing upon the spot.

*Océano* (ocean), near San Luís Obispo.

*Ochumnes.* This is a name of Indian origin, but the meaning of it has not yet been ascertained. It is one of the numerous group of Sierran Indian names ending in the suffix *"umne,"* which Professor Kroeber thinks may mean "place of." If that be the case, *Ochumne* may mean "place of the village of Ocho." It is in Sacramento County.

*Ojai,* the name of a former Indian village in Ventura County, popularly translated as "nest" or "big tree," neither of which can be looked upon as authentic. According to Professor A. L. Kroeber, the meaning of the word *Ojai* is "moon."

*Los Ojitos* (little springs). See page 44.

*Ojo de Agua* (spring of water). See pages 45 and 240.

*Ojo de Agua de Figueroa* (spring of Figueroa), the last word being a surname. The Figueroa family were among the earliest settlers.

*Ojo Caliente* (hot spring).

*Ojo de Agua del Coche* (spring of the pig).

*Olancha,* in Inyo County, just below Owens Lake, was possibly named for the Olanches Indians of southeastern California.

*Olema.* See page 167.

*Oliveras* (olive-trees), in San Luís Obispo County. Olivera is also a surname.

*Los Olivos* (the olives). See page 86.

*Olla* (a round earthen pot). In a deep ravine in the Santa Cruz Mountains a mule which was carrying the camp cooking-pot fell. On account of this accident the place was called *El Barranco de la Olla* (the ravine of the cooking-pot) by the Portolá party. This name is an example of the trivial origin of many of the names.

*Olompali* was named for a former large Moquelumnan village in Marin County, about six miles south of Petaluma. It means "south."

*Omo,* in El Dorado County, is the name of a Moquel village.

*Oro Fino* (fine gold), in Siskiyou County. See page 188.

*Oro Grande* (large or coarse gold), forty-nine miles north of San Bernardino. Also in Madera County.

*Oro Loma* (gold hill). This name is a particularly bad attempt at giving a Spanish name with-

out sufficient knowledge. It should be *Loma de Oro* (hill of gold). It is in Fresno County.

*Oro Rico* (rich gold), the name of a mine near Sonora.

*Oroville* (gold-town). See page 208.

*Ortega,* a street in San Francisco named for *José Francisco de Ortega,* a sergeant in the Portolá party, first to see the bay of San Francisco.

*Oso Flaco* (thin bear). In San Luís Obispo County.

*Los Osos* (the bears). See page 98.

*Otay,* or *Otai,* was the name of a former Indian village near San Diego. It may have first been applied to the Otey or Otay land grant. Otay is named from a Diegueño Indian word meaning "brushy." See page 168.

*Otero* (literally a "hill, or eminence," but probably a surname here).

*Pachappa,* near Riverside, Indian name, meaning not ascertained.

*Pacheco* (a surname). See page 168.

*Pacoima,* near Los Angeles, an Indian word, meaning not ascertained.

*Paicines,* also spelled *Pajines.* See page 118.

*Pájaro* (bird). See pages 111 and 240.

*Pala.* See page 26.

*Palmas* (palms).

*Dos Palmas* (two palms), in Riverside County, so called from two giant palms near a spring.

*Palo,* literally "stick," was used by the Spaniards in the sense of "tree."

*Palo Alto* (high tree). See page 125.

*Palo Blanco* (white stick, or tree).

*Palo Cedro* (cedar tree), in Shasta County.

*Palo Colorado* (redwood tree). These trees were first observed and named by Gaspar de Portolá, the discoverer of San Francisco Bay.

*Dos Palos* (two sticks, or trees). See page 205.

*Paloma* (dove, pigeon).

*Palomares,* named for the family of Francisco Palomares, a resident of San José and an Indian fighter of 1833.

*Palo Prieto* (dark tree) Canyon. It is in San Luís Obispo County.

*Palou,* a street in San Francisco named for Fray Francisco Palou, founder of Dolores Mission and author of the first book ever written in California, *Las Noticias de la Nueva California.*

*Palo Verde* (green tree), in Imperial County.

*Panamint Range.* See page 232.

*Panocha.* See page 118.

*La Panza* (the paunch), in San Luís Obispo County, so named by some hunters who placed the paunch of a beef to catch bear. *La Paleta* (shoulder-blade) and *El Carnaso* (loin) were put out in other places, and the names still remain.

*Las Papas* (potatoes) Hill is in the San Fran-

cisco district. *Papa* (potato) is provincial and American.

*Paraíso* (paradise). See page 118.

*Paraje de Sánchez* (place or station of Sanchez).

*Pasadena* (crown of the valley). See page 64.

*Paskenta,* in Tehama County, is Indian and means "under the bank."

*Paso* (pass).

*El Paso* (the pass), of the Truckee River.

*El Paso Peak* (the pass peak), in Kern County.

*Del Paso* (of the pass), near Sacramento.

*Paso de Bartolo* (pass of Bartolo), the last a Christian name.

*Paso de Robles* (pass of the oaks). See pages 93 and 239.

*Pastoría de las Borregas* (pasture of the ewe-lambs). A sheep ranch in Santa Clara County.

*La Patera* (a place where ducks congregate). In early days the fresh water swamps near here abounded with ducks. La Patera is a flag station in Santa Bárbara County.

*La Paz* (the peace). Probably a peace arranged with the Indians, or it may have been named for La Paz in Lower California.

*Pecho* (breast) Rock is so named from the shape of the rock. It is near San Luís Obispo.

*Pedernales* (flints). See page 81.

KAWEAH MOUNTAINS

"Kaweah, or Kawia, was the name of an Indian tribe near Fresno."

*Peñasco Rocks* (rocky hills) is in Fresno County.

*Los Peñasquitos* (the little cliffs), in San Diego County.

*Penitencia Creek* (penitence creek). The reason for this name has not been ascertained. It is in Santa Clara County.

*Peralta* (a surname), that of a pioneer family.

*Peras* (pears) Creek, in Los Angeles County.

*Los Perros* (the dogs), possibly Indian dogs.

*Pescadero Point* (fishing-place point). See page 168.

*Petaluma.* See page 189.

*Picachos Mountains,* a ridge east of San Francisco Bay. *Pichacos* are frequent, isolated, conical peaks.

*Picacho* (top, sharp-pointed summit) is the name of a post village in Imperial County.

*Pico* (a surname), ten miles from Los Angeles. José María Pico of Sinaloa was the founder of this family, and its most notable member was his son, Pío Pico, at one time governor of California. According to Bancroft, the character of Pío Pico was a mixture of good and bad, in which the good predominated. "He was abused beyond his deserts; he was a man of ordinary intelligence and limited education; of a generous, jovial disposition, reckless and indolent, fond of cards and women; disposed to be fair

and honorable in transactions, but not strong enough to avoid being made the tool of knaves. He did not run away with large sums of money obtained by sales of missions, as has been charged." Also the name of a street in Los Angeles.

*Pico Blanco* (white peak), a noted mountain in the Santa Lucía Range, near Point Sur.

*Piedra* (stone, rock), near Fresno.

*Piedras Blancas* (white rocks). See page 98.

*Piedras Grandes* (big rocks).

*La Piedra Pintada* (the painted rock). See page 84.

*Pilar* (literally "pillar of stone"). Point Pilar may have been named for *Nuestra Señora del Pilar* (Our Lady of the pillar), from a church at Saragossa, Spain, where there is an image of the Virgin on a marble pillar. Pilar is also a surname, that of a pioneer family, for whom this point may have been named. The Portolá party of 1769 gave the name of *Nuestra Señora del Pilar* (Our Lady of the pillar) to a place in this vicinity, lending color to this theory of the origin of the name of Pillar Point.

*Pilarcitos* (little pillars).

*Pilitas* (basins or water-holes in rock).

*El Pinal* (the pine grove), in San Joaquín County.

*Pino Blanco* (white pine), in Mariposa County.

302

*Pino Grande* (big pine), in El Dorado County, near Placerville.

*Pinole* (parched corn ground into meal). Point Pinole was so named because the expedition under Lieutenant Vallejo had nothing to eat but pinole while they waited at that spot for the return of the *cargadores* with provisions from Monterey. See page 168.

*Piñón* (pine kernel) also the scrub pine, a very picturesque tree bearing a delicious nut).

*Point Pinos* (point of pines). See page 110.

*Tres Pinos* (three pines). See page 120.

*Pintado* (painted, mottled).

*Pinto Range* (painted or mottled range). See page 233.

*El Piojo* (the louse), in Monterey County, a short distance south of Jolón.

*Piru,* near Camulos, the name of a former Indian village. It is the name of a plant.

*Pismo.* See page 99.

*Pit River.* See page 210.

*La Pita,* in San Diego County. *Pita haya* is the fruit of the cactus called "prickly pear."

*Placer.* See page 214.

*Placerita* (little placer) Canyon is in Los Angeles County.

*Placerville.* See page 215.

*Planada* (a plain, level ground), seventy-four miles from Stockton.

*Plano* (a level surface), in Tulare County.

*Plano Trabuco* (plain of the blunderbuss), a valley in Orange County. This name no doubt originated from the story of the party of Spaniards who lost a blunderbuss in that region.

*La Playa* (the beach), in Santa Bárbara County.

*Pleito* (quarrel, lawsuit, bargain). See page 114.

*Plumas* (feathers). See page 211.

*Las Plumas* (the feathers), near Oroville.

*Polvadero* (dusty) Gap is in Fresno County. Polvadero is probably a coined word from *polvo,* dust.

*Pomo.* See page 189.

*Poncho* (cloak, blanket).

*Poonkiny* (wormwood). Poonkiny, sometimes misspelled Pookiny, is from the Yuki Indian language.

*El Portal* (the gate), the entrance to the Yosemite Valley.

*Portolá* (a surname). Much argument has arisen in regard to the spelling and pronunciation of this name, but that the form here given is the correct one is proved beyond dispute by original letters signed by Portolá's own hand still existing in the archives of Mexico, as well as by its use in documents by many of his contemporaries. See page 168.

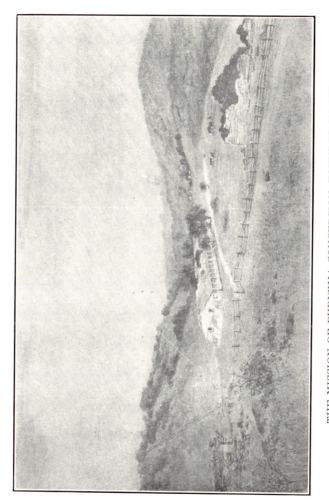

THE MISSION OF PURISIMA CONCEPCION, FOUNDED IN 1787

Two towns, one in San Matéo County and the other in Plumas County bear the name of Portolá, one of the most famous in the annals of California. See pages 168 and 240.

*Posa* (well, pool, also spelled by the Spaniards *pozo, poso*). The fact that *posa* also has the meaning of "passing bell for the dead" has caused some rather ludicrous mistakes. For instance, *La Posa de los Ositos* (the pool of the little bears) evidently refers to a place where some bears were seen drinking, and certainly would be absurd translated as "the passing bell of the little bears." When used as names of places the connection makes it quite clear that they were so called in reference to pools of water present on the spot.

*Las Positas* (the little pools).

*Las Positas y la Calera* (the little wells, or pools, and the lime-kiln).

*Poso* (pool, or well), in Kern County, and *Poso* in San Luís Obispo County.

*Los Posos* (the pools, or wells), in Ventura County.

*La Posta* (person who rides or travels post, post-house, military post, etc.). In the case of La Posta, 170 miles from the Mission Tule River Agency, it probably means post-station.

*Potrero* (pasture, generally for horses). See pages 36, 165 and 169.

*Potrero* de los Cerritos (pasture of the little hills).

*Potrero Chico* (little pasture).

*Potrero Grande* (big pasture).

*Potrero de los Pinos* (pasture of the pines) is in Riverside County.

*Potrero y Rincón de San Pedro de Reglado* (pasture and corner of St. Peter Regalato). St. Peter Regalato was a Franciscan and was especially distinguished for his sublime gift of prayer. This was the name of a land grant.

*El Potrero de San Carlos* (the pasture of St. Charles).

*Potrero de San Francisco* (pasture of St. Francis). This district still goes by the name of "the potrero" in the city of San Francisco.

*Potrero de San Luís Obispo* (pasture of St. Louis the Bishop.)

*El Potrero de Santa Clara* (the pasture of St. Clara).

*Poway,* in San Diego County, is an Indian place name.

*Pozo* (pool, well). See page 99.

*Prado* (meadow), in Riverside County. See page 64. This place was so named on account of its resemblance to a prairie.

*La Presa* (dam, dike). See page 36. This place is so called from the Sweetwater irrigation dam located there.

*Presidio* (garrison, prison). See page 169.

*Prieta* (dark), a place north of San Francisco.

*Los Prietos* (the dark ones).

*Providencia* (providence).

*Pueblo* (town).

*Los Dos Pueblos* (the two towns). See page 83.

*Puente* (bridge), near Los Angeles. See page 64.

*Las Puentes* (the bridges). See page 119.

*Puerco Canyon* (dirty or muddy canyon). It is in Los Angeles County.

*El Puerto* (the port), of San Diego.

*El Puerto Creek* (the pass creek) is in Stanislaus County. In its original Spanish form it was called El Arroyo del Puerto (the creek of the pass). It is one of the Coast Range streams, and, rising in these mountains, flows down through cañons until it reaches the San Joaquín. It takes its name from a natural pass through which it makes its way to reach the level land of the west side.

*Pulgas* (fleas). See pages 64 and 161.

*La Punta* (the point), in San Diego County.

*Punta Almejas* (mussel point).

*Punta Año Nuevo* (point New Year). See page 114.

*Punta Arenas* (sandy point). See page 240.

*Punta de la Concepción* (point of the immaculate conception).

*Punta Delgada* (thin or narrow point). See page 187.

*Punta Gorda* (fat or thick point). See pages 86 and 187.

*Punta Guijarros* (pebble or boulder point).

*Punta de la Laguna* (point of the lagoon). See page 188.

*Punta Loma* (hill point), near San Diego. See page 35. It should be *Punta de la Loma.*

*Punta de Pinos* (point of pines). Near Monterey. See page 110.

*Punta de los Reyes* (point of the kings). See page 169.

*Punta de las Ritas* (point of the rites). See page 87.

*Purísima Concepción* (immaculate conception). See page 87.

*Purísima Point* (point of the most pure). On the Santa Bárbara Coast.

*Purísima* (most pure), in San Matéo County.

*Point Sal* (a surname). See page 88.

*Point Sur* (south point). See page 120.

*La Quemada* (the burned place), from the verb *quemar* (to burn). This name refers to a custom prevalent among the Indians of burning over large tracts of land for the purpose of killing the underbrush and encouraging the growth of grass, which resulted in attracting game. The diaries of the Spaniards refer frequently to this

custom, and speak of finding a great deal of country burned over in this way. One writer has offered to his astonished readers the translation of *La Quemada* as "the over-full, having enough to eat."

*Quién Sabe* (who knows), a familiar expression among the Spaniards.

*Quintin.* See page 172.

*Quinto* (a surname). Simón Tadéo Quinto was one of the members of this pioneer family.

*Raimundo* (Raymond).

*Ramírez* (a surname), near Marysville.

*Ramona* (a Christian name), well known as that of the heroine of Mrs. Helen Hunt Jackson's romance.

*Rana* (frog) *Creek.* In Monterey County.

*Ranchería,* a word meaning "settlement," but generally used by the Spaniards to mean an Indian village.

*Ranchería del Baile de las Indias* (village of the dance of the Indian women). See page 77.

*Ranchería del Corral* (village of the yard).

*Ranchería de la Espada* (village of the sword). See page 79.

*Ranchería del Río Estanislao* (village of the river Stanislaus).

*Ranchita de Santa Fé* (little ranch of holy faith).

*Rancho del Puerto* (ranch of the pass).

*Ratón* (mouse).

*Real de las Aguilas* (camp of the eagles).

*Redondo* (round). See page 63.

*Refugio* (refuge) is in Santa Bárbara County. Refugio is also a Christian name.

*Represa* (dam), so called on account of a dam at that point, west of the state prison at Folsom.

*Del Rey* (of the king), also known as *El Rancho Nacional* because it was used to provide meat and horses for the military. This ranch was in Fresno County.

*Reyes* (kings). See page 169.

*Ricardo* (Richard) is in Kern County.

*Rincón* is the interior angle formed by the junction of two walls or lines, and is one of the terms used in the apportionment of land grants.

*Rincón* (corner) is in San Bernardino County.

*El Rincón* (the corner) is in Los Angeles County, and comprises rich agricultural land on either side of the Santa Ana River.

*Rinconada* is the corner formed by two houses, streets, roads, or between two mountains, or a corner section of land in a grant.

*Rinconada del Arroyo de San Francisquito* (corner of the creek of little St. Francis). Land grant.

*Rincón de los Carneros* (corner of the sheep). Land grant.

*Rinconada de los Gatos* (corner of the cats—wild-cats). Land grant.

*Rincón de la Brea* (corner of the asphalt). Land grant.

*Rincón de los Bueyes* (corner of the oxen). Land grant.

*Rincón del Diablo* (corner of the devil). Land grant.

*Rincón de los Esteros* (corner of the estuaries). Land grant.

*Rincón Point* (corner point). See page 88.

*Rincón de la Puente del Monte* (corner of the bridge of the wood, or hill). Land grant.

*Rincón de las Salinas* (corner of the salt marshes). Land grant.

*Rincón de las Salinas y Potrero Viejo* (corner of the salt marshes and the old pasture). Land grant.

*Rincón de San Francisquito* (corner of little San Francisco). Land grant.

*Rincó del Sanjón* (corner of the slough). Land grant.

*Río* (river).

*El Río* (the river), often improperly run together as Elrio, is the name of a village in Ventura County.

*El Río de los Berrendos* (the river of the antelopes). See page 30.

*Río Bravo* (turbulent or wild river). It is in Kern County.

*Río Grande* (big river).

*Río Jesús María* (River Jesus Mary). Land grant.

*Río Lindo* (beautiful river). It is in Sacramento County.

*El Río de los Molinos* (the river of the millstones). See page 63.

*El Río del Nido* (the river of the nest), referring to the nest of an eagle once seen in a tree on the banks of this stream. The name is now shortened into Río Nido, or Rionido.

*Río Oso* (Bear River), should be *Río del Oso.*

*El Río de Santa Clara* (the river of St. Clara). Land grant.

*El Río de los Santos Reyes* (the river of the holy kings). See page 201.

*Río Seco* (dry river).

*Río Vista* (river view). See page 208. Improper construction. It should be *Vista del Río.*

*El Rito* (the rite, ceremony).

*Rivera,* literally "brook, creek," but also a surname. The Rivera family were among the pioneers. See page 65.

*Roblar de la Miseria* (oak grove of poverty, wretchedness). It is likely that in this grove the Spaniards suffered from a shortage of food sup-

plies, and named it in memory of their sufferings. Land grant.

*Los Robles* (the oaks), ten miles from Los Angeles.

*Rodéo* (cattle round-up). See pages 170 and 240. The town of Rodéo was first laid out to maintain a large packing-house for meat, but this was abandoned, and it has become an oil-refining town.

*Rodéo de las Aguas* (gathering of the waters). See page 65.

*Del Rosa* (of the rose), in San Bernardino County. If this is not a surname it is improper in construction, and should be *De la Rosa.*

*Los Rosales* (the rose-bushes). See page 36.

*Rosario* (rosary), or a procession of persons who recite the rosary. Also a Christian name.

*De Sabla,* in Butte County, is a family name.

*Saca de Agua* is a term usually employed to mean a place where water is taken out for irrigation. Sometimes the word *saca* is used alone.

*Sacate* (grass, hay).

*Sacramento* (sacrament). See page 195.

*Sal,* in the case of Point Sal, a surname. See page 88.

*Salada* (salted, salty, saline land). It is in the salt marshes on the shore of San Matéo County.

*Salazar* (a surname), that of a pioneer family.

313

*Salida* (exit, out-gate), village in Stanislaus County, seven miles northwest of Modesto.

*Salinas* (salt-marshes). See pages 110 and 240.

*Sal si Puedes* ("get out if you can"). See page 89.

*La Salud* (health). See page 127.

*San Andreas* (St. Andrew). See page 233.

*San Andrés* (St. Andrew). See page 233.

*San Anselmo* (St. Anselm). See page 170. St. Anselm was born in Italy of noble parents, and became a monk at the age of 27. He was a man of great intellectual attainments and rose to a high position in the church, finally becoming Archbishop of Canterbury. He is noted for his theological and philosophical writings, and for his mild, gentle, but firm character.

*San Antonio* (St. Anthony).

*San Antonio de Padua* (St. Anthony of Padua). See page 105.

*San Ardo* (St. Ardo) is in Monterey County. St. Ardo, in Latin *Smaragdus,* was a Benedictine monk who wrote a life of St. Benedict which is considered reliable. He died in 843.

*San Augustine* (properly Agustín), born in Numidia, was the son of Santa Mónica. "In his youth he was so devoted to pleasure that his mother feared the destruction of his character," but he became converted by the preaching of St. Ambrose, and it is thought that the *Te Deum* was

314

composed in honor of the occasion of his baptism. It is told of him that "while walking on the sea-shore, lost in meditation on his great theme, the *Discourse on the Trinity,* he saw a little child bringing water and endeavoring to fill a hole which he had dug in the sand. Augustine asked him the motive of his labors. The child said he intended to empty all the water of the sea into this cavity. 'Impossible!' exclaimed St. Augustine. 'Not more impossible,' answered the child, 'than for thee, O Augustine, to explain the mystery on which thou art now meditating.' St. Augustine is the patron of theologians and learned men."—(*Stories of the Saints.*)

*San Benito* (St. Benedict). See page 119.

*San Bernabé* (St. Barnabas, or Barnaby). This saint was a native of Cyprus, and a cousin of St. Mark. "He labored with Paul at Antioch, and tradition says he preached from the gospel of St. Matthew, written by the Evangelist himself, which he carried always with him, and that it had power to heal the sick when laid upon their bosoms. He was seized by the Jews and cruelly martyred, while preaching in Judea."—(*Stories of the Saints.*)

*San Bernardino* (St. Bernardinus). See page 57.

*San Bernardo* (St. Bernard). There were two saints of this name, one born in 1190 at Fontaine,

and the other in Savoy. The latter, St. Bernard of Menthon, is famous as the founder of the St. Bernard hospitals in the Alps, where "the monks, assisted by their dogs, search out and care for travelers who are lost in the passes of the mountains, where the storms are severe, and the cold intense."

*San Bruno* (St. Bruno). See page 170.

*San Buenaventura* (St. Bonaventure). See page 73.

*San Carlos* (St. Charles). See page 104.

*San Clemente* (St. Clement). See page 65.

*Sandia Canyon* (watermelon canyon) is in Riverside County.

*San Dieguito* (little St. James).

*San Diego.* Although the dictionary meaning for *Diego* is always James, in the case of the saint it seems to be more properly translated by the Latin Didacus. See page 20.

*San Dimas,* "probably St. Dismas, is popularly supposed to have been the good or converted robber on the right side of Christ on Good Friday. In places he is celebrated by the Latins on March 25. The Greeks have him on a much later date."—(Fray Zephyrin Engelhardt, O. F. M.) *San Dimas* is the name of a post-village in Los Angeles County.

*San Domingo,* more properly *Santo Domingo* (St. Dominick). St. Dominick was a Castilian of

316

high descent, and was the founder of the Dominican Order of preaching friars, who were bound by vows of absolute poverty.

*Sanel,* the name of a former Indian village called variously Se-nel, Sah-nel, Sai-nel and Sanel. "Sanel is derived from *cané* (sweat-house), and was the name of a very large village situated south of the town of Sanel, on the eastern side of Hopland Valley."—(Barrett, in Univ. Publ. in Arch. and Ethn.)

*San Emygdio,* "English or Latin *St. Emygdius,* Bishop and Martyr, feast August 5. The Roman Martyrology has this on him: 'St. Emygdius, Bishop and Martyr, was consecrated Bishop by Pope St. Marcellus and sent to preach the Gospel at Ascoli. He received the crown of Martyrdom for confessing Christ, under Diocletian.' He is invoked against earthquakes."—(Fray Zephyrin Engelhardt.)

*San Felipe* (St. Philip). See page 131.

*San Fernando* (St. Ferdinand). See page 52.

*San Francisco* (St. Francis). See page 134.

*San Francisco de las Llagas* (St. Francis of the "stigmata"). See page 129.

*San Francisquito* (little St. Francis). Land grant.

*San Gabriel* (St. Gabriel). See page 51.

*San Gerónimo* (St. Jerome). See pages 170 and 240.

*San Gorgonio* Mountains and Pass are in the Coast Range of Southern California. Their patron saint, Gorgonius, suffered martyrdom in 304 at Nicomedia during the persecution of Diocletian. Gorgonius, who had held a high position in the Emperor's household, was subjected to most frightful torments, and was finally strangled and his body thrown into the sea. It was, nevertheless, secured by the Christians and was afterwards carried to Rome.

*San Gregorio* (St. Gregory). See page 170.

*San Ignacio* (St. Ignatius). St. Ignatius Loyola was the founder of the order of the Jesuits. "In his youth he was a page in the court of Ferdinand the Catholic, and later a brave and gay soldier." He became a permanent cripple through being severely wounded in both legs. While confined by these sufferings, he devoted himself to reading the life of Christ, and was thus induced to take up religious work. After some years of study, he induced five men to join him in forming a community under the title of the "Company of Jesus," whose especial duties are "first, preaching; second, the guidance of souls in confession; third, the teaching of the young."

*San Isidro,* also spelled *Ysidro* (St. Isidore). There were two saints bearing this name. St. Isidore the ploughman could neither read nor

318

write, but performed many miracles. His master objected to the time wasted by Isidore in prayer, but his objections were silenced when he found, upon entering the field one day, the plough being drawn by two angels, while St. Isidore knelt at his devotions. The other St. Isidore was Bishop of Seville, and in the church in that city bearing his name, there is a "magnificent picture which represents him dying on the steps of the altar, having given all his property to the poor." See page 240.

*San Jacinto* (St. Hyacinth). See pages 65 and 240.

*San Jacinto Nuevo y Potrero* (New St. Hyacinth and the horse pasture.) This is the combined name of two land grants. It is in Riverside County.

*San Jacinto Viejo* (St. Hyacinth the Old).

*San Joaquín* (St. Joachim). See pages 197 and 240.

*Sanjón* (deep ditch or slough). Also spelled *zanjon.*

*Sanjón de los Moquelumnes* (Moquelumne slough).

*San José* (St. Joseph). See pages 123 and 240.

*San José de Buenos Aires* (St. Joseph of good airs).

*San José y Sur Chiquito* (St. Joseph and little

south). These are the names of two creeks near Monterey.

*San Juan* (St. John), the name of a small town in San Benito County where the famous Mission of San Juan Bautista is situated, of a picturesque stretch of road running from that place to Monterey known as the San Juan Grade, and of a land grant in Sacramento County and a range of hills in Santa Clara County. In the spring time one may drive for many miles along the San Juan Grade through variegated beds of wild flowers which line the road on either side.

*San Juan Bautista* (St. John the Baptist). See pages 113 and 240.

*San Juan Cajón de Santa Ana* (St. John canyon, literally "box," of St. Anne). Deep canyons were often called *cajones* (boxes).

*San Juan Capistrano*. See page 28.

*San Juan Point* (St. John Point). See page 66.

*San Julián* (St. Julian). This seems to have been a favorite name for saints, since there were twelve who bore it. Only two, however, are of special importance, St. Julian Hospitator, and St. Julian of Rimini. The first had the fearful misfortune to kill his own father and mother through an error, and to make reparation, he built a hospital on the bank of a turbulent stream in which many persons had been drowned. "He constantly ferried travelers over

THE TALLAC TRAIL TO TAHOE

the river without reward, and, one stormy night in winter, when it seemed that no boat could cross the stream, he heard a sad cry from the opposite bank. He went over, and found a youth, who was a leper, dying from cold and weariness. In spite of his disease the saint carried him over, and bore him in his arms to his own bed, and he and his wife tended him till morning, when the leper rose up, and his face was transformed into that of an angel, and he said: 'Julian, the Lord hath sent me to thee; for thy penitence is accepted, and thy rest is near at hand' . . . . St. Julian is patron saint of ferrymen and boatmen, of travelers and of wandering minstrels." Little is known of St. Julian of Rimini except that he "endured a prolonged martyrdom with unfailing courage."—(*Stories of the Saints.*) See page 240.

*San Justo* (St. Justus). Little authentic is known of this saint, except that he was the fourth archbishop of Canterbury, and died there about 627.

*San Leandro* (St. Leander). See page 171.

*San Lorenzo* (St. Lawrence). See page 171.

*San Lucas* (St. Luke). See page 119.

*San Luís Gonzaga* (St. Louis Gonzaga). This saint, also known as St. Aloysius, was the son of a noble Italian lady, the Marchese di Castiglione. "He entered the Society of Jesus when not yet

eighteen years old, and became eminently distinguished for his learning, piety and good works. He died at Rome in 1591 of fever, which he contracted while nursing the sick."—(*Stories of the Saints*.)

*San Luisito* (little St. Louis) Creek. It is in San Luís Obispo County.

*San Luís Obispo* (St. Louis the Bishop). See pages 92 and 240.

*San Luís Rey* (St. Louis the king). See page 25.

*San Marcial* (St. Martial) was the Bishop of Limoges, and is especially noted for the conversions he accomplished, in particular that of the beautiful virgin St. Valerie, who suffered martyrdom for her faith.

*San Marcos* (St. Mark). "This evangelist was a disciple of St. Peter. He founded the church at Alexandria, and on account of his miracles the heathen accused him of being a magician; and at length, while celebrating the feast of their god Serapis, they seized St. Mark and dragged him through the streets until he died. Then immediately there fell a storm of hail, and a tempest of lightning came with it which destroyed his murderers." His remains were removed in A. D. 815 to Venice, where the splendid cathedral of St. Mark was erected over them. Many legends are told of this saint, among them the story of

his having saved the city of Venice from destruction by demons, who raised a great storm and came in a boat for that purpose, but were driven away by St. Mark, who went to meet them and held up a cross.

*San Marino,* near Los Angeles, was named for a saint who was born in Dalmatia in the fourth century. He was a poor laborer and was employed in the reconstruction of the bridge of Rimini. His piety attracted the attention of the Bishop of Brescia, who ordained him as a deacon. Marino retired to Mount Titano, and gave himself up entirely to religious practices. His cell attracted others, and this was the origin of the city and republic of San Marino, the smallest republic in the world.

*San Martin* (St. Martin).  See pages 132 and 240.

*San Matéo* (St. Matthew).  See page 171.

*San Matéo Point* (St. Matthew Point).  See page 66.

*San Miguel* (St. Michael).  See page 95.

*San Miguelito* (little St. Michael).

*San Nicolás* (St. Nicholas).  Little that is authentic can be obtained concerning the history of this saint, but there are numerous legends of miracles performed by him, several of them connected with raising children from the dead, and similar stories.  St. Nicholas is the chief patron

of Russia and of many sea-port towns, and is the protector against robbers and violence. He is also the patron of children and schoolboys in particular, and of poor maidens, sailors, travelers, and merchants.

*San Onofre* (St. Onophrius). See page 66.

*San Pablo* (St. Paul). See page 171.

*San Pascual* (St. Pascal). This saint was a Spanish peasant, born in Aragón in 1540. He was a member of the Franciscan order, and was remarkable for his unfailing courtesy and charity to the poor.

*San Pedro* (St. Peter). See page 66.

*San Pedro, Santa Margarita, y las Gallinas* (St. Peter St. Margaret, and the chickens), combined names of three land grants.

*San Quentin* (St. Quentin). See pages 172 and 240.

*San Rafael* (St. Raphael). See page 159.

*San Ramón* (St. Raymond). See page 173.

*San Simeón* (St. Simeon). See page 99.

*San* (more properly *Santo*) *Tomás Aquinas*. San Tomás Aquinas is the name of a public highway which runs southward from the Payne road in Santa Clara County. It was named from the creek, which rises in the Santa Cruz Mountains and empties into Campbell Creek. The titular saint of this stream, Santo Tomás Aquinas, was born in the little city of Aquinas near

324

Naples, Italy. He was of noble descent, and nearly allied to some of the royal houses of Italy. He was born in 1225, and, in spite of the opposition of his family, entered the Dominican Order in his seventeenth year. He became a profound theological scholar, and accomplished an amazing amount of literary work, through which he exerted a tremendous influence on religious thought. He was canonized in 1323.

*Santa Ana* (St. Anne). See page 45.

*Santa Ana y Quién Sabe* (St. Anne and "who knows"), combined names of two land grants.

*Santa Anita* (St. Annie, or little St. Anne).

*Santa Bárbara*. See page 69.

*Santa Catalina* (St. Catharine). See page 48.

*Santa Clara* (St. Clara). See page 122.

*Santa Clara del Norte* (St. Clara of the north).

*Santa Cruz* (holy cross). See page 112.

*Santa Cruz Island*. See page 79.

*Santa Fé* (holy faith), near Los Angeles. See page 240.

*Santa Gertrudis* (St. Gertrude). St. Gertrude the Great was a benedictine nun and mystic writer, born in Germany in 1256. She is especially noted for her learning and religious writings, all of which were written in Latin. She was charitable to the poor and had the gift of miracles.

*Santa Inez,* also spelled *Ynez* (St. Agnes). See pages 89 and 240.

*Santa Lucía* (St. Lucy). See page 99.

*Santa Margarita* (St. Margaret). See page 100.

*Santa Margarita y las Flores* (St. Margaret and the flowers),combined names of two land grants.

*Santa María* (St. Mary). See page 90.

*Santa Mónica* (St. Mónica). See page 47.

*Santa Paula* (St. Paula). See page 90.

*Santa Rita* is the name of a village in Monterey County, near Salinas. The patron saint of this place was born at Rocca Porena in 1386 and died in 1456. Her feast day is May 22, and she is represented as holding roses, or roses and figs. When but twelve years of age Santa Rita was compelled by her parents to marry a cruel, ill-tempered man. This man was murdered, and after his death, his widow desired to enter the convent at Cascia, but was at first refused admission on account of her widowhood. She was finally received, however, and so many miracles were reported to have been performed at her intercession that she was given in Spain the title of *La Santa de los Imposibles* (the saint of the impossibilities).

*Santa Rosa* (St. Rose). See page 178.

*Santa Susana* (St. Susanna). This saint, who was remarkable for her beauty and learning, was a relative of the Emperor Diocletian, who desired her as a wife for his adopted son Max-

imus. St. Susanna, having made a vow of chastity, refused this offer, and Diocletian, angered by her refusal, sent an executioner to kill her in her own house.

*Santa Teresa* was born at Avila in Castile, March 28, 1515. During her earliest youth, through reading the lives of the saints and martyrs, she formed a desire to take up religious work. In accordance with this desire, at the age of twenty years, she entered the convent of Carmelites, and chose as her life work the reforming of the order of Mount Carmel, as well as the establishment of a number of convents for men. She revived the early rule in the Order of going barefoot. Santa Teresa had distinct literary gifts, and her history of her life is a work of absorbing interest, which is still read with genuine pleasure by students of the literature of Spain. She attained a position of such authority in that country that Philip III chose her for its second patron saint, ranking her next to Santiago (St. James).

*Santa Ynez.* See Santa Inez. See pages 89 and 240.

*Santa Ysabel,* also spelled *Isabel* (St. Isabella of France), who founded the convent at Longchamps, was sister to the saintly King Louis. She was educated with her brother by their mother, Blanche of Castile. St. Isabel dedicated

her convent to the "humility of the Blessed Virgin," and gave to it all her dowry. As long as the convent existed the festival of this saint was celebrated with great splendor.—(*Stories of the Saints.*)

*Santiago de Santa Ana* (St. James of St. Anne). Land grant.

*San Timotéo* (St. Timothy). St. Timothy was the beloved disciple of St. Paul, whom he accompanied on many journeys. It is said that he was Bishop of Ephesus, until at the age of eighty years he suffered the cruel fate of being beaten to death by pagans.

*San Tomaso* (St. Thomas) was a Galilean fisherman and one of the apostles. "So great was his incredulity that he has always been remembered for that rather than for his other characteristics," and it was in this way that the familiar expression "a doubting Thomas" arose. At the time of the ascension of the Virgin, Thomas refused to believe in the event, and the legend relates that in order to convince him the Virgin dropped her girdle to him from the heavens. Three other saints also bear this name, St. Thomas á Becket, the celebrated English historical character; St. Thomas Aquinas, a grandnephew of Frederick I and a man of great learning; and St. Thomas the Almoner, who was so charitable that "as a child he would take off

his own clothes to give away to children in the street." It is related of the last named that he wore the same hat for twenty-six years, and that his whole life was "but a grand series of beneficent deeds. When the hour of his death came he had given away everything except the pallet on which he lay, and this was to be given to a jailer who had assisted him in executing his benevolent designs." There is a remarkably beautiful picture of him by Murillo, representing him as a child, dividing his clothing among four ragged little ones. A number of places in California are named for San Tomás Aquinas.

*San Vicente* (St. Vincent). Three saints bear this name. St. Vincent of Saragosa was martyred during the persecution of the Christians by Diocletian. Legend has it that his remains were guarded by crows or ravens, and when in the year 1147 Alonzo I removed them to Lisbon, two crows accompanied the vessel, one at the prow and one at the stern. In pictures St. Vincent is always represented as accompanied by a crow or raven. St. Vincent Ferraris was born at Valencia in 1357. He was a celebrated preacher and missionary, and "so moved the hearts of his hearers that he was often obliged to pause that the sobbing and weeping might subside." The third of this name, St. Vincent de Paul, was the son of a Gascon farmer, and his charities

were so various and so many as to cause his name to be revered by all, irrespective of religious differences. He established the Hospital La Madeleine for the Magdalens of Paris, a foundling hospital, and numerous other charities. In truth, the practical good done by this man during his life makes him well worthy of the title of "saint."

*San Ysidro.* See San Isidro. See page 240.

*Saticoy.* See page 67.

*Sauce* (willow). *La Cañada de los Sauces* (the valley of the willows) is in Santa Bárbara County.

*Saucito* (little willow).

*Saucos* (alder-trees).

*Sausal* (willow-grove). Properly spelled *Sauzal.*

*Sausalito* (little willow-grove). See page 157.

*Sausal Redondo* (round willow-grove). See Redondo Beach, page 64.

*El Segundo* (the second), so called because at that place the Standard Oil Company's second refinery on the Pacific Coast is located. Modern.

*Sepúlveda,* name of a Spanish pioneer family of Los Angeles.

*Sequoia,* the giant tree of California, was named for the Cherokee, Sequoyah, who invented an alphabet for his tribe. Sequoyah, also known as George Gist, or Guess, was the son of

a white man and a Cherokee woman of mixed blood, and was, after all, more white man than Indian. He had a natural genius for mechanical invention, and, having been crippled for life in a hunting accident, he occupied his time in devising the alphabet, which was accepted with such enthusiasm by his people that every Cherokee, of whatever age, had learned to read and write in a few months. Sequoia, although not a place name, is given here for the interest it may have for tourists and other persons unacquainted with the origin of the name of the famous "big trees."

*Serena* (serene). See page 90. This name is spelled on some maps as *Sereno,* but is called *Serena* by the people of the neighborhood.

*Serra* (a surname). See page 67. On the pages of the history of California, no name shines with a whiter luster than that of Junípero Serra. With his scholarly attainments, he might, had he chosen to remain in his own land, have aspired to the highest honors in the church, perhaps even to the Papacy, but he chose, instead, to leave all this behind him and to devote the rest of his days to the upraising of the heathen in far distant America. Feeble in body but strong of soul, he suffered every hardship without complaint, and in the hour of his death it was found that he had given away everything that he pos-

sessed to the poor Indians, even to his under-
clothing, which he removed for the purpose, so
that he might not die in it. So strong was the
power of his will that he rose from his bed but
a few hours before the end, and walked unaided
into the chapel, where he joined, "in a high clear
voice," in the singing of his own death mass. It
is fortunate that his devoted companion, Father
Palou, has left a complete record of his life and
death, to serve as an inspiration to all Californians. This priceless document, yellowed with
age, is now in the care of the parish church at
Monterey. *Junípero Serra Boulevard* in San
Francisco enshrines the memory of the saintly
man who first lighted the torch of civilization in
California.

*Sespe,* named for a former Chumash Indian
village said by Indians to have been on Sespe
Creek, in Ventura County.

*Shasta.* See page 182.

*Sierra* (saw, saw-toothed mountains). See
page 209.

*Sierra Madre* (mother mountains). See page
209.

*Sierra Morena* (brown range) is the name of a
spur of the Coast Range commencing about ten
miles south of San Francisco and running
through San Matéo County into Santa Clara
County. This mountain range, which contains

some very charming scenery, may have been so named on account of its color, or it may be the namesake of the *Sierra Morena* of Spain. The name is sometimes spelled *Moreno,* and one of the possibilities is that it was named for the pioneer Moreno family.

*Sierra Nevada* (snowy mountains). See page 209.

*Sierra Pelona* (bald mountain range) is in Los Angeles County.

*Simi,* in Ventura County, is an Indian place name.

*Siskiyou.* An Indian name of undetermined origin. The theory that it is derived from the French *six Cailloux* (six stepping-stones) is one of those labored and far-fetched solutions which have absolutely no basis in fact, but are mere products of the imagination. See page 184.

*Sis Quoc,* a town and river in Santa Bárbara County, named from *Souscoc,* a former Chumash village near the Santa Inez Mission.

*Sobrante* (residue, surplus), a term applied to a piece of land left over after measuring off land grants.

*Sobrante de San Jacinto,* residue of the grant called St. Hyacinth.

*Solano.* See page 192.

*Soledad* (solitude). See page 110.

*Somis,* in Ventura County, is an Indian place name.

*Sonoma.* See page 175.

*Sonora.* See page 233.

*Soquel,* or *Souquel,* was probably derived from *Usacalis,* a Costanoan Indian village situated in 1819 within ten miles of the Santa Cruz Mission.

*Soscol.* See Suscol.

*Sotoyome,* a former Indian village near Healdsburg. The derivation of the name is uncertain.

*Stanislaus.* See page 198.

*Suerte,* a word of many meanings (luck, chance, lot of ground). In the apportionment of land by the Spaniards a *suerte* was a cultivable lot of land granted to colonists near the pueblos and within the four leagues assigned to the pueblo. Each *suerte* consisted of two hundred *varas* of length and two hundred of breadth, a *vara* being about thirty-three inches. Thus one *suerte* is one lot (of land), and not, as one writer has translated it, "one chance." *Dos suertes* is two lots.

*Suisun.* See page 193.

*Suñol* (a surname). See pages 173 and 240.

*Sur* (south). For Point Sur see page 120. In this vicinity the scenery is remarkably picturesque.

*Del Sur* (of the south) is in Los Angeles County.

*Suscol* was the name of a Pooewin tribe who lived in a village on the east bank of Napa River. See Soscol.

*Tahoe.* See page 217.

*Talega* (bag, or sack) Canyon. It is in San Diego County.

*Tallac,* an Indian word, meaning not ascertained.

*Tamalpais.* See page 153.

*Tambo* (South American for inn, or hotel), so called because in early days there was a stopping place in this vicinity for travelers crossing the continent. Near Marysville.

*Tasajara,* the name of a resort near Monterey, is probably a corruption of *tasajera,* a place where jerked meat is hung up to cure. Tassajara in Contra Costa County, and Tasajero Creek in Contra Costa and Alameda Counties are probably different spellings of the same word.

*Tecolote* (owl).

*Tehachapi.* See page 208.

*Tehama.* See page 190.

*El Tejón* (the badger) is in Kern County. Tejón Pass is badger pass.

*Tembladera* (quagmire) Slough. It is in Monterey County.

335

*Temblor* (earthquake) Range is in Kern County.

*Temécula.* See page 37. Temécula is in the southern part of Riverside County.

*Temescal* (sweathouse). See page 53.

*Tenaya Peak,* in Yosemite Valley, named for Ten-ei-ya, chief of the Yosemite Indians.

*Tequisquite* is an Aztec word, probably meaning salt-petre.

*Terra Bella* and *Terra Buena,* in Tulare and Sutter Counties, are perhaps misspellings of *tierra bella* (beautiful land) and *tierra buena* (good land).

*Tia Juana.* See page 37.

*Tiburón* (shark). See page 159.

*Tierra* Seca (dry land).

*Tocaloma.* See page 173.

*Todos Santos* (all saints).

*Todos Santos y San Antonio* (all saints and St. Anthony).

*Tolenos,* in Yolo County, is probably a misspelling of Yolenos, from the Indian *Yolo.*

*Toluca,* near Los Angeles, is probably derived from *Tolujaa,* or *Tilijaes,* a tribe among the original ones at San Juan Capistrano in 1776, although there is also a place named Toluca in Mexico.

*Tomales.* See pages 173 and 189.

*Topo Creek* (gopher creek).

*Toro* (bull). See pages 67 and 120.

*Toros* (bulls).

*Tortuga* (turtle, tortoise).

*Trabuco* (blunderbuss, a sort of wide-mouthed gun). See page 67. Trabuco Canyon is in Orange County.

*Trampa del Oso* (bear trap).

*Trampas* (traps, snares), perhaps named in reference to traps which were in common use among the Indians to catch game, as well as their human enemies. In Contra Costa County.

*Tranquillón Mountain* is in Santa Bárbara County. *Tranquillón* is a mixture of two kinds of grain, such as wheat and rye, called in English "mastlin," or "maslin." The origin of the name in this case has not been verified.

*Tres Ojos de Agua* (three springs of water).

*Tres Pinos.* See page 120.

*Tres Vias* (three roads) is in Butte County. It refers to three railroad tracks which encircle a triangular piece of ground.

*Trigo* (wheat) is 128 miles from Stockton.

*Trinity County.* See page 185.

*Trinidad Bay* and town. See page 185.

*Triunfo* (triumph) is in Ventura County. This place was named by the Portolá party in honor of the day of their arrival, which was the fiesta of *El Triunfo de la Cruz,* commemorating a great victory of the Crusaders over the Turks.

*Trópico* (tropical), near Los Angeles.

*Truckee.* See page 216.

*Tulare* (place of rushes). See page 202.

*Tularcitos* (little rushes), little Tulare ranch.

*Tulucay Rancho,* near Napa State Hospital, is derived from the Indian word *tuluka* (red).

*Tunitas* is a place near San Francisco on the Ocean Shore Road. The tunita is a beach plant sometimes called the "beach apple." *Tuna* is the Spanish name for the common cactus known as "prickly pear."

*Tuolumne.* See page 221.

*Tustín* (a surname), a place in Orange County, near Santa Ana. Fernando Tustín was one of the early settlers, and came to California in 1845.

*Ukiah.* See page 189.

*Ulloa,* name of a street in San Francisco, is in honor of Francisco De Ulloa, one of the early Spanish navigators on the west coast. He first explored the coast of Lower California and proved that it was not an island.

*Urrutia Canyon* is in Fresno County. Urrutia is a family name.

*Usal,* in Mendocino County. This is an Indian word, possibly derived from *yosal,* or *yusal,* the name of a tribe of Pomos, living on the coast from Usal northward. Pronounced Yusawl.

*Las Uvas* (the grapes). See page 121.

*Vacaville.* See page 208.

338

*Valencia Peak,* near San Luis Obispo. Valencia is a surname, that of a family of Spanish pioneers. A street in San Francisco also bears the name.

*Valle* (valley).

*Vallecito* (little valley) is the name of places in Calaveras and San Diego Counties. See page 234.

*Los Vallecitos de San Marcos* (the little valleys of St. Mark).

*Vallejo* (a surname). See pages 174 and 240.

*Valle Mar* (sea valley), on the Ocean Shore, near San Francisco. Improper construction. It should be *Valle del Mar* (valley of the sea).

*Valle de San Felipe* (valley of St. Philip).

*Dos Valles* (two valleys).

*Valle de San José* (valley of St. Joseph).

*Valle Verde* (green valley). See page 67.

*Valle Vista* (valley view). See page 67. Improper construction. It should be *Vista del Valle* (view of the valley).

*Vega,* an open plain, or tract of level land. Vega is also a surname.

*Las Vegas* (the plains). Frémont refers to the *vegas* of the Southern Central Valley in these terms: "We encamped in the midst of another very large basin, at a camping ground called *Las Vegas,* a term which the Spaniards use to signify fertile or marshy plains, in contradistinction to

*llanos,* which they apply to dry and sterile plains."

*Vega del Río del Pájaro* (plain of the river of the bird).

*Venado* (deer) is in Sonoma County.

*Ventana* (window), the name of some volcanic cones and a creek in the Sur country in Monterey County. It was so called from an opening in one of the hills which resembled a window.

*Ventura* (fortune). See page 91.

*Verano* (summer) is west of Napa.

*Verde* (green), twelve miles from San Luís Obispo.

*Verdugo* (a surname in this case). See page 67.

*Los Vergeles* (flower gardens, beautiful orchards).

*Vicente Point* (Point Vincent). See page 68.

*Viejas* (old women) Mountain and Valley, in San Diego County. It is quite likely that this name was given because the Spaniards saw some old Indian women in the neighborhood, but this is merely conjecture.

*Viento* (wind) is in San Bernardino County.

*Las Virgenes* (the virgins). See page 240.

*Visitación Valley.* This name may have originated in a fiesta of the church called La Visitación, in reference to a visit made by the Virgin to Saint Elizabeth on July 2nd. The valley, which now forms a district of San Francisco,

may have been discovered on that day, and so named in consequence.

*Vista* (view), in San Diego County.

*Bella Vista* (beautiful view).

*Buena Vista* (good view).

*Chula Vista* (charming view). See page 32.

*Vista Grande* (large view) is in San Matéo County.

*Monte Vista* (mountain view). Improper construction. It should be *Vista del Monte* (view of the mountain).

*Río Vista* (river view). See page 208. Improper construction. It should be *Vista del Río* (view of the river).

*Vizcaíno Cape,* named for the celebrated Spanish explorer Sebastián Vizcaíno, who touched at various points on the California coast in the year 1602.

*Volcán* (volcano).

*Wahtoque,* or *Wahtoke,* was the name of a powerful Indian chief or medicine man.

*Wawona,* in Mariposa County, where the famous "big trees" are situated, is of unknown origin. It does not appear to be Indian.—(Kroeber.) See page 234.

*Weitchpec,* near Hoopa Valley, Humboldt County. "The Weitspekan family consisted of the Yurok tribe alone, inhabiting the lower Klamath River and adjacent coast. The name is

adapted from Weitspekw, the name of a spring in the village. At the site of the present post-office of Weitchpec was one of the most populous Yurok villages, and one of only two or three at which both the Deerskin dance and the Jumping dance were held."—(A. L. Kroeber in *Handbook of American Indians.*)

*Yallo Bally Mountains.* The two peaks, known as North and South, between Trinity and Tehama Counties, are named from the Wintun Indian words *yola* (snow) and apparently *boli* (spirit), thus meaning "spirit of the snow." The belief that peaks were the abode of spirits was common among the Indians of California.—(Kroeber.)

*Ydalpom* (pronounced Wydal'pom), in Shasta County, is derived from an Indian place name, probably meaning "north place."

*Las Yeguas* (the mares), referring to a pasture where mares were kept.

*Yerba Buena* (good herb). See page 146.

*Yokohl,* in Tulare County. This was the name of a Yokuts tribe formerly living on Kaweah River, Tulare County.

*Yolo.* See page 192.

*Yorba* (a surname). This was the name of one of Captain Fages' original Catalán volunteers. Yorba is near Los Angeles.

*Yosemite* (grizzly bear). See page 224.

342

*Yreka.* See page 185.

*Yuba.* See page 191.

*Yucaipe,* in San Bernardino County, is an Indian place name.

*Yuma,* in Imperial County, is named for the Yuma tribe, but the origin of the word is unknown.

*Zamora,* probably named for the province of the same name in the ancient kingdom of León, in Spain. There is an old proverb about this place which says: "No se ganó Zamora en una hora" (Zamora was not taken in an hour), the same idea as expressed in "Rome was not built in a day."

*Zanja* (ditch, trench) is in San Bernardino County.

*Zapatero Creek* (shoemaker creek).

*Zapato* (shoe) Canyon. It is in Fresno County.

## THE END

*Printed by* BRUCE BROUGH PRESS, *San Francisco, California*